From Death Row with Love

Margôt Aczel

Pirata Publications

First Published in Great Britain by Pirata Publications 2003

Anglesey House, Marine Crescent, Deganwy, Conwy LL31 9BY

ISBN 0 9545196 0 4

Acknowledgements.

I would like to declare my love and gratitude to my parents, Caradoc and Elizabeth Jones, who gave me a wonderful start in life. Through their love, guidance and support I have had the strength to deal with life's tribulations.

My heartfelt thanks to Richard Mercer for many hours spent encouraging, advice about the computer, typing out excerpts from Ted's letters and using the scanner.

Thank you also Richard and Carrie Aczel for your precious time and advice.

A special thank you to Anthony Vent, your expertise in many fields of publishing, including editing, was of enormous value

Many thanks to Carlos, Natalie and Jeanette at IDEA for designing the cover.

Thank you to Marie Iddon for your help and good company.

Thanks to Inmaculada Moya García for your assistance.

Thank you Sister Jennifer for so much. Always being there for me.

Thank you David Aczel & Elaine Markey for help on the computer and some of the artwork.

My grateful thanks go unceasingly to Michael and Ruth Blackburn for their enthusiasm and care. For Michael's knowledge and precision in countering my lack of such.

How can I ever thank Sister Joy for introducing me to this world of prisons? I also thank her for being my sister in spirit.

My thanks to Ted for sharing his life with me and who opened his heart to God's love.

My family have also been of paramount importance in the months of writing, thank you for your patience and understanding.

None of this would have happened but for the unstinting help, encouragement and tremendous love that I received from John, my best friend and husband. Thank you from the bottom of my heart, dearest John, the finest of husbands.

For John, my husband.

A Letter from Cormac Murphy-O'Connor, Archbishop of Westminster

Dear Margôt,

Thank you for sending me details of your book. It is clear that your encounter with Ted has been a life-changing experience. His story, and the story of your friendship are deeply moving. By telling that story with all its wrongs, its pains, its honesty and the glimpses it gives of the surprising and life-giving mercy of our loving God, I pray that you will touch people, particularly people who are prepared to support the idea, which we reject, of a life for a life.

With my prayers and best wishes to you and to Ted in Jesus Christ.

Yours sincerely

Cormac Murphy-O'Connor
Archbishop of Westminster

Sue Lusk, Texas Coordinator for Human Writes Magazine.

More than 3,800 people are currently awaiting death by execution in the United States. Many have been held in small soulless cells on Death Row for over twenty years awaiting their fate.

The State of Texas has the highest rate of executions, far exceeding all other States in the US. Death was administered by hanging and later, by the electric chair. When capital punishment was declared 'cruel and unusual' by the US Supreme Court in 1972, there were 52 people on Death Row in Texas. All sentences were commuted to life under this new statute and Death Row was cleared by March 1973. Revisions to the Texas Penal Code came into effect in January 1974 whereby executions were once again permitted to resume and at this point, Death Row was re-opened. In August 1977, Texas adopted a new method of execution; changing from the electric chair to lethal injection, which is the method still used to this day.

In 1998, a group of seven prisoners made an escape attempt from the prison where Death Row was housed. This gave the authorities the chance they had been looking for to move the entire male Death Row population to a 'supermax'-type security prison, the Polunsky Unit, which is where they are housed today. This is a harsh environment and prisoners spend 23 hours a day in total isolation in a 6ft x 10ft (1.5 x 2.7 metre cell). The only window is a slit measuring

3 inches high x 3 feet long, which is located high in the wall. Cell doors are solid steel and there is minimal human contact.

During my eight years of involvement with Texas, I have come to know most of the prisoners on Death Row, and some of their families too. In so many ways their families and loved ones walk through every day of their sentence with them. As the reality of execution gets nearer it is sad to watch the light of hope fade from their eyes.

Whilst we should never forget that for all crimes there is a victim, it has been proved that some innocent prisoners have in fact also been executed. Many, too, find themselves on Death Row due to years of abuse suffered during childhood, where the release from the emotional torment has been found in drug, or alcohol abuse, which in turn has led to a crime being committed.

I have asked myself on many occasions, what does executing this prisoner actually achieve? Occasionally, there is relief for a victim's family, although many have not found this to be the case.

Last year I watched a mother led away from her son having said her last goodbye a few hours before his execution. She was physically supported on either side, as her legs could not carry her, and her sobbing echoed around the room long after she had gone. She, too, is a victim; a victim of the system that allows this to keep happening. Perhaps the most poignant of all memories is of two mothers who, in 1997, watched a young man die, each from a different side of the execution chamber. One was the mother of the prisoner; the other of his victim. Afterwards, they both cried and hugged each other ... that day they were both united in the pain of the children they had lost.

As you read this book, I hope that you too will learn more about the reality of Death Row, and through the story of Ted Cole written by his long term friend, come to know the human side of those who society condemns in this way ... the real people they have become and who are destined to become another execution statistic in the Texas system.

Introduction

I have written this book because I am sure that people like myself do not know what prisoners on Death Row are like. When I visited Ted I was amazed, horrified, humbled and elated.

Amazed - that Ted was not some monster. Amazed - that he talked and practised repentance, forgiveness, love of God, compassion and redemption. Horrified - at the appalling conditions in which these inmates are kept. 5ft by 9ft (1.5 x 2.7 metre) cells. This was the size of the cell that Ted occupied at Ellis One. Solitary isolation is twenty-three hours a day. Horrified - at the cruelty of shackles, chains, handcuffs, and electric probes around their waists. And yet humbled by the goodness that emanates from the men that I have met. Some of these men, to whom I have written, are now dead, killed by the State of Texas. Others are waiting to die, who die inside themselves each day in anticipation of their final day. Elated - that love, compassion, confession, forgiveness and hope are evident in the men that I visit on Death Row.

The tension between good and evil is stretched tight on both sides of the fence, but I found a man on Death Row who has changed my life. Like Ted, I too have searched and found truth that helps me to live each day to my best. Each day is a battle one way or another for us all, but as Ted says I can go off on holiday, or play tennis, swim or sail and forget my troubles for a while. He is unable to do this and so suffers that much more intensely each day.

Through God men have found hope where there was only despair. Some of the men are abandoned, or worse, no longer thought about. They have been despised and rejected, thought of as getting their 'just deserts'. They are mostly penniless - there is no one on Death Row with money.

Many men are underprivileged, ignorant, uneducated, they can be from dysfunctional families, or with no families at all. Many have been abused since they were born and have brain tissue damage which demonstrates this. Their actions in later life may result from the computer of the brain responding negatively to certain stimuli. Therapy and rehabilitation could help. In the Gospels, the Shepherd looked for his lost sheep. He spent time searching for them. He did not reject them. He rejoiced when they were found. No one is totally evil. We are all worthy of redemption. God is good. God works miracles every day, especially on Death Row. This is the hidden face of the U.S.A. 2003.

The excerpts at the beginning of each chapter are from the poems written by Ted Calvin Cole, T.O. Carm.

Margôt Aczel
Benalmádena Costa
Spain
June, 2003

Chapter 1

Destination Death Row

Have you ever wondered about the meaning of life?
Have you ever asked yourself, "Why am I here?"

The gates clanged shut behind me. I walked down the path and entered Death Row alone. The guard behind the desk took my passport, my driving licence, my return ticket to Manchester and my car keys. A number was given to me, 21. I was now a prisoner. No escape. Above the door was written

"No Hostages Rescued".

Standing nearby, in the hall, was another visitor, a tall, thin, very good-looking young man. He looked distraught. A number was called and he moved away into another room.

"Number 21!"

This was my number and the guard indicated the way that I should go into a corridor and past a model of the whole prison. Nervously, I then went into a vast room with a huge cage in the middle. What on earth was I doing here?

No escape. There were chairs all the way down the side of the large cage that dominated the hall. Each chair had a number on the back. I had to find my number. I found it half way down the caged area. I sat down and looked about me. Inside the cage was an empty wooden chair facing me. That was where the person I was visiting would sit. I put my small purse containing $10, the only amount that was permitted, on the narrow ledge in front of me. The area from the ledge to the floor was encased with iron or steel. Above the ledge and up to the ceiling was wire mesh-reinforced glass.

My mouth felt dry and I was rigid with anxiety. The strain was overpowering then I remembered that I was allowed to buy a drink from the large dispenser. That was what the money was for. I was unfamiliar with American coinage. Quite an assortment of cold drinks; Coke, Pepsi, Root Beer. Perhaps Coke would be the best choice. The machine did not seem to work so I tried another one. A tall, white haired lady came up to me and said that many of the machines were empty most of the time. She indicated one on the other side of the room. Success. I bought two Cokes and a packet of crisps.

On this side of the hall the prisoners were in separate small cages. I was to learn that this was for "Lock Down" inmates, usually known as "Segregation". They did not have wooden chairs, but small steel stools that were attached to the floor. A guard and his handcuffed prisoner came through the corridor from the cells and stopped at a small cage. The prisoner went in and the gate was locked shut. The guard undid the handcuffs through a hole in the gate. Rubbing his wrists the inmate greeted his visitor with a smile. His visitor was the tall young man I had seen on the way in. With renewed apprehension I moved back to my side of the room, placed the drink and crisps where the guard indicated, and returned to my seat with my can of coke.

13

Opening the can in my nervousness, it splashed onto my dress. What was I doing alone, in a place like this? The chair was still empty. Who was I waiting for? I thought that the Lord must want me here for some purpose. When I am in trouble or need help I put my hands together, palms upwards and put myself in the hands of God. I really needed some confidence. I was here to visit a murderer, who did not receive many visitors, and I had to tell him that I could not come again the next day as had been arranged from Wales. I was very nervous. Would he become angry and cause a scene? What would I talk about for four hours? Up until now I had tried not to think about the situation too carefully because most people, especially my husband, had thought that I was mad coming to Texas, to Death Row, to visit a murderer... I had known that it was the right thing to do, but now it was crunch time. Now it had arrived. Now I must place all my trust in God. Had I done the right thing? I was frightened enough already. What if I could not cope with this man? What had I let myself in for?

Originally, I had intended to come to Huntsville as a travelling companion for my friend, Sister Joy, who is a nun. How was it that I was now sitting inside Death Row, on my own, waiting to talk for four hours, to an unknown convicted murderer? Was I safe? Safe from what I wondered?

Chapter 2

How It All Began

Teach me to walk softly,
To speak softly,
And to reach out tenderly
to those around me,

It had been a bright sunny August morning in 1997 when Joy phoned, "I want to ask you a question, and I need to see your face as I ask you".

Sister Joy and I had been at school together at Loreto College, a convent in Llandudno, North Wales. Although Joy was Baptist, and not a Catholic, she was impressed by the faith of her best friend, Mary Byrom. They enjoyed frequent discussions about religion as they bussed to and from school together. Joy went on to the Grammar School in Colwyn Bay. Mary and I stayed on at Loreto until the end of our school days.

We met up again in college in Liverpool, where Joy was my "College Mother". This was a position to help new students find their way around college in their first few days. By this time Joy had become a Catholic, and was interested in becoming part of a community of nuns. She later joined the White Sisters Community and went as a missionary Sister to Africa, which she loved.

After five year's teaching, I exchanged the hills and sea of Wales for a post in Wimbledon, Surrey, where I met my husband, John. We set up home in Cobham, Surrey, and had three boys, James, Richard and David. After nearly thirty years there, I returned to Wales for two weeks each month as my father was ill. Spasmodically, Joy and I had kept in touch. She had returned from Africa, to other appointments, and had also returned to Wales to nurse her parents.

During this nursing period in 1987, Joy saw a BBC documentary called Fourteen Days in May, about the last two weeks in the life of a young black man called Edward Earl Johnson, on Death Row, Texas.

The camera crew and the presenter felt sure of his innocence, but he was executed. At the end of the film a caption read: Any person over the age of eighteen, who would like to write to a Death Row prisoner, can do so by sending their details and address to Life Lines in Cambridge, England.

Joy had no doubts about the injustices and brutality of capital punishment, a system contrary to Protocol 13 of the Council of Europe's Human Rights Convention – abolition of the Death Penalty in all circumstances. The American Supreme Court had lifted a 10-year moratorium on Capital punishment in 1974 and some states were now employing injection, electrocution, gas, hanging and the firing squad to despatch prisoners.

Joy had spare time in the evenings, after her father, who was in his late nineties, went to bed early. She felt that writing to a

Death Row prisoner was something she could do. She wrote, if somewhat intermittently, for 7 years to Leslie Gosch. They continued writing even after her father died at 99¾ years of age.

Joy is a deeply spiritual person with a great gift for dealing with people. She can make them feel really special - as they are, she would say. She helped Lesley with happy, prayerful letters. Under threat of death he had little time left. In August 1997 he wrote to Joy asking her to visit him on Death Row. Money from the sale of his father's house would pay for her airfare. He also wanted her to come, see and tell the world just what was going on in Huntsville, Texas.

The letter was a shock. She had never contemplated going to visit Lesley. But, she could not refuse a dying man. If she could find someone to accompany her she would go.

Her flat in Rhos-on-Sea is just 10 minutes from our house on the promenade in Deganwy. We had coffee in our upstairs sitting room, with its beautiful view of the Menai Straights, Puffin Island and Anglesey. Joy quickly came to the point:

"Margôt, how would you like to come with me to America? I want to visit a man on Death Row in Texas who is going to die soon and he has asked me to visit him."

I had immediately agreed. Deep down I knew that this was good, something that I could do. Then I had another thought: When Joy goes to Death Row I can do some shopping!

That afternoon we booked our flight to Houston, Texas, and organised a car to hire. We would go at the end of September and

17

the beginning of October. A few days later Joy came to me and asked,

"Margôt, how would you like to visit someone who does not get any visitors?"

Well, when she put it like that, what could I think except good-bye to the shopping? The prison bureaucracy began. I wrote my name, age, address and country and sent it to the prisoner I was to meet, Lesley's friend - Ted Cole, Number 000906, Death Row, Ellis 1, Huntsville, Texas. He added my name to his visitors' list and sent it to the warden's secretary, who agreed the days of my visit.

My husband, John, said, "You are going to need counselling before you go and after you come back."

But somehow I had confidence. Joy knows what she is doing. She had told me as much as she could about Lesley. One of Joy's priest friends advised, "Just be yourselves, let love direct your steps".

These words strengthened my resolve. What had been done in the past was the past. It had brought them to this. Now was where they were. I would go with love and listen.

The weeks flew. David was going to university. Accommodation had to be found. Books had to be bought, all the preparations for a young man leaving home for the unknown world of higher education.

My husband and I took David down to Exeter. After the inevitable hitches accommodation was duly found. A new exciting life for David and back home for John and I. It was now almost the time of departure for Joy and I.

John was very busy but had time to worry about what we were letting ourselves in for and kept telling me. Fortunately, I was also busy with all the practical things to be done at home. I had the shopping to do, meals to make for John and my aunt Tanya who would look after Barney, the dog. I had no time to worry. Lastly, but very time consuming, I had to explain to friends where we were going and why. Most found our trip a little weird.

Finally we were off. John took us to Manchester Airport and away we went to Houston, via Amsterdam. This meant a delay and therefore, a longer journey. By the time we arrived at our hotel, we were ready for bed. On the flight we talked about what we could possibly be in for regarding "The prisoners". We had no idea. We could not imagine what they would be like either in looks or in conversation. Joy had no information to pass on to me regarding Ted, only that he was Lesley's friend. I decided to enjoy the experience, take care with the driving and let events unfold. We were still talking as we prepared for bed and I felt that when I woke up it might all be a dream.

The next morning the courtesy coach took us to collect our hire car and we headed out to Huntsville. It was a straightforward road but we seemed to be going slower and slower as though we did not want to get there at all. Nearing Huntsville, a huge white statue loomed larger and larger on the right hand side of the road. It had been erected in honour of Samuel Houston, Houston's founder. There is a museum behind it and an area of natural beauty where amongst others Blue Bonnets and Red Indian Paintbrush, the beautiful flowers of Texas, grow.

We were to stay at Hospitality House, a refuge for "Hurting families", arranged by our English friend, Sue Lusk. Sue was the Texas Coordinator of Life Lines, the English magazine for people who write to Death Row prisoners. Sue had been delighted that we were going.

We found a single-storey, wooden building with a garden and car spaces. Hospitality House is in a quiet road just off the main street. 300 Baptist men had built it in twenty-four hours. It is stocked by people's generosity, and is manned by volunteers, apart from the Warden, Bob, his wife, Nelda and Jean, a helper. Bob opened the door and welcomed us into a large, bright room. Tables and cosy chairs were in abundance. Jigsaw puzzles on one or two of the tables were left unfinished. There was an area with baskets of toys, small chairs, and tables for children. On the walls were beautiful original paintings of American scenes. On a wall near the men's sleeping area were poems that had been written by prison inmates. It was tranquil. No television or radio - just serenity. From this room one went into a large, well-stocked kitchen, including two sinks, two huge cookers and enormous fridges.

We passed into the corridor that led to the sleeping accommodation. Our room had a two-tier bunk bed, a chest of drawers and a shelf under which was a hanging space with wire coat hangers. A curtain and a wall separated us from the next two bunk beds. I had the top bunk, as Joy did not like the height. There was a very small room near the communal ladies' shower and bathroom. We peeped in. It was a prayer room. An open bible resting on a stand, a table with a box of tissues and a sofa were all that it contained, but the aura was unmistakable.

John rang the next morning just as we had finished a biscuit made by Jean. Every weekend homemade bread rolls, called biscuits, are served for breakfast. John was so happy that we were still in one piece. I was happy to hear from him. We went to the local Church for Mass. What amazed us was that no one said a word or uttered a prayer for the people in prison or on Death Row. Next week's execution was not even mentioned. The priest was totally charming when we spoke to him, but was not particularly interested that we had come all the way from Wales just to visit people on Death Row.

There are 68,000 prisoners in Huntsville including 460 on Death Row. Most local people are connected in some way with the many penal institutions. I would have thought that the presence of such an institution would have been at the forefront of everyone's minds - especially in the local Church.

Chapter 3

Execution Vigil

Love sees beyond the surface-
Love looks from heart to heart.
It sees the truth that's hidden,
And it tears the lies apart.

We endured Prison Service bureaucracy again when I phoned the prison Warden to confirm the permission to visit 906 Cole. September had almost ended and October began in the same week. I learnt when I phoned the Warden to arrange the visit, that I would be limited to two, four-hour visits, one on Wednesday and one on Thursday. Unfortunately we were not allowed to visit Lesley and his friend Ted for the last two days of September, as they were in the same week as our agreed visit for October.

Either the goal posts had been moved or we had not been told of this new rule. In any case, we would not be permitted to visit Lesley and Ted for these last two days of September. To make matters worse I was very nervous on the telephone. First we had to buy a phone card from the Post Office. At Hospitality House we had to operate one of these cards when we used the phone, but there are so many numbers to key in one can easily make a mistake, as I did. Eventually it was sorted out.

We eased our disappointment in the form of a shopping trip. In fact it was a valuable exercise in assessing local mood and opinions. With the forthcoming executions that were reported in the press, we were surprised that the death penalty was not on everyone's lips.

When assistants said, "I just love your accent, where are y'all from? What are y'all doing here?" there was a startled silence to our response of, "Oh, we are visiting prisoners on Death Row."

This seemed to be a taboo topic. When Joy asked one assistant if she believed in the death penalty, the assistant did not know what to say and eventually responded, "I guess I do".

Most people we met said, without thinking, that they supported the death penalty. Only one lady said that if it had been her son who had committed the murder then she would be against it, but if he had been the one to be killed then she would want the death penalty. It took courage to ask these questions but we found the general feeling, sadly, to be pro death penalty.

An execution was set for Tuesday evening. In previous years the execution would take place at midnight but this was changed to six o' clock to allow the victim's family to watch.

We wandered round this town that, since Texas became a state, had been chosen as the site for the first penitentiary, The Huntsville Unit - "The Walls." Huntsville is now established as the home of the Texas Department of Criminal Justice. It is therefore the home to legal killing by the State of Texas. Until 1964 this was undertaken by electrocution, now they are executed by lethal injection.

The museum in a side street is dedicated to crime memorabilia. "The Texas Thunderbolt" or "Old Sparky" is there, built by an inmate and first used in 1924. There are graphic descriptions and details of how it misfired, how many times and how many different ways that it frizzled and fried its occupants. The Curator, an ex-teacher, seemed to take a vacuous delight in her new employment. It was obvious that she had not given it much thought. Our questions about the morality of the death penalty, miscarriages of justice and the death of innocent people fell on deaf ears.

"No one on Death Row is innocent," she retorted.

I rather wished she had stayed teaching little ones the difference between right and wrong. I felt that some love and a place to talk with the present generation would have been appropriate instead of glorifying the dubious deeds of the past.

The newspapers had given a brief summary of the life of a man who was about to die that evening. Joy and I decided to take part in a vigil for the man. We knew where to go, just round the corner from the town centre to "The Walls", this dreaded place where so many people are killed…. legally. Already there was tape tied across the road. Heavily armed guards hovered around in the beautiful afternoon sunshine.

After meeting so many people that day who were pro-death penalty, it was with some relief when we saw a small group of protestors gathered there. One lady was voicing the injustice of the system through a megaphone. She began to sing a melodious hymn.

I felt encouraged. Joy began to speak to some of the bystanders whilst I took up the other end of a large banner that said.

"Texas - Killing Capital of America".

A tall, young Dutchman was holding the other end of the banner. He had been returning to Huntsville for the last few years to visit a young American he had corresponded with and befriended. Unsure when his friend would die, he travelled over from Holland each year.

At a quarter to six, the victim's six witnesses were escorted out of the holding room across the street and entered "The Walls". Then the six witnesses of the man about to be killed stumbled up the steps and into the unknown. The protestors fell silent. Could this be really happening?

The sun shone. A squirrel darted across the grass on to the road. He suddenly stopped, looked about him and scrambled up a tree, curious at seeing all these quiet people standing so still. He was not to know that the State of Texas was preparing to take a life.

Some cars passed, their horns blaring as they read our placards. Other drivers just revved their engines hard. Some people leant out of the car windows and shouted pro death penalty statements as they went by.

At about 6.30pm, relatives and friends were escorted down the steps from "The Walls". The difference between them was easy to see. The victim's entourage walked tall and aggressively, whilst the family of the person just killed appeared, holding each other for support.

We fell silent and helped to fold up the banners and placards. Most of the protestors were from Houston. The group including retired people, housewives, thoughtful students, a university professor, a few foreigners, came every time that there was an execution. We shook hands, said goodbye, we turned the corner, walked down the road, past all the lovely, well-tended gardens as though we were in a dream. I could not believe that a man's life had just been taken. We were both silent, trying to collect our thoughts

However, the dream soon ended when we arrived back at Hospitality House. Bob said that there was a message for Joy to ring Lesley Gosch's lawyer immediately. It transpired that Lesley had been transferred to San Antonio to be given an execution date by the judge. It had happened that day, so through the attorney, he wanted to tell Joy that he would not be on death row for her visit the next day. This was a major bombshell for us. We had come all this way and now he had been spirited away. Was this done deliberately, we asked Bob? No, he assured us it could happen at any time. The authorities have their own schedule. They take no one into account.

What should we do? I was due to go to Death Row the next day to meet someone that I had never known about, let alone written to, until a few weeks before. Now I was going to have to go on my own to meet him on Death Row. This was not the scenario that I had envisaged.

I had thought that Joy and I would drive to the prison together, walk in together, face the authorities together. Most of all I had thought that we would meet our prisoners together. But this was not to be. I would go on alone and continue with the plan. I had no choice. I would not go back on my word, no matter how nervous I felt of this hitherto unknown world of prison and inmates. I would soon learn.

I hardly slept that night. In the early morning Joy made tea. We sat and talked whilst we drank it. The dormitory was now ours. The lady who had occupied the other half had only been there for the weekend whilst she visited her husband in "Population", the name given to prisoners who will be released after having served their sentence.

As the other ladies had done, I dressed with great care. Like all Huntsville prisoners, the men on Death Row always wear white. The guards wear grey uniforms, so visitors try to dress brightly. The prison dress code is no shorts, see-through blouses or tank tops. Skirts must be below the knee. I put on a vivid green silk suit with tiny royal blue flowers dotted about here and there. It sounds awful, but it was not too bad and it was also comfortable.

I had agreed to follow a German family in their car. They knew the way to Ellis One. They had arrived the day before, from Germany, with their baby. Elsa, the mother, had first visited her correspondent when she was single. Then she brought her husband. Now they came to show the new baby to their friend. I waved goodbye to Joy. She was particularly upset. She was not going to see Lesley on Death Row this morning. We had arranged with Bob that we would leave that afternoon and go the 400 miles to San Antonio to see Lesley. Meanwhile, alone, I had to see Ted on Death Row.

Chapter 4

My first visit to Death Row

Give it all away, my friend;
Just give (then give some more!),
And pretty soon the Lord of Love
Will knock at your heart's door.

The road was very quiet at 7.10 that morning when I left Hospitality House. Out of Huntsville into the countryside, driving along tree lined lanes, with the mist rising high in the fields. Horses were grazing, ghostly in the mist. Suddenly the sun, seemingly huge and very close, lifted gracefully above the trees. It climbed into the sky on my right hand side. I was nervous. I felt that I was someone else driving the car as I passed various departments of correction, knowing that I was going to enter one similar. Shadowy white clad figures moved in lines, working in the misty fields, flanked by guards on horseback with rifles.

Suddenly the lead car turned left into a wide drive with well-tended borders of multi-coloured flowers along the grass verges.

'Ellis One Unit Texas Department of Corrections' - the notice read as I drove up a long drive, passing a guardhouse and slowly pulling into the huge car park full of pickups.

High, wire fences surrounded the tall grey multiple storey buildings. Watchtowers stood at regular intervals along the

29

perimeter. A female guard manned the one nearest to the entrance of Death Row. She lowered a bucket down from the tower above me for each new guard as he arrived for duty. With a cheery "Good morning" to her, he deposited his car keys into the bucket. She hauled it up to her tower and took out the keys. She then placed them out of sight in the security of her glass observation room. The guard produced his papers out of a plastic see-through bag, which the officer in the ground hut glanced at as she crossed his name off her list. She then pressed a button to open the gates. He passed into the prison for duty.

I joined a small group at the wooden hut outside the prison. The visitor's name and their passport or identification number was written down and phoned through to the main prison reception. The sun was very strong, even though it had only just gone 8 o'clock. When it was my turn, I went into the hut. The young female officer was chewing gum as she wrote down my name, passport number, and the name and number of the prisoner I had permission to visit. Then she picked up the phone, dialled and waited until it was answered. She repeated my details, said "Thanks" and put down the phone. She shouted, "Next!"

That was my dismissal to move out of the shed and wait outside for my next instructions.

The German family I had followed stayed in their car to feed and change the baby. As I waited for verification, the only other person who was left outside with me was another German lady. She told me that to fund her visits, she paints pictures on glass, which are very popular in Germany. She stays with the mother of her "friend". She had been many times and once came with a German T.V. crew who made a film about the unacceptable conditions of death row. Eventually my name was called. I said goodbye to her and walked through two sets of gates. The second gate could only be passed through once the first gate was closed. Each gate closed with a foreboding clang that quite startled me. I continued through the second gate, and along a path between well-tended borders of pretty flowers into the stark main building.

I felt quite detached as if I was entering a new world, a world where I had no say in anything. I had to obey the rules. I must do exactly as I was told or I would rue the consequences. Nobody smiled at the reception desk as I passed over my passport, driving licence, return ticket to Manchester and the car keys. A small purse with $10 is all that I was allowed to carry in with me. A man dressed in white passed me sweeping the floor accompanied by an officer as I waited again for instructions. The receptionist called out my name and number. She indicated the doorway through which I had to pass. Now I was sitting nervously on my hard chair in this bleak prison.

Suddenly a guard stood in front of me. He had with him a tall thin man who sat on the chair behind the glass.

"Hi, I'm Ted," he said, as the guard strolled away.

"Hello, I'm Margôt," I said somehow as my mouth went dry. I told him immediately that the visit for the next day was off, and

31

the reason why. He looked at me and said in a Texan drawl, "Don't worry, it's all in God's hands."

I could not believe what I was hearing. He had just repeated my silent heartfelt prayer.

"Thank you," was all that I could muster with relief, but I was then able to concentrate on making this an enjoyable meeting for a man who knew that he was going to die at an appointed date and time. I felt chilled at the thought. He was so alone.

"What do you do all day?" I asked.

I learnt that he was on a voluntary "Work Programme". He made the right hand trouser pocket of the guard's uniform in the Death Row garment factory. Although unpaid it meant that he exchanged his cell for an air-conditioned room, and could chat to other inmates for a few hours once a day. Another bonus was that his cell was unlocked, so he could go to the yard for exercise if he wished. He said,

"It gives a structure to the day and makes us slightly human. Mail time at 5.00pm is the best part of our day. That is when the mail is distributed. All of us who can read and write look forward to receiving letters. Some inmates, who have no family, or whose family has abandoned them for one reason or another, send mail to themselves by sending for free catalogues, free offers, etc."

Once a week they can order from a prison shop called the "Commissary" necessities such as soap, toothpaste, tins of food, etc., which they can eat at night, as prison mealtimes are rather strange. They have breakfast at 3.30am and lunch at 11.00am.

The last meal of the day is at 4.00pm, so by early evening Ted is hungry. Ted worked from 10.00 am until 2.00 pm, consequently, he missed lunch. He does not eat meat now and the frozen (never fresh) vegetables are usually overcooked. He therefore did not mind missing lunch, as long as he was able to have something like tinned soup or beans in the evening, bought from the Commissary.

Ted's step-dad occasionally sends money for him to buy things from this state prison shop. His step-dad seems very good to him. Ted frequently runs out of stamps or writing paper, and then has to wait until his step-dad sends him some more money.

As Ted explained, a new ruling meant a drop in the quality of their lives:

"There was a time when we would get together for dominoes (we're not allowed to have playing cards) and everyone would bring something to drink or snack on, but now it's against regulations for a prisoner to give or share anything with anyone. Anything! If we're "caught" giving anything to anyone, whatever was exchanged can be confiscated as contraband and both inmates can end up going before the Disciplinary Committee on a charge of "trafficking and trading." Most of the officers don't bother enforcing the rule if the items involved are things like books, magazines, newspapers, a cup of coffee or tea; mainly, I think because they don't want to do the paperwork that goes along with it. The rule constantly hangs over our heads, though, and one never knows when he might somehow manage to get on the "wrong side" of an officer who will be more than happy, to use the rule against him.

"Some of the officers are just plain sadistic, though. There's one female officer who works in the evenings, and if she happens to be working our cellblock when it's our turn to go to the commissary, she's just overjoyed! We're not paid for our work and everyone here doesn't have money, of course, so some people go to commissary every week while some hardly ever go. And when it's our turn to go, most of us like to treat ourselves to some sort of ice cream and those who have a little money to spare will sometimes buy extra for folks who have none. But not when that woman's working! She will actually walk up and down the tiers to see who's got what, and she's quite up front about it: if you didn't go to the commissary, you'd better not be eating ice cream! Can you imagine what it's like to be a fully-grown adult and having to hide and keep a watch for the "Police", just so you can have a bit of ice cream? You would think that these officers would have better things to do with their time, wouldn't you? But, anyway, we no longer share cookies, coffee and tea when we get together for dominoes."

Smoking is now forbidden on Death Row as it is bad for their health! Even a man on his last day is not allowed a cigarette.

Ted is interested in Sant Mat, an Indian mystic. His friend, Lesley Gosch, Sister Joy's correspondent, and who had now been moved 400 miles away, also follows his teachings. Sant Mat's supporters fast and meditate. They observe a strict lacto-vegetarian diet with absolutely no meat or eggs, the premise being that it is wrong or sinful to profit from any loss of life. They keep a daily 'self-introspective' diary, which is divided into columns for "thought", "word", "deed" and "diet". They pay a "tithe" of each day's time (2¼ hours) and devote it to meditation, but extra time is also advisable.

Ted had clear ideas about his spirituality:

"I was raised Protestant - Baptist, to be exact - I'm also familiar with the teachings of the Catholic Church, but I don't really claim any particular religion for myself. Instead, I follow the spiritual discipline of Sant Mat, which is a life-philosophy, and not a religion. Religion, of course - if genuinely embraced and practised - is a life-philosophy and should be a total, minute-by-minute way of life and not just something to be picked up and carried to church on Sundays, which is what most religions are to their adherents.

"That's the main reason I got away from the traditional and established religions: if they can't seem to bring about a genuine change in their own "good" members, what possible hope could they offer to someone like me? Of course, that was back before I realized that it's true that God will come a hundred (thousand? million?) steps toward us if we'll just take that first real step toward Him - but we have to take that first step on our own. He won't force us to come to Him. But I don't want to debate "my" faith against anyone else's faith; there's too much of that in the world already, and it only serves to divert the attention to people who might otherwise be trying to come closer to their Creator."

Ted gets up and meditates in the night because with the constant key rattling to open and close doors, which are made of steel poles, the noise during the day until the lights go out is horrendous. The TVs are on constantly and are situated around the tiers, so that each cell can see and hear at least one of them.

Ted sits on the floor near the bars to look out at TV if he watches anything at all, until about 11.30pm to midnight when the films end, and the shouting of the inmates from cell to cell has abated. There are a lot of young men on Death Row and they do not want to think. They just want to chill out every night and forget their situation. Sometimes Ted will watch a film, but mostly he reads or writes letters.

Each day a vote is taken for the programmes that they wish to see the next day. It works quite well. They usually want to see cowboy, Sci-Fi, or horror movies. Ted is not interested in the many adverts and their unreal world of "happy families". There are at least four TV sets, all blazing out the same false message adverts of loving Mommies, caring Daddies, perfect children, always doing the right thing and being oh, so happy! They live in beautiful spotless houses with fantastic kitchens and wonderful food.

But in Ted's experience life is very different: "I don't suppose I actually know what real poverty is. I don't remember ever being hungry as a child, although I know we were poor. There were many, many, evenings when our supper was only a bowl of beans and a couple of tortillas, and more often than not our clothing was bought from the "Goodwill" or the "Salvation Army". But I was fed and clothed and I knew a lot of children in the neighbourhood who had much less than I did. There is also a poverty of love and affection, though, and many of the financially poorest families were richer than mine.

Fortunately, family isn't something I have to worry much about. My Mom and Dad separated when I was six."

He was then put in a children's home, which he had loved because he had good friends and something positive to do. He was treated well. There had been many problems at home resulting in Ted finally jumping through a plate glass window. He did not dwell on this topic. It was said in such a matter of fact way that I did not like to ask why. At the home he was given jobs to do that he loved. He helped with the haymaking and cleaned up the yard. Each day he fed the chickens.

He was sad to leave it all when his Mom came four years later when he was ten years old, with his sister and a man whom she said was his new dad. He didn't even have time to say goodbye to his friends who were out in the fields. That made him really sad. He remembered dragging his suitcase bumpity-bump down the stairs of the empty house where he had been happy and that had been his home.

They moved to the city, but Ted had loved the country. His school grades plummeted. His new dad just worked and watched TV. There were to be no fishing trips, no talk, no sport - just work. He liked the high life and Ted began to "party".

Ted's sister, Cathy and her youngest son Everett had Aids. They were being treated at John Hopkins Hospital, Baltimore. They don't often write to him and even missed his birthdays and Christmas. Cathy had visited him once or twice in his 12 years on Death Row.

She still said she loved him, but he had never even seen Everett. Ted told me all this without any reproach or self-pity. They were the facts of his life. Ted has two brothers, Michael who is in prison in Texas, and Keith, who lives in Oklahoma.

Ted was imprisoned for the first time at 16, for a murder during a bungled robbery with others. After five and a half very difficult years in prison where he suffered both physical and mental abuse, he was very distrustful of others. He was released on parole in 1978. He was given a cheque for $200 and bought his own bus ticket. He was still unqualified. He told me that people in similar situations would live in the bins for a month or two, and then would end up where they had left off previously, back with the same bad influences such as gangs, again.

I asked Ted if he had any education whilst in prison, or had he been allowed to learn a skill that would have helped him when he was released, such as carpentry, plumbing or brick-laying? He told me that during the seventies when he was in prison: "Texas started an "Inforex Rehab Program" - using Inforex machines to transfer information from paper deeds of cars and trucks and boats to magnetic tape. They offered a one- year course on the Inforex system and a certificate of "qualification". I took the course for the required year and then put in another year training new operators and transferring countless titles of deed.

"When I was released - "rehabilitated" and trained and experienced in a useful occupation, I went out with my little certificate to find myself a job. The first place I went to was the phone company and the man in charge of personnel actually thought one of his friends had sent me as a joke! I told him that I was an Inforex operator with two years' training and would like a job. He looked at me for a minute and said, "This is a joke, right?" Then he got up from his desk and opened the door, motioning me out, he said something like, "I don't know who sent you but I'm a busy man and I don't have time for this." I was too shocked to be angry. I hadn't even gotten around to telling him I was an ex-prisoner!"

Well, operating on the assumption that a place that kept lots of records would need Inforex operators, I next went to the city water department and told their personnel manager that I had experience with the Inforex system and would like a job. He looked at me kind of strangely and asked if I was serious. I told him I certainly was. He asked my age and I told him I was twenty two, he sort of chuckled and said, "Son, you aren't old enough to have experience with the Inforex system. Nobody's used that for nearly ten years!"

Now, I suppose it is possible that the folks in charge of the prison Inforex programme didn't know that the system was ten years obsolete - but I doubt it."

He spent another five and a half years in prison before he found himself on Death Row:

"There are many people who are able to turn their lives around in prison, I was not one of them. Since the age of sixteen, I have spent my entire life (except for about three and a half years in the early Eighty's and almost six months in the late Eighty's) in prison. Those years behind bars didn't slow me down enough to think about who I was or where I was headed. The people who were in charge of the prisons honestly believed that it was their job to make prisoners so miserable that we wouldn't "want" to come back to prison. As if anyone truly wants to come to prison in the first place! But all they succeeded in doing was to create a new WORSE person. I took all of my anger and hatred and hurt and spite and I hid it deep down inside myself and nourished it and fed it. Hate was all I had left, so I clung to it and made it strong and it protected me from hurt."

When Ted came to Death Row hate still predominated his innermost feelings. He was very angry with himself and life. He took a long hard look at himself and tried to find out what had brought him to this dreadful point. I asked Ted had he thought about the death penalty when he committed murder? No, he admitted, that had never crossed his mind. It all happened so quickly. It was a question of drink-fuelled passion taking over, and with no other thought until it was too late.

This revelation reinforced my belief that the death penalty does not act as a deterrent to impulsive, let alone premeditated murders. Ted says:

"All of my problems in life: drugs and alcohol and crime can be traced back to my family and early childhood, children need love and support not just material support, but emotional support. In fact, I would say that a child who is loved and generally cared for and who knows that he or she is truly wanted and respected as a member of the family, any family, will never need or even want to look for love and acceptance and protection elsewhere. But if they can't find that at home or school or church or somewhere then they'll find substitutes and alternatives that provide the security and acceptance they need by gangs or else they turn to drugs and alcohol to deaden the pain of being alone. Every time I hear or see on the news about another school shooting or a murder or robbery committed by a child I just want to slap their parents senseless. Kids don't just wake up one morning and decide it might be fun to be a criminal. It takes years of neglect and frustration and even of desperation to turn a kid into a criminal.

Only a selfish parent, wrapped up in their little private world, could miss all the signs that are begging for help, love and understanding. I'm not saying that my screw-ups are my parent's fault, only that my actions and decisions have always had their roots in my childhood, including my later teen years from 16 to 21, which were spent in prison."

In Texas murderers are executed. In Europe they receive a prison sentence, during which time they are rehabilitated, for example, by re-education. In Europe they are not isolated and are able to worship in the chapel, have tuition, meet their visitors unshackled and be treated humanely. With good behaviour, they can be released earlier. In England "The Criminal Cases Review Commission", an independent body, reviews old cases. It has the power to bring old cases back to the courts and consequently,

41

some prisoners have been released after a fresh approach has been taken. From June 2002, UK law states that a minimum term, which is now reduced to 12, from 15 years, must be implemented in the majority of murder cases. The situation, as Ted explained, was very different in America:

"Here when the courts say "without parole", that's exactly what they mean. Now, in an ideal society that cared for each and every individual we could be provided with decent jobs that give some sort of meaning to life; jobs that would pay wages comparable to what anyone else doing that job would get, and that would give every prisoner a chance to earn and keep his human dignity and self respect and was given a purpose and reason for existing, while still being kept separate from the law abiding society."

All through his prison years Ted's Mom visited him constantly. While on Death Row, he asked her, "Will you be there at my execution?"

"No, son, I can't do that, I will hear about it all on TV." she replied.

"Where is she now?" I asked. He said that she had died, just last year, from cancer. "Oh! Ted, I am so sorry. I'll be your Mom."

I couldn't bear the thought of one of my sons having to ask me that same question and thought of the agony that she must have endured in seeing her son in this position. I thought of Ted's sadness watching his beloved mother each time she visited him, knowing that she too was under the threat of death. Then when she died, it must have been terrible being unable to go to her funeral. These and many more sad thoughts flashed through my mind as I instinctively offered to be his substitute Mom.

But Ted's step-dad had visited him over the years, sending money whenever he could for the meagre necessities of Ted's life on Death Row. Ted was very grateful to him.

The young German family were sitting talking to their friend nearby. The baby had been put on the floor to stretch.

I said to Ted, "Do feast your eyes on that little darling. I am sure that you do not see many little children." Then, I remembered and said, " I am going to be a grandmother next month" and annoyingly I burst into tears.

I felt mortified by my lack of control and resolved never to let go again. I would have to be strong from now on. Ted was rather embarrassed, but he did look and said, "What a precious little child."

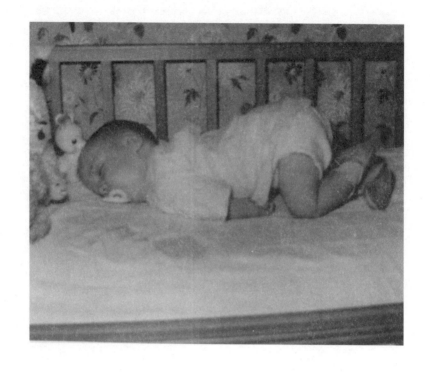

Ted at about three months old. Ted writes, "You see?
Once upon a time, there really were carefree days."

Chapter 5

Talking to Ted

Teach me to wait on You, Lord,
When my patience begins to fray
You alone have perfect timing,
Yours alone is the perfect way.

Ted continued answering my questions and told me that he shared his cell with Garry Miller. Fortunately they became friends, and had then been together for six years. Their "home" in Ellis One measured only 5ft by 9ft (1.5 x 2.7 meters). There was no air-conditioning in the cell, but if you had the money, a fan could be bought from the Commissary. Many of the cell windows were broken and never repaired. This is fine in summer, but dreadful in winter when it can get really cold at night. The floor and three of the cell's walls were concrete. The wall containing the door had open bars, affording no privacy whatsoever. This cell, "home", "house", there are many names given to it, contained two bunk beds, a washbasin and a lid-less lavatory. There was little room for personal belongings. In any case, the guards came in quite often and trashed the room, tearing down pictures from the walls, throwing them on the floor and stamping on them. This caused some men to get "real angry," especially if it was a particularly precious picture or photo.

Did Ted ever exercise in the open air I wondered?

"For outside exercise, we have a small 60' x 30' exercise yard that is attached to our dayroom. It has three brick walls and one wall of chain link fencing, which also covers the top. We have access to it seven days a week from 7am to 9pm, but I don't usually go out much. There is often a basketball or handball game in progress, and anyone who is not playing either stays off the yard or spends his time dodging balls and players. There is just too much chance of confrontation at those times, sort of like wandering on to a battlefield.

I take advantage of the yard at three different times; when it is too hot and humid for anyone else, when it is too wet or cold for anyone else, and when there is a football or baseball game or a blood and guts movie on TV. At these times there are generally only two or three others out besides me. So I do get outside exercise, though probably not as much as I should. I much prefer to stay indoors with my books and letters and lessons."

Ted and Garry made rosaries. They bought the materials and assembled the rosaries with tweezers, as they were not allowed any tools. They sent them to convents or hospitals by the parcel-load to be distributed. I did not think that the recipients realised that Ted and Garry paid for all that themselves as nothing was given to them in regards help or finance. Postage was especially expensive. They seldom received any thanks. Ted explained:

"We order our material from Our Lady's Rosary Makers. Garry always sends a dozen rosaries to a Franciscan Monastery in Chicago, but I pick a different person each month to send my dozen to. It's just a way for Garry and I to give our support to Christ's church."

Ted said he would send me one. I asked him if he knew their meaning or what they represented. He did not, so as he encouraged me, I told him that they chronicle the life of Our Lord, Jesus Christ, who Christians believe is God made Man, and who came on earth to save us, rose from the dead and ascended into Heaven. Ted saw similarities between the rosary and the prayer beads, called a mala, that are used in Eastern religions, and in Sant Mat where a prayer is also offered at each bead.

The guard came and spoke to Ted. Apparently we had 5 more minutes left. Four hours had raced by. I said that I would try and return the next day. I did not know how, but the visit had not been cancelled officially. Ted thanked me for coming. He did not get to see many new faces. It was also interesting to meet someone from overseas. If it were possible we would meet again the next day, I was not to worry, it would all work out.

Was it time already? Ted rose as soon as he saw the guard appear to escort him back to his cell. He raised his hand slightly in farewell. I waved back. I watched until he disappeared. I knew I must return the next day. Far from being lady bountiful, I was the one who had benefited from the experience of meeting this interesting individual. I had felt uplifted, meeting, listening and talking to him. The time had passed so quickly. It had seemed like four minutes rather than four hours. He had not made any excuses for himself, which I would have hated.

How was it that I had been so remiss in my thinking? How had I never given any thought to the plight of these individuals? They sat in their cages day after day, year after year. How was it that the world gave no thought to the condition of men sitting here waiting to die? How could we treat people so cruelly? The very fact that they were sentenced to death was unbelievable. Now I understand what the author of Dead Man Walking, Sister Helen Prejean, meant when she said:

"How can it be right to kill people, who kill people, to show people, that killing people is wrong?"

I had just met a man who was going to be put to death - legally! This was crazy. He was not mad. I am not mad. Just what was happening?

They say that love and time heals wounds and changes people. I'm not the same person I was ten years ago. Even my clothes are of a different style. I look at photographs of what I wore then and smile. My mind has also changed with my experiences. Hopefully I have matured.

People on Death Row have also changed. They are not the same as they were ten, eleven, twelve years ago. Repentance, sorrow, the need to make reparation is present in us all. We all expect to be forgiven of our sins. Life is sacred. God is compassionate even to hardened criminals. Surely, the State of Texas is above revenge?

On the way to the bins to dispose of my tins, I saw the tall young handsome man again. He was visiting a distinguished

48

looking white haired man who was in the end cage. There was more family here now. Two girls were crying. The man in the cage looked calm, the young ones looked ashen. I left that sad place, collected my passport, tickets, and car keys and walked out into the burning sunshine. The gates clanged shut behind with the same loud noise, but this time I was not afraid. In fact I wanted to return.

What a journey this man Ted had made! I wanted to hear more. He was so honest telling me about his life. He had come such a long way. Each day he had to confront himself. There was no escape. He had to try to accept himself and live as best he could with this death threat hanging over him, knowing that it would not go away. How could he still be sane? How could he have grown so much? This was a really good man to whom I had been speaking. He was not acting, one could tell the difference.

The steering wheel was too hot to touch, so I sat for a few minutes with the air conditioning on high. It would be good to return to Death Row the next day, if only to confirm what I had seen and felt today. Here was a very special person and a very different one from the one who had entered prison all those years ago.

One cannot forget the families of the murdered. Just to come to terms with the violent death of a loved one is bad enough. It must seem almost impossible to forgive the murderer.

In America there is a wonderful organisation called "Families of Victims of Crime Against the Death Penalty". Its aim is to heal the venom and hate built up after such crimes have been committed to their nearest and dearest. Some don't forgive and are encouraged not to by a sensationalist media always referring back to the past and demanding "an eye for an eye". Thereby keeping alive, for exploitation, the bitterness that does not affect them emotionally. This rancour is debilitating. It can often lead to long-term illness. It takes time, possibly a lifetime, and a great deal of love, to nurture mercy, compassion and forgiveness.

The murderer's family are also victims. They are often forgotten victims, jeered at and hounded. It takes courage to cope with this public humiliation. How must the families feel if the "murderer" is found to be innocent after his death? That must also be hard to forgive and rationalise.

Forgiveness is God-given. It takes love and time. It is not easy to understand, but the Holy Spirit does give us strength if we ask, persevere and have faith.

The morning mist had lifted. The landscape shimmered in the heat and the cattle sheltered under the trees. My nervousness had been replaced by an unexpected humility. This kind of suffering was happening to a minority daily. There was no one on Death Row with money Ted had told me.

I found my way back to Hospitality House to a worried Joy. She needed to know if we were going to be allowed to see Lesley once we got to San Antonio. We needed a phone-card to call the County jail. The Huntsville Post Office was the nearest place to buy them, so I drove there and with Bob's directions, I found it quite easily. Betty Mathews, a Death Row Chaplain and her friend, whom I had met at the vigil the night before, were in line at the Post Office. They asked whether we were going to the vigil that night. I told them the story of our San Antonio journey to visit Lesley so they would understand if we did not turn up.

Handing over the phone card to Joy back at the house, I attacked some food. I was starving. Joy came off the telephone. The news from San Antonio was positive. We would be able to see Lesley. But Bob intervened and said that we would arrive too late now to get to see Lesley tonight.

"It would be much better," he said, "if you stayed the night here in Hospitality House again, Margôt could then go and see Ted early in the morning. Then both of you, could go straight away to San Antonio to see Lesley."

So it was agreed. I was going to see Ted again. What a change from that morning! Now, I was looking forward to returning to Death Row.

I must have talked for at least two hours with Joy about my experience on Death Row for it was now time for the execution vigil. We again walked round the corner and crossed the busy main road to "The Walls". The first people I saw standing there was the same handsome looking family I had seen that morning at Ellis One. Suddenly, I realised with a shock that the gentleman who had smiled at me then in the end cage was going to his death that night at 6.00pm. No wonder the family had looked so unhappy.

The relations who did not go into "The Walls" as witnesses were sitting on the grass under a tree, one with a babe in arms.

51

They had some supporters round them who made a fuss if anyone tried to approach or take a photo.

It was the same scenario as before. The families of the victim walked first across the road into "The Walls", followed by the family of the man about to die. The tall, handsome man I had stood behind in the queue to get into the prison that morning was now going up the steps of "The Walls" to see his kinsman die.

We, outside, stood waiting and praying, holding candles hoping that there would be a stay of execution. Suddenly, the guards emerged from the door leading from "The Walls" followed by the haughty, congratulatory swagger of the victim's family, and then the sad, dejected relatives of the perpetrator's family. The tall young man was supporting an older lady, maybe his mother. She had difficulty managing the steps. I felt very sad and uncertain that this could be happening to these people today, but it had just happened. The bored guards standing around treated this as routine. A man had just been legally killed. Their attitude suggested that he deserved it, so why the fuss? This patronizing attitude is a result of their training to treat prisoners with little or no respect. This was wrong. It could be likened, in my imagination, to the Christians in Ancient Rome being thrown to the lions.

Only one TV camera and presenter was there to record the death of a citizen. They managed to look fairly uninterested. This was another routine job. The people they interviewed, depending on their views and relationship, if any, to the victim, looked animated or concerned, and seemed to enjoy the brief moment of airtime.

The banners were again folded and collected. People drifted away. The busy guards took down the yellow tape, which separated the public from the witnesses in front of "The Walls". Normality returned quickly and easily to this little stage.

"The Walls", also known as "the killing house", in Huntsville, Texas. It is within these walls that all state executions are undertaken. It formerly housed the notorious electric chair "old Sparky", which is now thankfully a museum piece. Note the anti – Death Penalty demonstration in progress. September, 1997.

Chapter 6
Silence

From the world I receive
Scorn and derision
They see the man who was...

The next morning I was glad of the companionship of Heidi, from Germany, on our drive to the Ellis One Unit. She always stayed at Hospitality House as she had been coming for a few years to visit her friend on Death Row. She could not understand American thinking. According to Amnesty International statistics, 26% of the men on Death Row were innocent. Many had learning difficulties. All had a history of dysfunctional family life from birth and many had a history of sexual abuse from childhood. She was not making excuses, but mostly they did not stand a chance in life at all, she said. I was learning a lot.

We travelled the same route as the day before, but this time I was looking forward to the encounter with Ted. On arrival we saw a queue of people waiting to enter the prison. We parked, and thank goodness, Heidi was with me. The guards, who could have been much more pleasant, told me that I did not have a "special" visit, just a two-hour one. They intimidated me so much that I did not reply. But Heidi would have none of it. She stormed up to the guard and said,

"This lady has come all the way from England therefore she is down for a "special".

A special visit lasts for four hours for people who travel further than 500kms, I learnt much later. An "ordinary" visit lasts for only two hours. Quite a difference to a prisoner who does not receive many visitors and for the visitor who has come a long way! The guard picked up the phone and spoke to someone inside at reception. After a while I was given the all clear for a "special". One good turn deserves another. I was very grateful to Heidi and said that if our exit times coincided, I would drive her back to Hospitality House. She was returning to Germany that evening.

Eventually my name was called and I could proceed through the first and second gates, both of which clanged behind me, as before. This time I was eager to go up the path and into Death Row. What a change! This time I did not feel like one of the prisoners but as someone going to meet a friend. Heidi was already in the reception area and was just coming away from the visitors' restroom, which I did not know had existed.

Today I had a different number, but it was the same procedure as the day before. I entered the hall via the same doorway, with the writing above it. Well there we are; I am on my own. I was not disturbed by the thought.

The prisoner is only collected when the visitor is in the building. Then a guard is sent along to the cellblock and the prisoner is strip-searched before being handcuffed and escorted down to the visiting area. This all takes a long time and depends on the mood of the guard. There is no privacy. A male or female guard can make the strip search. The prisoners are totally at their mercy.

Ted likes root beer, so I went to get sustenance for him from the drinks dispenser. Perhaps he is not allowed to buy it in the Commissary. As I sit waiting for Ted, I watch the various prisoners as they pass in front of me to go to their respective seats. I look into their faces. Do I see a murderer? No, I see ordinary men.

The visitors are varied; a lawyer; a priest or a family member. Some visitors are old. Some are young. A lady sitting near me is very sad. She is trying not to cry as she waits for her man to arrive. The noise level is getting annoying, the crashing of steel doors, the voices raised in anger or laughter and the shouts of the guards to each other. This is a stressful situation. Suddenly, Ted and his guard arrive in front of me and the noise disappears as I concentrate on talking and listening to him.

It was with smiles and genuine pleasure that we greeted each other. I was really pleased to see Ted and continue our conversation. I had not had such a deep talk for a long time. That might sound really strange. I have a busy family life with responsibilities and pressures. Maybe I had not had the time, opportunity or the necessity recently to examine my life and ask myself,

"Where am I going? Am I going in the right direction? Could I put more of God into my life?"

Ted had more time to ask himself these questions. He had been on Death Row for two months when he wrote a poem. Initially he had been very angry, with the world, authority, and the law, in fact with everyone, including himself. He is a sensitive man but also, I suspect, quick tempered. His early poems show his anger at finding himself in this position. "Silence" won him an award and was published.

Silence.   *Ted C. Cole*   *8.1.1988*
I sit here — alone
not just by myself,
but really alone.

I hear others around me.
They speak and say nothing;
They hear, but don't listen.

I talk to myself,
I talk to the walls ...
I only hear echoes of Silence.

I sit here — alone —
waiting, day after day,
to hear a voice that will
say something.
I'm tired of waiting.

Someone,
Supposedly much wiser than I, once said:
"Silence is Golden."
The man was a fool.

Ted told me that: "Silence was scribbled a very short two months later after first arriving here on Death Row in June 1988. At that time I still had no personal "property" – I had a pencil and some papers and a cup to drink from, and I had a few photographs to remind me of all I'd just thrown away. I was lonely and depressed. There was absolutely no one I could turn to. I couldn't even afford postage to write to Mom.

"I was trying to come to some sort of inner acceptance. It occurred to me that there are three different types of silence: there is the purely objective lack of sound that is sometimes experienced by a lucky few individuals; there is a mystical sort of silence, in which one turns away from and overcomes the outer physical senses and so is able to hear that "still, small voice" within; and there is a third, terrible silence whose clamour is almost deafening – the "silence" of a madhouse or a prison. It's constant, unceasing talk with absolutely nothing of consequence ever being spoken. Now I look for that second mystical silence. I found it once – a wonderful and awesome place of peace and solitude, but it's eluded me ever since.

"The silence I wrote of then would be more properly termed a total apathy. No one cared and no one cared that no one cared! But now, almost ten years later, I know that as long as I can turn within for consolation I don't have to turn to anyone around me. Am I still angry? No, I'm frequently frustrated, but that's just part of life. Except in very rare instances, though, my anger has diminished to almost nothing."

Ted was pleased that I liked his poetry. Bob had shown one to me on the wall at Hospitality House that Ted's mother had placed there before she died. His Mom was always his biggest fan. As Ted was to later write, his poems were more than simply an emotional outlet:

"I've often wondered whether my poems ever had any effect on the people who heard them, or if people simply considered them to be a silly way to pass the time of day. ...I've always wanted to be a "somebody" - to be able to leave this world knowing that my brief presence made some sort of positive impact on at least one person."

That morning, when Ted realized that I was able to visit, he asked the guard for a favour. He gave him a rosary and asked that it be taken to the reception desk at the front door with my name on it. I would hope to pick it up when I left. This was a big request. The guards are told to treat all prisoners as though they, the prisoners, had raped the guards' mothers. Consequently, a bad attitude prevailed. One or two of the guards had the sense to see that not all the prisoners were evil. Some guards though, relish their jobs. Human nature being what it is, some enjoyed their power over the less fortunate and helpless.

I asked Ted about his lawyer: "My Attorney, as he is called in here, is Carlton McLarty and he's one of the best Appeal Attorneys in Texas. The problem in my case is the Judge. You see Carlton is my "Attorney of Record" and he is the only one who is recognized by the court to act on my behalf. However, when he accepted a position with the Federal Public Defenders Office back in 1993, he became unable to represent anyone below the federal level. But as long as the Judge insists on keeping Carlton as my Attorney of Record, no one else can represent me, either! Officially (on paper at least) Carlton is my Attorney legally, even though he's one of the very best at his job, he can't touch my case. The Judge refuses to respond to requests from me, from Carlton and even from the District Attorney for the state! It's his court, and he can handle things anyway he wants to for just as long as the people keep electing him to the bench. There is not a thing I can do about it."

I could not understand the ethics of the American legal system that had resulted in Ted being without a lawyer all this time. It seemed to me from his statements that power and popularity from the electorate seemed to be of tremendous importance and the driving force of the legal system, rather than justice. I felt horrified that a man in line to be executed had no legal help. He had been forgotten, was this deliberate I wondered, Ted did not know if this was an unusual occurrence. He tried to pass it off as amusing, I realised that was his way of telling me something important. I did not know how to tackle this situation.

I said to Ted that Joy and I were invited by Lesley to tell the world what was going on in Texas prisons and that was what we would do. We would expose this amoral state of affairs as well as we could, as soon as we could.

I went out to the reception area a couple of times on Ted's advice, to check that the rosary had arrived. At last I was able to put Ted's mind at rest. It was waiting for me, having been carried by the accommodating guard, scrutinised and passed by the relevant authority. "It is made of rose quartz. It is one of my best!" Ted said.

I promised that I would write to him, although I'm not a good correspondent. Ted said that I must put his number on the envelope, with the address, otherwise it would be thrown away – 'junked' or sent back home, depending on the mood of the mailroom assistant. Some people put their block, cell and tier level on correspondence, but it isn't really necessary. They change cells quite often. Their number is the important factor. The mailroom will do the rest on arrival, after they have opened, read and censored all the incoming mail for each Death Row prisoner.

Ted had told his cellmate, Garry, all about my previous day's visit. They wondered if he could send Garry's name and number to me, in case someone in the Catholic community would write to him.

Garry had become a Catholic three years ago. He had had visits from Deacon Tom McKinney, the new Death Row Chaplain at the Ellis One Unit. The Deacon actually requested that he be assigned to Death Row from the local church. Ted told me:

"The Death Row Chaplaincy is not an easy job to do, so he either has a genuine desire to help, or he just doesn't know what he's gotten himself into. Only time will tell, I guess".

61

Ted wished that he could go to a quiet, serene place that could be set aside and reserved for prayer and meditation. I wished that for him too. I was shocked that "murderers" were not allowed to go to the chapel on the premises, or that they did not have their own chapel.

"I wish the administration would allow us to have small statues or candles or icons, or even a small crucifix to hang on the wall. Just something that could be kept in a prominent place to be a constant reminder that there's more to our world here than mere concrete and steel".

I told Ted that in November, the next month, I was fortunate enough to be able to go to Medjugorje, a small village in Herzegovina. Jennifer McGlade, a friend from our convent school days, had visited there before and had often urged me to try and make the pilgrimage with her. It had happened that one stressful day that Spring, just after I had recovered from a bout of bronchitis, we met as we shopped in Llandudno. I agreed with her, I needed to go to Medjugorje on a Pilgrimage. She booked us for the following November. I never thought then that I would be going to Texas the month before.

I said to Ted that I would offer the visit for the abolition of the death penalty in America, especially Texas. At this point, Ted told me that he was not happy with the thought of life imprisonment under the harsh conditions, in which he was living. He felt that those petitioning on behalf of Death Row prisoners were not aware of the daily torments of living in this kind of prison. Many prisoners had tried to commit suicide, or drop their appeals, because of the inhumane treatment from the justice system, the penal system, administrators and the guards on a daily basis. This surprised me. This thought had not occurred to me, but when he explained it that way I realized that it is more courageous to try and live under these conditions than to commit suicide.

Ted outlined his thinking to me: "Thanks to the scare tactics used by today's politicians, the only alternative that most people will accept to the death penalty is life without parole. In an ideal society that might not be too bad. We could be provided with decent jobs that give some sort of meaning to life. But this is not an ideal society. People don't care, and I don't believe they ever will. Human life means nothing unless it's a member of his or her own family or circle of friends." Ted neatly sums this up in his poem, A Garden In Which To Roam (See Poems).

Again the four hours sped by. I was really sad to see the guard arrive and say,

"Five minutes more, Cole".

It was time to say goodbye. I promised to write. I much prefer to talk on the telephone, which, of course, was impossible. Prisoners do not have access to the telephone unless it is to the lawyer or sick relative and that depends on whether one has the money. It is usually reserved for last words just before execution, on a reverse charge call, if one has any family or friends left by then.

The authorities try to discourage visits. It is another way to break a man's spirit. Visits can be cut short with no explanation and no warning even after a long, expensive journey has been undertaken.

I put my hand on the glass to say goodbye, as the guard came to escort Ted back to his cell. I could not believe that life for Ted would be back to that tiny, shared cell. Here was I going out into the bright, strong sunshine, with a rosary clutched in my hands that had been made by a man with tweezers who was going to be killed soon. Life on Death Row had certainly brought Ted very close to God. He had accepted his sins with remorse and sorrow. He had asked God to forgive him. He had left behind anger, hatred and recriminations. He had opened his soul and focused on purity and truth. Despite the daily indignities he had found some peace in his monastic lifestyle.

What a revelation! Never in my life had I thought that I would visit a prisoner on Death Row, let alone find such a lovely person. I hoped that Ted's struggle to find an inner calm would set an example to others as an alternative way to handle the situation they were in, guards and prisoners alike. It cannot be easy for the "Gestapo", as Ted sometimes calls the guards, when he "has the blues".

Some guards, unable to cope with the situation, had left Death Row. We heard this from a lady who worked in a Huntsville photography shop. Her father had been a prison guard. He left as it made him ill to see good people treated so badly, and the not so obedient, treated inhumanely. It was unnecessary, amongst many other insults, to 'trash' an inmate's prized possessions, rip photos off the wall and stamp on them. They were already paying the ultimate punishment for their crimes. There was no need for the guards or administration to mete out further vindictive treatment.

Prisoners who react negatively to the situation are placed into dungeons within the prison. Their only contact with anyone is to be given food each day. Food comes in the shape of a loaf containing all the necessary minerals and vitamins. They are given this at a set time each day and then they are left in solitary confinement for long periods. This can be for weeks, rather than days, so one can only imagine the atmosphere down there. Ted had not been in trouble for bad behaviour himself but was punished only when everyone else was in trouble. The whole unit was then put on "lock-down" which meant no recreation outside or inside, no work, and being left in the cell for periods of up to twenty-four hours, for weeks sometimes. During this time, their food consists usually of frozen sandwiches three times a day. It also means no shopping at the Commissary, so if one runs out of something that is just too bad. Stamps, envelopes and drinking chocolate powder seem to be the main things that Ted runs out of.

As before, when I left the prison, the car was too hot to sit in and it was impossible to touch the steering wheel. Betty Mathews, a Chaplain who came frequently to Death Row, had given Heidi a lift to the airport. I hurried back as Joy was waiting for me to start our long journey to San Antonio. With a shock I realized I was originally only coming here to accompany Joy. What a great deal I had encountered, learnt, and hopefully, would live up to in my correspondence with this gentle man.

Ted writes, "The good ol' days? This was taken just before I was taken to the Children's Home."

Chapter 7

San Antonio Jail

Dear Lord Who dwells within us all,
Ignore my word, I pray
And hear instead, O Perfect One,
The things my heart will say.

Lesley, the prisoner to whom Joy had been writing, had been taken to San Antonio, where the judge gave him an execution date. It was televised to gain maximum publicity for the elected judge.

When we arrived at the busy Jail, the main police station in the centre of San Antonio, Joy stepped forward and spoke pleadingly with the kindly looking Hispanic policeman in charge,

"We have come all the way from England, please may we have longer than half an hour with Lesley Gosch?"

I was unaware that we were only allowed half an hour. I had assumed that Joy would have longer. The man looked at us carefully then he said to me,

"And I suppose that you also want extra time, too?" I agreed readily. He nodded and let us through the security gates. Inside another guard asked,

"Have you anything to deposit?" He pointed to a notice that read, "All Weapons To Be Left Here".

The instruction was also illustrated, so you couldn't mistake the message, but we had nothing to deposit.

At the top floor, we gave Lesley's name and ours to the guard who told us to sit and wait. We managed to find chairs even though there were many people in the waiting room. From where we sat, we could see along a corridor, into the room beyond where young offenders came up from the cells wearing bright orange jumpsuits, standard jail clothes. They were searched before being escorted to one cubicle out of a line of small, three walled areas that had a stool screwed to the floor and a telephone attached to one of the wooden partitions. No ceiling, lots of noise.

Their parents, wives or girlfriends were then allowed into the other side of the glazed partitioned cubicle. For Death Row prisoners though the procedure was different. In the room where we sat there were three doors leading into three booths. Eventually, when Joy's name was called to meet Lesley she was told to enter the first cubicle through a door to the left of where we were sitting.

Lesley arrived via a back door to her booth. He also wore an orange jumpsuit and was handcuffed behind his back. He was un-cuffed and the door behind him was locked. He sat on a stool in a very small area. Joy could not hear what Lesley said as there was very thick glass between them and no telephone. She came out of the cubbyhole and spoke to the guard. She told him that they could not hear each other.

He called for Lesley's guard on his telephone and Lesley was re-handcuffed and moved to the next cubicle. That was just the same, the guard then apologetically explained that Death Row prisoners were not permitted telephones to communicate directly with the visitor. This deliberate petty mindedness amazed us. Communication was extremely difficult. Joy had to bend down and try and speak through thick glass re-enforced with steel wire. Conversation was almost impossible as neither could hear the other clearly. It amounted almost to lip-reading she told me later.

As I sat waiting outside Lesley's room, I observed the many sad people, mainly Mexican or coloured, who came and went. A young white female visitor slithered into one of the cubicles. She was struggling to co-ordinate her movements. Was she drunk or on drugs? A downcast mother and father sat near me, the only other white visitors. They could not meet anyone's eyes. People would come in and sit down to wait for their names to be called.

When the officer, sitting on a high dais with his back to a wall, called out the names, those people went along a small corridor and sat down in the room beyond, picked up the telephone and spoke to their offspring. At least at this stage in their incarceration they had a telephone even though their time to visit was limited to half an hour.

I wondered what sadness or circumstances had brought them here. Where would they end up? Not on Death Row I hoped. The room filled up. There were no seats left. People had to stand. Some looked weary as though they had come straight from work or because they had travelled a great distance. They could also have felt weary having been in similar situations previously.

69

"Gosch, second visit,"

a loud voice called out over the hubbub. It brought me back to earth. It had been an unspoken agreement between Joy and I that she would have the extra time allocated to me by the guard on the front desk. I had not expected to be called. I quickly jumped to my feet and went into Lesley and Joy's cubicle. It was hot and stuffy. Joy looked tired. Lesley could hardly see me. He had a small face behind thick glasses and very dark hair. Rotund, came to my mind as I looked at him. I said, "Hello."

This was the first time that we had met. I was very anxious though, as the guard outside the room was expecting someone to leave this room soon. I told Joy that I would disappear downstairs whilst she had the second hour here with Lesley. I would wait for her in the main reception area. She did not realise that an hour had passed, but was pleased to have more time. She asked if I would like to stay and have a word with him. I would have enjoyed that but I felt somehow that the guard would not allow it. As it was, we were on extra time.

On reflection, I realised that I was intimidated by the surroundings and did not wish to overstep the rules. Perhaps no one would have noticed if I had stayed. I said a rapid "Good luck and farewell," to Lesley whom I knew to be embroiled in legal work trying to overcome his dreadful sentence. I quickly slipped out of the stuffy cubicle, over to the lift, which took me down to the ground floor and the general waiting area.

The drab hall was full of noisy people, talking loudly. Policemen, with guns in holsters round their hips walked briskly through, some sauntered looking at everyone. I sat down on a vacant wooden bench. Bright lights. Small high windows. Old, torn posters on the parchment coloured walls. Cigarette smoke. The clangour and clank of lift doors moving, wide steps leading up somewhere, it was a tense, raucous atmosphere. I needed to relax, to try and be peaceful.

The benches filled up, a graceful Mexican lady, with beautiful teenage twins, spoke to me. Her name was Maria. One of the twins went upstairs to the jail. Her boyfriend had been arrested. Because I did not understand Spanish, it was difficult to communicate with her in detail. We managed to pass some information to each other mostly by signs and a cocktail of Spanish and English words. It was a heartfelt time and I was warmed by the confidences that she shared.

It must be hard if one does not read English, or has little education. They were trying to find a lawyer/attorney. The only lawyer her boyfriend would be given would be a court appointed attorney (who for various reasons could not find any other work). This work is poorly paid. Good lawyers can command huge sums elsewhere.

It would be very difficult, if a lawyer did not speak Spanish, to understand a client without an interpreter. There were other 'Foreign Nationals' residing in Texas who must find it equally difficult to communicate with the authorities.

71

Maria wished that she and her family could leave Texas for one of the other American States where they did not have the death penalty. She was very sad.

Joy arrived after an hour. She said that she felt exhausted, but happy to have met and at least spoken with Lesley for two hours. We left that busy nerve centre of people who had been arrested on suspicion, fighting for their rights. We went outside into the evening sunshine and rapidly left San Antonio in our car. Under happier circumstances, I would have liked to explore this beautiful, historical city steeped in the lore of the "Battle of the Alamo".

We drove along the freeway without speaking for many miles. I began to relax in the companionable silence and the motion of the car. I always enjoy driving and especially in the evening when the road was fairly empty. Also I wanted to be near Houston airport for our flight home the next day.

At about midnight we finally decided we would begin to look for somewhere to sleep. The Motel we chose had friendly staff and they gave us a large bedroom. Sitting down later with a cup of hot chocolate ready for bed, we talked at length about our experiences of that long day.

The next morning we slept late. After a breakfast of coffee and doughnuts, we took some photographs by the Motel pool with the assistance of the jolly receptionist who seemed to find our accents amusing. We set off on our last leg of the Texan journey to find Houston Airport and the car hire depot. Because we had difficulty finding the latter we arrived late to book in at the airport. Consequently we were allotted seats that were separated by many rows. It was suggested that when we embarked we should ask our steward if someone would change places so that we could sit together.

This was duly done but the people on either side of me, for various reasons, did not want to change seats. Consequently, they were very nice to me afterwards. The rather large man on my left began to tell me about his holiday. He'd been "huntin' and shootin'" in the mountains and staying in deluxe log cabins with the best guides possible. Very necessary he thought, when chasing big game. After he had exhausted his monologue, he asked condescendingly and with that 'ready to be bored' tone of voice, "What have you been doing in Houston?"

I had been reticent about mentioning our visit. Now I let him have it right between the eyes. "We have been visiting someone on Death Row."

He was amazed. When he said that he was a lawyer in Brussels for European Human Rights I was the one to be amazed! We had a mutually informative conversation for the rest of the journey to Schiphol. He promised to look into the situation. Who knows, perhaps he did.

After our arrival at Schiphol airport, we had a six-hour wait for a connecting flight, which meant that we could continue discussing our amazing meetings in the Texan prison. For the last lap of our journey home Joy and I were able to sit together and talked, it seemed, non-stop. John was delighted to see us back safely and he drove us home with evident happiness.

Two friends of Joy came to see us in Deganwy for tea on our return. Piadad, a nun from Joy's Community of White Sisters, was shortly going to open a new house or Community in the Philippines. Paul, a vicar, had been given a year's sabbatical from his parish. They had met while on a three-month retreat at St. Beuno's, a Jesuit retreat house in St. Asaph. Paul's wife, very understandingly, supported his wish to spend some of his sabbatical in fasting, contemplation and prayer.

They listened raptly to our experiences. They compared Ted's cell and his achievement at fasting, contemplation and prayer with awe. How different to accomplish these things in the quiet, peaceful surroundings of a detached country house with only birds and cattle to break the silence.

As Ted had told me on my visit, "You would think that after being surrounded by noise for 10 years that I'd be used to it but unfortunately that's not just the case. Being in a constant din, everything does tend to sort of merge into the background and I can ignore a lot of it. Come to think of it, I can't remember what true "silence" is anymore!"

We had been back a few days when I invited Joy to a Noson Goffie, at the home of Ivor and Lily, our neighbours on Deganwy promenade. This was a Welsh coffee evening. All the proceeds were going towards a new chapel roof. It was well attended. One of the guests was the Liverpool Daily Post Features

Editor, Iorwerth Roberts. During our conversation, I told them where we had been. He was most interested and a few days later a reporter showed up on Joy's doorstep. The resulting article started some media interest as the story of Lesley Gosch, a prisoner on Death Row and the nun from Wales, was taken up by the Welsh press, TV and radio stations. Somehow we were doing what Lesley and Ted wanted - to tell the world what was going on in Texas.

"This one was taken on Mother's Day by a guard at the Ferguson Unit of the Texas Department of Criminal Justice. I was 17 years old, doing my first stretch in prison for murder. Not a happy time for either one of us, but mom and I managed to get through our 2-hour visit without too many harsh words being said."

Chapter 8
Medjugorje Pilgrimage.

Poets say that love is blind,
But I know that isn't true.
Love sees with much more clarity
Than most mere mortals do.

I had left Ted on October 3rd 1997. As promised, he immediately wrote a letter containing a self-typed pamphlet of his poems. He wrote on the flyleaf:

To my newest friend Margôt With Love From Death Row.

He said "I mainly just wanted to let you know that you may do whatever you wish with my poems. My major interest was in simply writing down what I felt within; that having been done, I leave them in the hands of fate. I would only ask that, should the opportunity ever arise for any of them to be published for pay, all profits from them should be given to a children's charity. I doubt that such an opportunity would ever present itself, but one never knows. Please feel free to share the poems – and even my letters, for that matter – with whomever you care to."

Ted also sent me his cellmate's details: Garry D. Miller, No. 947, in the hope that I might be able to find someone to correspond with him from the Catholic community. Subsequently, Garry received a letter from Charlotte Dugdale, a student from

76

Treaddur Bay, Anglesey. They enjoyed writing to each other from 1997 until he was executed in December 2001.

In his letters, Ted told me about his prison address 'H-17, 3-11'. 'H' is for House. '17' is the Wing. '3' is the tier. '11' is the cell. They are all moved around frequently, so this information is often wrong before he receives my letters. 'Death Row' is not needed on the address, as their ID numbers are different from any other Texan prisoner. Prisoners are not allowed to receive blank postcards or anything with staples. Books can only come from specified outlets, such as Dillon's in Nottingham, England, which has permission from the Ellis One Warden to send books to prisoners direct. This is the dictate of the Governor, or Warden of this particular prison.

In my letters I try to give Ted a description of my life and how I live it. This gives him a window into the outside world and something else to think about, besides prison life, the bad treatment of the guards and the inevitable death sentence, hanging over him like the Sword of Damocles.

Ted wrote and thanked me for A Simple Prayer Book, which he was enjoying reading. He had been unaware that there were so many different prayers for so many different occasions. He also thanked me for the Daily and Sunday Missals. These books contain the order of service and the prayers that are said at Daily and Sunday Mass for three years. In the Daily Missal, the name of the Saint of the day with a small explanatory history is included. The texts are absolute gems taken from the Bible. Each word and sentence means so much. One lovely example from the Daily Mass is, "Protect us from all anxiety".

He did not realize that Mass was celebrated daily and with different prayers added each day according to the liturgical season.

Ted was enthusiastic about meeting the new Catholic Chaplain, Deacon McKinney, whom Garry had talked about:

"I went to Communion services yesterday morning and had a chance to meet and speak with Deacon McKinney. He actually seems to have a genuine desire to help those of us who truly want his help. He's going to start an RCIA [Right of Christian Initiation] class soon – he's only waiting for a couple of his outside volunteers to finish a special class so they're qualified to teach it. This will be the first time that there has been a RCIA class here for Death Row. Can you believe it? I'm looking forward to getting started with it."

Ted said that religion and spirituality were not high on the administration's list of priorities as far as Death Row prisoners were concerned, and that there was a need for a Warden who believed in Redemption for Death Row prisoners, as well as a chapel and a religious inspirational library.

Deacon McKinney rang Benedictine monasteries all over the country trying to find groups or organizations with the funds to send books, tape players and cassette tapes for the Death Row men. Ted and Garry also wrote begging letters to Bishops and Archbishops telling them what they needed to send to Deacon McKinney. Religious bookstores were another target for used or damaged books to be purchased at a discount. The Catholic Home

Study Courses sent some lessons for Ted to study, which he enjoyed. He said he would be sad when they finished. The begging letters and a request for a catalogue about religious books were fruitful. On 20th December he received a package from "The Pauline Books & Media" which contained some interesting religious books. His favourite was Common Mystic Prayer by Gabriel Diefenbach, O.F.M. Cap.

In November 1997 I went on the Medjugorje pilgrimage that I had told Ted about. This was my first visit to Yugoslavia. It had been organised by Tony Hickey of the Manchester Medjugorje group. Sister Jennifer had been several times before, usually in the Spring.

Jennifer McGlade, a friend from our convent school days in Llandudno, had become a nun and then a teacher. Eventually, she took the headship of our local Catholic school, Stella Maris. Under her leadership the school thrived. My mother used to say that Sister Jennifer was very well liked and that the local children were fortunate to have such a good teacher and school.

It was deep cold winter in November when Sister Jennifer and I went to Medjugorje. This is where the apparitions of Mary, the Mother of Jesus, began to occur on Wednesday 24th June 1981. Her message to the world is that God exists, for us to be at peace, and to reconcile our differences. On the 10th anniversary of the apparitions war broke out in Yugoslavia. Three of the six visionaries continue to have apparitions. About 20 million people from all over the world have been to Medjugorje to pray and say the Rosary together. They try to meet at least one of the visionaries whilst they are there.

From Split airport in Croatia we travelled by luxury coach along a breathtakingly beautiful route, through small villages, then up a mountain road that climbed and twisted higher and higher. On one side were the ragged grey mountains on the other there was a sheer drop into an icy blue sea.

We eventually left this main road and headed into the hinterland. We passed into a war-torn countryside of burnt out cottages and derelict farms. There were no cattle, just a few thin goats on the roadside, plucking at the grass that grew around abandoned cars. We were now in Bosnia. Our guide told us that every family had lost someone in the war. Medjugorje itself had not been bombed. There was now a lull in the fighting.

Night had fallen by the time we arrived at our destination. We had been divided into small groups. Sister Jennifer and I were in a guesthouse near to the church in the middle of Medjugorje. We shared a simple room. We had an excellent evening meal with the other guests. Our itinerary was produced. Our pilgrimage had begun.

Evening prayers were said in an elevated outdoor arena. It had a roof and tiered seats around three walls. Wide steps led the way to the seats and to the central space where Mass could also be celebrated. After prayers and petitions, we wandered towards the sound of a guitar and a man singing. He sat near hundreds of flickering candles in red holders. Pilgrims huddled around him and joined in the popular hymns and songs of devotion. The stars were very bright in the dark, inky sky as they looked down on this peaceful scene.

The next day was windy as we made our way to the vast, tented arena to hear about the six Visionaries. As an international pilgrimage centre, Medjugorje is only some twenty years old, so we had to sit in an enormous marquee, or exhibition tent as a more stable structure has yet to be built. It was filled with hundreds of rows of chairs. Meetings in different languages were given there at specified times. It had a noisy loudspeaker system that fought with a screaming wind that had found its way in through gaps where thick ropes tied each section of the tent together. In hot weather these flaps would all be rolled up to allow fresh air to circulate.

Our own Manchester Pilgrimage, and the many other English speaking or understanding pilgrims assembled there, heard that the main message of Medjugorje is:

Prayer. It is so essential to pray, pray and pray, especially for world peace.

Father Slavko Barbaric, the Visionaries' priest, addressed us. His message was compelling:
"He who prays surrenders his past, his present and his future into the hands of the Father, who reigns over time and space and who knows us and loves us. And this is what faith really is – to surrender one's heart and whole life to God. When we think like this, it becomes clear that the calls to prayer are primarily for our benefit - therefore we must respond."

A congregation of hundreds listened intently. It was heartening to hear that we must not be afraid. He pointed out that, "In the Biblical texts we find 365 times the call: Do not be afraid! I am with you! God does not want man to live in fear, because man is not well when he is afraid. Therefore Mary can tell us: He who prays, does not need to be afraid, because prayer is the meeting with God. Thus all the sacraments are an aid to deliverance from fear, and especially the sacrament of reconciliation, when we know that God forgives us through the priest and we are then at peace with him. Peace returns, fear departs."

Later we heard Vicka, one of the Visionaries, speak outside her house. We stood packed into the narrow lane. Many stood on walls to catch a glimpse of her. Her interpreter told us many things that Mary, the Mother of Jesus had told her. Above all, she said, we must talk to Jesus and thank Him. We must have hope. Mary thanked us for coming to Medjugorje in response to Her call. We must pray, pray, pray. She would be with us all, at all times.

After a light lunch, each day, time was our own. Mary, the Mother of Jesus, appeared to the Visionaries at the top of mount Podbrdo. As a group, we climbed Podbrdo following the Way of the Cross with a leader. The first time I saw it I thought that I would never climb that vertical mountain. I thought that I would leave it to others to climb. But somehow I found myself walking there with Jennifer and our group.

It was rough underfoot. Stones rolled under our tread. Some people scrambled up. Some plodded. Some had sticks. Some walked bare foot up and down. Others ascended arm in arm, supporting each other. I was very impressed. How brave they were. It was something that I would never be able to do. However, the next day, I found myself supporting an elderly lady up and down the steep path. My asthma had not been a problem. Miracles happen all the time.

On the mountaintop a huge cross has been erected. It can be seen for miles. Called Krizevac, it is said to light up at certain times, although there is no electricity on the mountain. Some people also see the sun moving in circles. One of the recurring messages from Gospa, the Croatian for Mother of God is, "Peace, pray for peace."

This was so relevant as from the summit we saw aeroplanes and helicopters circling in the distance; our local guide explained that the political situation was critical at the moment.

Nearly everywhere we went people prayed fervently, saying the Rosary, aloud or silently, walking alone or in groups. It is that kind of place. The 6 p.m. Mass at the parish Church of St. James, run by the Franciscans, was packed. Some people went nearly an hour early to make sure of a seat. The area around the outside of the Church was also crowded. On one side of the pale cream square, under the trees, were small wooden Confessional booths. Lists of languages, in which confessions could be heard, were pinned up on each door. Before and after Mass the queues to go to confession were long outside each cubicle as people waited patiently in the cold.

Another day our party took a coach to hear Father Slavko eulogise in his own Church. He was lively, charismatic, and interested in everything. He was a most compelling speaker, full of sincerity and humility. The message that I left with was, "Do not be afraid. Spend time to listen to God. Help each other."

Death Row was on my mind constantly during my pilgrimage. People I had met in the hotel said that they would pray for the prisoners. A lady there from Ireland said that she thought Ted's poems were beautiful. She wished she could send them to her friend in prison on the Emerald Isle. Ted had been with me throughout. I had spoken to several priests about Death Row. I left a letter for Father Slavko. I just wanted them all to pray for the situation in Texas. I especially prayed for a dedicated, permanent Chaplain and a Chapel or place of reflection for the men.

The weather had been pleasant for a couple of days, quite warm with bright sunshine. Just before we left the temperature plunged, it became very cold, with snow visible on the surrounding mountains. The sun vanished and I was glad to be going home to a temperate climate and to see John.

The plane landed safely in warm Manchester. Our companions bade farewell as we dispersed for destinations North and South. Jennifer and I were met at the airport by her best friends, Ruth and Michael Blackburn, who drove us home to Wales we had such a lot to tell them about that inspirational place, Medjugorje. It had left a tremendous impression on me. I will never forget that it was a privilege to have been invited there. Nor will I ever dismiss from my memory the warmth of the people I met and with whom I shared a few days of intense prayer.

It was on November 24th 2000 that suddenly, near the panel of the Resurrection and after leading the "Way of the Cross" for the parish as he did every Friday, Father Slavko died. He was 54 years of age. A wonderful way to die for him, but a tragic loss for his world wide flock. He was a remarkable man.

Chapter 9

Confidences shared

Thank you for another day
To spend here at Your feet;
Thank You for another chance
To hear Your words so sweet.

Meanwhile life in Texas continued normally. Ted was pleased that he had obtained perfect scores for his home study course. The results came through on 18th December 1997. The next day was also his last day at the garment factory until after Christmas. His yearly wages were a hamburger, chips and banana pudding:

"This year, Mrs. Ringo, the Garment Factory Accountant, has volunteered to cook special 'Soya burgers' for those of us who insist on sticking to our vegetarian diets. It ought to be interesting. I don't think I've ever eaten Soya bean substitutes before. Mrs. Ringo claims we won't be able to tell the difference, but we'll just wait and see. Garry and I have also figured out how we will be spending the next few days over Christmas filling the hours and staying out of trouble: making small gifts for our friends in Wales. I won't tell you what they are, but they're wooden and useful. I do love surprises."

These surprises turned out to be small rosary boxes, filed into shape, beautifully lined and decorated, made from scrap wood.

Ted compared the scraps of wood to how he felt as an outcast, of no further use, on the scrap heap of life, in prison. I keep it on my dressing table at home.

They were not looking forward to Christmas, but he went with Garry to a Mass in the days before Christmas:

"We went to Mass this morning - a real Mass for a change! Father Stephen Walsh, a Franciscan friar from Boston, came down for his monthly visit to Death Row. I always seem to get more out of the mass when he's the celebrant. He promised to bring me a copy of the Catechism when he returns next month. I don't want to wear out Garry's."

"I'm really not too crazy about this time of the year. It's rather difficult to stay in the true spirit of Christmas when one is totally surrounded by people who try so hard to pretend they're strong enough to do without Christmas. Especially when their strengths seem so frequently manifest in the form of vulgarities, bullying, and sacrilege. Keep a special prayer in your heart for those here who don't know God as his Son."

Ted saw Lesley, who was spending a great deal of time corresponding with his attorneys and family. He seemed to think that his attorney would still be able to do something for him at the last minute. Without an official stay of execution from the Court, the administration had to move him to 'lockdown' by 15th December, 30 days before his execution date, 5th January 1998. 'Lockdown' meant confinement in a 8' x 5' box, on constant 24 hour watch by the guards and with nothing to do. He would only be allowed out of his cell, for an hour a day Monday to Friday. Ted said that he had been through this process twice himself, and probably that Lesley would soon be "climbing the walls".

Ted wrote: "I guess it's at times like these, that a person's faith in the Almighty is tested. Lesley has been through this before, but this time, we just wait and watch and pray. I should be allowed to visit him in the next few days."

Ted and Garry could not find any carols on the radio. It supplied mostly modern hillbilly and rock n' roll stations. He really liked the programmes, recorded in London, that the local university radio station broadcasted. I had never heard of them, but he and Garry listened twice a week. They heard lots of different kinds of music; panpipes, folk and ballads, harps, and even Gregorian chant.

Yvonne Hughes, a disabled friend of Joy's, writes beautiful poetry and has published a book called Low Clouds in High Places.

She lives in St. Asaph in North Wales, from where she is able to walk slowly up the mountains and contemplate life. Some of Ted's Death Row friends loved her poems and likened her freedom of spirit trapped in her ailing body, to their freedom of mind, but with their bodies trapped within a prison cell. Yvonne initially had problems with the morality of this comparison. She felt they had put themselves into that position, whereas her disability had been imposed upon her. With time, she recognised that they had disabilities too but of the unseen variety.

Ted and Garry had visits from the Evangelists, who come round every Christmas. Ted said:

"The Evangelists who visit with us don't need to knock! They just wander from cell to cell peering and gazing into the cells and asking stupid questions. The two questions that I have never heard them ask anyone: "Are you busy?" and "May I talk with you about Jesus?" The closest they came to that latter question was "Are you saved?" and when one considers that we are all sitting here on Death Row, that question taken at face value, doesn't really mean much!"

However, as Ted observed some guests are more welcome than others:

"As I sit writing this, I'm able to observe a little boy – perhaps two or three years old – wearing a bright red jacket, dancing around on the sidewalk near the out-door visiting area. It isn't often we are able to see children in here – I never realised until I came here how much effect children had on my life. Without them around, life seems to have a large empty spot!"

They were looking forward to Christmas Day Mass by a visiting Jesuit priest:

"It is very rare that we are actually able to go to Mass on Christmas Day. Let's hope that it happens. Perhaps God will work some major miracles in this place someday!"

Just five days before Christmas Ted had some upbeat news:

"The third good thing today was my receiving a visit from my step-dad. He got here late and was only able to visit for an hour and a half before he had to leave (visiting hours are over at

5.00p.m.), but we had a very good visit. He's met a lady – a widow and a Catholic. I think it's great. He's a Baptist, but she said it doesn't matter and he shouldn't worry about it. She won't ask him to convert unless he feels an inner urge to do so. She insists that they be married in the cathedral at home, but then he can go to his church on Sundays and she'll go to hers. There's just one problem with their little romance: her eldest son holds a sergeant's rank here in the prison system (but not on this Unit), and he doesn't know about me yet.

"She's been wanting to come visit with me, but she's afraid if her name is put on my visitors' list in the State's computer her son will somehow find out, or else his superiors will discover that his family has connections with an inmate on Death Row and it might hurt his chances for promotion. I think I'll send her a rosary for Christmas, just to say, "Hello".

"Dad didn't have much to say about my sister Cathy. She's almost completely surrounded herself with parties, drugs and alcohol, and doesn't seem to have much use for the family any longer. No one knows whether or not the AIDS treatments are helping her and my nephew because she won't discuss it with anyone, but at least she is continuing the treatments. My nephew, Everett, is only 10 – I can't help but worry about him. Cathy is an adult and can live her life in any manner she pleases, but Everett has no control of his life at all. Please ask Sister Joy and the others to remember both of them in their prayers."

Lesley's execution date had been set for 5th January 1998. That day, Joy and I went to St. Beuno's, a Jesuit retreat house in St Asaph. Gerard Manley Hopkins, the Jesuit poet, had lived there from 1874 to 1877. Amongst other poems, he wrote there were: The Wreck of the Deutschland, Penmaen Pool and Valley of the Elwy.

Joy and I celebrated Mass together said by Father Michael Ivans, a Jesuit. He is very ill with a brain tumour and lives each day as his last. With Lesley due to be executed that night, the Mass was very special for the three of us.

That evening, Joy and I organised a Vigil for Lesley at St. Joseph's Church, Colwyn Bay. A large group came to pray and the media attended. We had prayers, readings and music. It was very emotional.

We finished putting away the chairs, blew out about 100 candles, had coffee, and had just said goodbye to everyone, when a message came through from the Western Mail newspaper office to say that Lesley had been given a reprieve. It was 1.00a.m. six hours ahead of Houston time. The journalist had telephoned the prison especially to find out Lesley's outcome. It was great news until we realized that it was only temporary.

Ted's first letter of 1998 was on January 16th: "Garry and I both paid special attention to the media, TV, radio and print, and neither of us ever heard or read a single word about Lesley. There was quite a bit on the news about Karla Faye Tucker and the death penalty and women, even right up to just a half-hour or so before

91

Lesley was to be executed, but not a word about Lesley himself. It's not really surprising, though, if you consider that executions in Texas have become such a commonplace thing that they're no longer considered newsworthy. You should also keep in mind that this is "prison country" and most of the people in this part of Texas either work directly or indirectly for the prison system, or else someone in their family does. I don't think they want to be reminded of things like last meals, last words and executions. I believe they need to be reminded, but I don't think a prisoner is the one to do it.

"According to the official rules and regulations, we inmates are not allowed to meet for any religious purposes without supervision and proper authorization. I once wrote to the Protestant chaplain, Chris Athey, concerning some of us getting together for prayer and general fellowship (listening to inspirational tapes or reading from spiritual books, or just sharing our religious and spiritual or prayer experiences) once or twice a month, and I was informed by him that I was welcome to come listen to him during his services when he was here, or I was free to read and pray alone in my cell. He is not a "gentle"-man and I don't think he'll ever have to face any accusations of being a Man of God. In fact, that's always been the problem with prison chaplains – they're paid by the State of Texas and their official duties are to keep us pacified and harmless; there are very few Men of God working in prison, at least here in Texas. Or so it's always been my experience.

"Have you been keeping up with the controversy over the upcoming scheduled execution of Faye Tucker? My feelings are divided. The centre of the controversy is the fact that she's a woman, which in itself shouldn't really matter. The other area of contention is that more than just a few people believe she has experienced a true religious conversion. If she's executed it will be the first time in Texas in over a hundred years. I'm a little disappointed that none of the public figures and celebrities who've taken up Karla's cause have bothered to mention that there have been many of the men on Death Row who have had, and continue to have true religious conversions. There are many men here who deserve just as much, or even more, the publicity and attention that Karla is getting from the media."

Ted was not too surprised that his copy of The Tablet, a weekly Catholic British journal, had not yet arrived, "Before any book or magazine can be delivered to an inmate by the mail room personnel it must be on an approved "reading list". In order to be approved it has to first be sent to a committee in Huntsville to be "reviewed" and then, depending on what (if anything) the committee finds "offensive or threatening to the prison's security", they then vote on whether or not it should be allowed in. The book or magazine is then passed on to another office where the name of the book, the publisher, and author is added to a list along with why it's being denied, or what pages are to be clipped, or if it can be allowed in with any censoring."

Ted continued with a description of his living conditions:

"My section of our cell is a combination bedroom, library, den, sitting room, kitchen, dining room and workshop, and my only piece of furniture is a narrow bunk bed that's bolted to the concrete wall. When I get ready to go from one project to another, say going from woodworking to bible studies, I have to clear away and clean up one mess before I can start another and anytime I leave my cell for any reason I have to have the cell cleaned up and everything I own packed away and out of sight. …I can almost understand why some inmates simply lie around all day reading books and watching television."

He also explained some of the finer points about "lock-down", the "Work Program" and "Administrative Segregation" (or "Ad/Seg"):

"Mainly it's just a matter of different privileges and more recreation time. 30 days before an inmate's scheduled execution date, the security officer will have the inmate moved back to Ad/Seg and placed in "close confinement". I suppose it's a reasonable precaution since their first concern should be the safety and well being of both inmates and staff and one can never know for certain how a person's thinking and behaviour might change as the time of the execution draws near. I don't particularly care for the procedure, since I believe a person in that situation (and I've had three "dates" of my own) doesn't really need to be locked in a cage with nothing to do except twiddles his thumbs and think. But, those of us who have managed to make prison our home aren't exactly famous for being reliable and rational thinking individuals, and it's always better to be safe than sorry, as they say. But anyway, that's what "lock-down" is."

On the 3rd February I was distressed to hear of Karla Faye Tucker's execution. She was the first woman to be killed in Texas since 1863 and the first to die in the USA in the past 15 years. I felt I knew something about this lively looking young lady from her appearance on British television. She had become a born-again Christian in prison and sought God's forgiveness. She deserved a second chance. She deserved to live.

I received a letter from Ted written on February 5th. He was quite candid:

"When Karla Faye was executed a couple of days ago, crowds of people actually cheered in the streets when her death was announced! I've killed twice in my life and I readily admit that in both instances the killing was senseless, selfish and cold-blooded. But I have never been so heartless as to publicly (or privately either) celebrate the killing of a person who has been strapped to a table and is unable to even move. They call me an animal, but I do know right from wrong."

Ted was disappointed about delays to his spiritual development:

"I think I may have bragged to you about our new Deacon/ Chaplain [Tom McKinney] just a little too soon. Our RCIA classes? We're still waiting; he hasn't mentioned it. He had arranged to meet me in one of our day rooms. That was three or four weeks ago. Well, the appointed day arrived, he didn't show up – and I'm

95

still waiting. He's never mentioned it. He told me last Saturday before Mass that some books I'd ordered from the "extension" magazine had arrived (why they were sent to him instead of me, I don't know) – I'm still waiting to get them. And the tape-program I was looking forward to.

"After all the letter-writing and begging that Garry and I did, and after getting a bit of interest stirred up, he's pretty much let the whole idea fizzle out. No matter what we want, or how we want to do it, in order for anything to become "official" it has to come through the Chaplain's office. By not doing his part, he effectively invalidates everything we try to do for ourselves! Fortunately, his superiors have a higher rank than mere prison officials, and I'll be more than happy to voice my opinions to them if I think something is amiss.

"I just finished the best book I've ever read dealing with the life of St. Francis. It almost makes me want to take vows and give away everything I own! He did it, and they said he was a saint; if I tried it, they would swear I was crazy. Maybe that's why they made him a saint – the only alternative would have been to declare him insane! I'm reading a book now about St. John Vianney. It's one of those I ordered from the Daughters of St. Paul, and it's also very good. I gave Garry the books I ordered for him, but I'll probably read them before he does. Our new rosary supplies came in yesterday, so now we've got plenty to do besides read."

I found his letter of March 4th particularly poignant. Ted's imprisonment meant he had been deprived of so many things, things which we, "on the outside", can so easily take for granted:

"I'm not a social person, though and never have been. I would much prefer to be alone with my thoughts and books than to go to parties or events with a lot of people. I've always enjoyed being out alone with two or three close friends, spending a long weekend camping or fishing or just stargazing. I love the crackle and flickering of a campfire and the night sounds of nature. Do you know, it's been more than 10 years since I've seen the stars."

Despite the limitations of his surroundings Ted was still optimistic, and as ever still searching:

"I'm hoping to find a prayer that "speaks to my soul" and I can make it for my own. I've found that having my mind repeat a prayer and meditate on it is a good way to replace all the mundane and useless (if not harmful) thoughts that flit though my head. The brain has to think… but it's a nice feeling to know that what it thinks is entirely up to you! And it only took me about 33 or 34 years to figure that out!!"

Ted was later to find a prayer called "God Be in My Head and in My Understanding". Ted explained:

"Now I have a prayer that helps me in times of loneliness and despair and when no one cares."

Lesley, meanwhile, was to have another two reprieves each lasting a month. During these hard times Joy and lots of our British friends had been bombarding him with mail. He occasionally wrote

97

back. Every time he came away from the killing room he felt as if he had been beaten all over with sticks. His mind numbed. He had now been strapped to the gurney, in preparation for death, several times. After these torturous experiences, all he could do was lie on his cell bed to recover (See Lethal Justice, Joy's book about Lesley). His latest execution date, Friday, April 24th, felt ominous. Was this really his last execution date? We decided to make a return visit to Texas. This was likely to be his last reprieve.

Our decision to return to Death Row was strengthened when I received Ted's next letter:

"I seem to spend a large portion of my waking hours just fighting depression and trying to keep myself busy. I am so tired of this place and these people. I feel like I'm drowning in a sewer with no respite in sight! This is not a good place to try and live a righteous and spiritual life, because the more I withdraw from worldly and immoral people, the lonelier I get. If there's any consolation in this, God is keeping it very well hidden."

We wrote and told Lesley and Ted that we would be returning. Lesley asked us to be witnesses at his execution. We said that we would willingly do this so that he would know that there were friends who cared about him when he died.

Joy and I flew to Texas in April. This time Lesley would be able to "entertain" Joy on Death Row, as he amusingly put it, instead of the County Jail. Here, they could finally talk and hear each other properly in the cubicles, which had been denied them in San Antonio.

Wednesday is "Media" day on Death Row for any inmates including those due to be executed that week. Journalists can apply to the Governor to be granted an interview with an inmate from noon onwards. Following the media coverage that we had engendered in our request to save Lesley, we had quite a following in Wales. Now it was Lesley's turn to be interviewed. Ceidiog, a Welsh TV reporter, who had been following the case, and had interviewed Joy and I on TV, had flown out to Houston to interview Lesley. He wanted to ask Lesley how he felt about his impending death in two days time. Ceidiog's interview would be filmed for Welsh television and was scheduled for that afternoon after our four-hour visit.

We went early in the morning of Wednesday, April 22nd, to get our visit in. As Joy saw Lesley, I was able to visit Ted. He had written to tell me that on his way to Catholicism, he had experienced, through his meditations and fasting, the most inspiring single event of his entire spiritual 'journey' to the Church. He had had a mystical experience, out of body and mind. It was during the time he was interested in Sant Mat. He was deep, deep in meditation and was inside a room (in his head). He heard a voice, which said, "I am not in this room".

This made him feel very desolate for he realised it was the voice of Christ. From then on he wanted Christ. His big search began.

This dramatic experience made him understand that he needed to completely change his attitude:

"What I experienced in my meditation was the greatest and most inspiring single event of my entire spiritual "journey" to the Church. It was the "true turning" point that caused me to finally reach for answers to my spiritual questions in Christianity".

He had been full of hate and struggling, but he filled his mind with God's love, concentrating on Jesus who had died for his sins. He had since read that there have been many people who have survived bad times, and risen above their problems to find peace and inspiration through God. Ted has been avidly studying the Catholic Faith, its traditions, truth and love. He was given a book of "St. John of the Cross" by one of the inmates and became totally engrossed in it. He decided he needed to read more about this wonderful character.

Ted had made a solemn profession of faith in the Roman Catholic Church on the 11th April 1998, six months after I first met him, in the St. Thomas the Apostle Chapel, at Ellis Unit. He received The Holy Sacrament of Confirmation in the presence of Father Ron Cloutier and Father Steven Walsh, volunteer chaplains. This was a culmination of his Catholic Home Study Correspondence course where he had an average grade of 99%, which he had started after I met him. He had studied very hard and read as much as he could about Catholicism. Ted had left school in his early teens so this was a remarkable achievement.

As Ted and I were sitting talking, Ted's spiritual advisor, Father Walsh, appeared. For his 76 years of age his appearance was youthful. A shock of controlled white hair covered a lively face with dancing, twinkling eyes. Not tall but slim, he walked with a purposeful stride in brown loafers and wore a long, brown habit tied with a cream girdle. Ted wanted me to ask Father Walsh to come over to our section. I went round to the other side where the men sat in locked cages. Father Walsh had just left a man and his family when I spoke to him. He came round, pulled up a chair and joined us.

Ted introduced me and said that I had helped him with encouraging letters and prayers all the way from Wales. Father Walsh was very happy with Ted and said he was an excellent student, very earnest and dedicated. I was delighted to meet him. He had played a big part in nurturing Ted's tranquillity and enthusiastic Catholicism, which helped Ted towards encouraging love over hate, and peace over anxiety. Ted said he was a strict disciplinarian with regard to spiritual matters. I asked Father Walsh if any of the inmates could ever become "Special Ministers". He immediately said no, shaking his head in a very definite way. I was surprised. I put that decision of his down to his strict obedience to the old fashioned way of thinking that only a priest can take a Eucharistic service.

I had hoped for a more positive approach in that he would give Ted encouragement and tell him that he would organise some preparation study for him. There is a shortage of sincere people to assist in prison ministry. On the other hand there is not much room for manoeuvre by the Catholic clergy in the prison system, it is all controlled by the administration. He left us soon after to visit the men in their cells.

Ted told me: "I don't know how he manages to keep his chaplaincy status. He doesn't know how to say "no" to any of the guys in here and if he has something that someone wants, he simply gives it to them: I can't remember how many times he's given away his own personal rosary, and he can't seem to keep a Bible or Psalter. Not long ago, more as a gesture than anything else, the Administration here suspended all his visiting privileges for four months because he gave an inmate his watch! He's now known among the staff as "Father Time". I don't think I've met anyone quite like him before, and I enjoy his company a great deal, even though I don't get to see him nearly as much as I'd like to.

"Most of the priests who are generous enough to visit and share our time with us are quickly disgusted by our behaviour. From among the usual 20 or 25 people who show up for Mass each Saturday, I would say there are no more than five or six who realise why we're there. All the others are there to visit or to conduct "business"…

"The other problem is communion. Even though there are only four or five, maybe six Catholics at each Mass, the Eucharist is taken by an average of 12 to 15 people. Our Chaplain has no idea of who is Catholic and who isn't."

Our drinks and crisps supplies needed replenishing, so as Ted was taken to the lavatory, I walked round to the drinks dispenser. En route I met Joe Cannon's tearful mother. She asked me to say hello to Joe, who was to die at 6.00pm. that evening. I knew her because she and Joe's stepfather, his sister and brother-in–law were all staying at Hospitality House.

Joe, aged 38, had been on Death Row for 23 years. Brain damage, after being knocked down by a car when he was 3 years old, had left him with a mental age of 6. His mother had begged the authorities, in vain, to put him into care. As he grew older, not knowing right from wrong, he would commit petty crimes. He might go to a house, take chicken from the fridge and then sit on their doorstep and eat it. She could not cope with the necessary fulltime supervision that he needed. But, to no avail, he wandered the streets and was easy prey.

When he was about 16 years old, attorney Anne Walsh took him into her home. She was very good to him. He integrated well with her family. One night, however, he got drunk, found a gun in the house and shot her dead. He told police he, "just went crazy." Although he was under 18 years of age Joe was eventually put on Death Row. He survived there because he had become institutionalised. He had become totally dependent on prison routine. He was given his medication, had companionship, and was unaware that he was going to be executed. But, now the day had come. His family were devastated and he would not understand what would be happening to him.

I went over to Joe's cage, smiled and said, "Hello, Joe. My name is Margôt."

He smiled back. He was fair-skinned, fair-haired, with a big, round happy face.

"How y'all doin'?" he said. I said I was fine, and asked how was he?

"Just great and good to see y'all!"

I told him that I was from Great Britain, but this was too much for Joe to take in. I left him to his fraught, loving family. He seemed not to have a care in the world. I wondered if any of the guards had any compassion for Joe when he went back to lock-down. Would they look kindly on him as they served his last meal? How would they feel as they finally tied this kindly middle-aged child down? What exactly did his death achieve? Away from society he was harmless. Like all legal killings, it costs far more to kill him than to keep him confined for the rest of his natural life.

Returning to my seat, Ted told me about another inmate with limited mental capabilities who, on the day he was to die, could not finish his last meal. He asked the guards to save it for when he came back from the 'other' cell. He didn't understand that he would never be returning for it. He would be dead.

Ted was to later develop his ideas in a letter to me:

"I know that everyone on earth is born on to Death Row – we just haven't been told the manner of the execution and the date, but we're all going to die. The only important thing is how we use the time between birth and death, and I believe we are all born into the time and situation where we can best fulfil our individual roles in God's divine plan. Those who are poor or ill have an opportunity to be living examples of humility and surrender while the rich and healthy are able to be examples of charity, selfless service and patience. All the opposites I can think of need each other in one way or another. But to put it into action in this place is more than I know how to do. It's as if for most of these people nothing has changed because of their conviction and sentencing – they're still predators looking for weaker victims. It's not their fault, because they were raised this way – it's all they know. It's how they were taught to survive in a world that doesn't care about them. The only difference between the inmates and most of the guards is the guards haven't been arrested yet!"

Ted had had no word from Cathy or his stepfather, and so was very pleased that I was visiting. He asked me if it would be possible to go and see Deacon Lopez to tell him all the complaints that he had discussed with me that morning. I promised that I would try. Our time up, the guard came for Ted and he was taken away. He knew that I would be visiting him the next day, Thursday.

I waited for Joy in the reception area. Caidiog and his cameraman, Marcus Havican, were just arriving to interview Lesley. We had a quick chat with them before Father Walsh fortuitously appeared, and we walked out into the enveloping warmth of the midday sun. I told him about my husband, John and my sons, James, Richard and David, Bee, my daughter-in-law, and Francesca, my granddaughter. I wanted him to know that I am an ordinary housewife with grown-up boys. I told him that I needed to find the presbytery belonging to the Church in Huntsville and to meet Deacon Lopez. He said that the Presbytery was where he stayed every month when he came to Death Row, and we should follow him in our car.

It was pleasant to sit quietly, to meet Deacon Richard Lopez and his friendly wife, Mary, in the peaceful, cool presbytery. It made all the difference to put a face to the name. I told them that Ted and Garry would love some help and communication from the parish. They needed their own Death Row Chapel. They would be very happy to build one. There was enough land, plenty of stones and a willing, free workforce on hand. Therefore, their lives would have some meaning, apart from the advantage of having their own chapel. All denominations could use it at different times, improving life for the clergy, to control the service and, for the inmates, more tranquillity.

At present the Mass and Eucharistic Services were hurried and felt to be insincere. They were said under difficult conditions. Nevertheless, the essence of spirituality, the food for their souls, the love, the words, all these were lost when the minister constantly looked at his watch and sighed.

I was very aware of Ted's grievances as he had described the situation graphically in letters written to me previously:

"I think a large part of the difficulty is that here we're constantly surrounded by active and "malignant" negativities. I can't seem to get away from all the worldly garbage long enough to catch my breath and get my bearings. The Mass isn't even a refuge! I can't really find any words to describe what our Masses are like, but imagine (if you can) a large room, which is normally a "den of iniquities", with a television, tables and steel benches. Now wedge a portable altar and a priest in one corner between the telly and a table, and scatter 5 or 6 Catholics around the room. Now fill the remaining benches and tables with 15-25 "tourists", with people "doing business", with whisperers and wanderers (literally!) who just don't have any place better or more interesting to be.

"Can you imagine someone walking up to read the bulletin-board (which hangs behind the altar) during the readings? It's happened. There's a latrine and water fountain in a corner of the room – can you imagine someone using the restroom during the Consecration? It's happened. Can you imagine someone slumped down in a bench with a cup of coffee, stockinged feet propped on a bench in front, during the Eucharistic prayer? That's happened, as well! I get angry and frustrated, and I've never been able to handle those emotions very well (obviously!)."

Ted had also told me:

"There are a lot of things I don't have, of course: a quiet place for prayers and rest and contemplation, a chaplain who understands his "job" and our needs, a supportive and encouraging community of Catholic believers. But I don't suppose those things are really necessary for a person to be a good Catholic. They would certainly be a big help, but they aren't absolutely necessary."

They needed more input from someone who could answer their exacting questions. They needed a special person who could organise their services with love, fervour and courage. Ted and

Garry had discovered something exciting in their newly found faith. From their viewpoint the only response from those supposedly "in the know" was lethargy and silence, to say the least.

Deacon Lopez and Mary listened silently. They knew that life on Death Row is difficult. They had tried hard in the past, even arranging for a Bishop's visit. They assured us they would try to "do" something. It is not easy to get help. Prison administration is beyond their jurisdiction. They can only go where they are allowed to go, only do what they are told to do. The prison board has its own chaplaincy – the Baptists. Theirs is the "official" religion. Their word is the law as regards religion or religious services go. Congregations in the town have their own problems but perhaps they fail to realise that the parish does not only consist of those fortunate enough to be outside prison walls. We left feeling sad and helpless. At least, we had tried to get the ball rolling. Maybe something would happen.

Chapter 10

Joe's Execution

I considered myself
To be sophisticated,
And avoided my more
simple neighbours...
God, forgive my ignorance

It took two hours, not the usual twenty minutes, to kill Joe Cannon that evening. The machine that pumps the three poisons separately into the victim's veins broke down. After Joe had been positioned on the gurney, and told to say his last words, the guards realized that the machine was not working. The needle was removed from Joe's veins and unhooked from the machine. His legs, feet and chest were unstrapped and he was brought down off the gurney. He sat around whilst the technicians fiddled with his killing machine. Unnerving at the best of times, but even more so when you are unsure just what is happening. Joe became confused and frightened.

With the machine repaired the whole procedure began again. Joe mounted the gurney and helped the guards tie his hands, legs and feet down with straps. A person in a white coat tried to find a vein in his arm. Joe tried to help. But by then Joe was so traumatized, a vein could not be found, so the needle was stuck into a vein in his neck. An eyewitness told all the news reporters this. Eventually he was pronounced dead. But what had the great State of Texas achieved? Joe was to be one of 44 mentally retarded people executed on Death Row between 1976 and July 2002. The press also seemed to find this distasteful. Instead of the usual bit reporting, they included the whole incident in full.

There was also drama outside "The Walls" where a large crowd had gathered. There were a few Texans who were opposed to mentally retarded people being executed, so unusually, they demonstrated. The Texan media were out in force. Groups like "Texas Death Penalty Abolition Movement", "Amnesty International" and "Victims Against The Death Penalty" attended. There were representatives from many European countries, notably Italy, none of which have had the death penalty for many years. They were there to show their disgust and disapproval of a barbaric and archaic punishment for convicted murderers, but especially those with low mental ages. Many young Italians came because they did not believe that the execution would really occur, and thought that their presence would alter the outcome of this case, and possibly future cases, but it did not.

The TV crews from around the world held impromptu interviews where the yellow tape was slung across the road. Behind the tape, apart from a few guards, the road in between "The Walls" and the "Waiting Rooms" was deserted. According to the authorities, it would never do for us to get close to the action.

Inside the "Waiting Rooms" facing "The Walls", Joe's mother stood with her friends. The rest of the family had gone in, but she could not witness her son's death. Finally, after two hours, the door from "The Walls" opened and the guards escorted the witnesses back down the steps and over the road. We all knew that Joe was dead.

Suddenly we heard the sound of an approaching ambulance, bells ringing loudly. The large, hitherto ambling guards, sped to drop the yellow tape. They bellowed to the bewildered mob,

"Move, c'mon, move. Hurry up there! Move out of the way. Can't you see that we're trying to save someone's life here?"

Bemused, slowly the crowd parted. The lone ambulance shuddered to a halt. Someone jumped out, opened the back doors and a stretcher, with a person lying unconscious, was quickly put inside. The doors closed and the ambulance, with much bell ringing, turned round and sped off into the darkness. The occupant bundled in so hastily had been Joe's mother. She had collapsed, not surprisingly, with a suspected heart attack and was being taken to hospital.

Many were disgusted with the whole business, yet very sad. Some were crying. Young people hugged each other in despair. They were amazed by the irony of the evening's events. Joe's life had been taken legally by the State of Texas. His homicide had resulted in his mother's collapse, and her possible death. So many victims! People walked about thoughtfully, talking amongst themselves or praying aloud. Eventually, the talking got louder as

TV crews worked furiously getting interviews for the world's news spots.

This did not look good for the people of Texas who were conspicuously under-represented at this gathering. In fact, there were hardly any there. Most locals had closed their eyes and minds to what was going on around them, or were ignorant of the facts. But, some Texans began making public for the second time that year their doubts about the death penalty. They did not like the thought of women, or the mentally retarded, being strapped down and killed. They felt as though they were under a microscope. The world was watching and they were unused to this bad publicity. Some Texans began to question the morality of their actions. As one person said to me,

"We do not go and burgle the house of a thief when we punish him. Equally, we do not rape the rapist. We find other ways of punishing them. We must do the same here in these cases."

Chapter 11

It isn't easy

It isn't easy for a man to be brave
When he stands in the shadow of the grave

Hospitality House was very quiet when we breakfasted the next morning. Joe Cannon's mother had been brought home from hospital sedated. She was still asleep. His sister and her husband were sitting close together talking. They would all leave for home with Joe's remains within the next day or so.

My second visit was sandwiched in between two killing days. Although I did not know either Joe or Lesley well, I was very badly affected by events. The pit of my stomach was churning as I walked into the visiting room of Ellis One. I felt as though I was walking in a silent cloud that wanted to crack into thunder and lightening. I wanted to scream.

My name was called. My number was allotted. My seat was found. All in a walking dream. What would I say to Ted today? How normal could I be?

Joy went to the other side of the room. Lesley, when he came, would be handcuffed and led to his cage and locked in there. He would sit on a small steel stool for four hours. It was preferable to having simply the company of guards.

As I waited for Ted, I examined a nearby table containing paintings, simple crayon pictures, leather goods and boxes, all made without the aid of tools. The tabletop was enclosed by dusty glass. No one had touched it for a long time. When he arrived Ted told me about the table. Its contents were made by the inmates for sale to try to earn some money. One of his friends, Clifford Boggess, had done very well with his self-taught paintings. They had been exhibited and sold in New York, which gave him some much needed money and attention.

I asked Ted how did he think Lesley might be feeling? Although Lesley's beliefs didn't quite coincide with church teachings, Ted had no doubt that Lesley, a Sant Mat follower, truly believed and trusted in God. Ted thought that the message for Friday 24th April, the following day, from God Calling, a book I had sent him, was very appropriate. It began:

"You can never perish my children, because within you is the Life of Life"

Caidiog had told us that Lesley's interview the day before had gone well. Lesley did not want to die, but was prepared. This all helped Lesley as he only had one day left. Lesley, like all inmates about to die, was in solitary confinement. This avoided self-injury and the risk of the State being deprived of its right to kill them. One young man, dangerously ill on "lock-down", was taken to hospital. Once he had recovered, he was returned to Death Row and then executed. With nothing to do, it is good for them to get out of the holding cell, where they are constantly watched. It would never do for the inmate to commit suicide.

As we were talking, two guards escorted Lesley down the aisle behind Ted.

"Morning, Lesley," said Ted loudly.

"Morning, Ted," replied Lesley just as resoundingly.

This went on all the way along the line of men, as Lesley passed the backs of his fellow prisoners. No one turned round, but they all knew when he arrived, and just when to say "Morning", exactly as he passed each cage and chair.

The guards opened the door of his tiny prison. He went in. It was locked. He put his handcuffed hands in a space through the bars and his handcuffs were removed. He had just enough space to move forward and sit on his stool, to face Joy through glass and wire.

Ted told me that most people liked Lesley. He had a great sense of humour and was a notorious practical joker. One day, when one of the officers was filling in official forms with Lesley, he chewed a big wad of gum around his mouth and asked with a Texan drawl, "What do you want us to do with your body when you die?"

"Resuscitate it," was Lesley's quick response. The officer nearly fell off his chair and swallowed his gum.

Lesley was not even averse to getting a laugh from his own physical disabilities, as Ted explained:

"One of the main things stressed to everyone who works in the garment factory – but especially to new guards and supervisors – is safety. I can remember many times when a new man would come to work and Lesley would take red paint that he had sneaked to work and he would pour it over the stumps of one of his hands. He would then go to the new supervisor and hold up a hand with no fingers and say,

"Excuse me, do you have a band-aid? I seem to have had an accident." Instant panic! Or he would take his food tray at mealtime and place his glass eye in the meat dish (it always worked best with stew or ground up meat), then show it to the officers on duty."

Ted was pleased and happy to have had a letter from his sister, Cathy. It was a positive letter. Blood tests for Everett and herself showed that the Aids virus was no longer in their blood. Although present in their organs, it was practically dormant, with the white blood cell count almost back to normal. She and her friend, Diane, had stopped partying two or three times a week, stopped smoking, and almost stopped drinking. She and Everett had started going to Church. Ted said,

"So, Miracles do happen from time to time." He wanted to meet Everett who was born just after his arrest.

Ted asked me if I would like to have the square flute that Lesley had made for him. Craft items had to be sold or mailed to someone outside the unit within 30 days of completion. Ted explained,

"We're not allowed to keep the things we make. We have to either sell them or send them to our families or friends."

Ted had already had it for four months. I said that I would be delighted to receive it. He had already sent me a little red angel at Christmas to remind me of our first meeting when we spoke about angels.

Lesley told Joy that he had spent his years on Death Row reading, painting and helping people with their law cases. Unlike many inmates who couldn't even read their own case files, he was educated. So he had done a lot of good work and he could have continued doing so, had he not been put to death.

Ted also admired Lesley and said of him, "He has what is commonly called a photographic memory, that gives him quite an edge over the rest of us when we start up some new study, particularly in languages or religion."

I went to buy some more crisps and a drink for Ted and in doing so, passed Lesley's cubicle, I said hello to him. Being partially blind, at first he had not seen me. I bent closer to the glass that separated us, and he recognized me when I said my name. He said hello and thanked me for the books that I had sent him over the years.

It is not allowed for one visitor to speak with another prisoner other than the designated one they have permission to see. I could have been thrown out, but as Lesley was going to die very soon, I felt compelled to speak to him. Perhaps, because Lesley was going to die soon, the guards made an exception or were not looking at their monitors. Anyway, we had a pleasant chat for a few minutes while Joy bought some snacks.

I returned from chatting briefly to Lesley and had handed the drink and crisps to the guard through a special little wire mesh flap. Ted continued our conversation,

"I heard from my "attorney-of-record-who-can't-touch-my-case because he doesn't handle State appeals", and he's decided it would be best for my case and for his career if I allow him to file the necessary briefs to force the judge to take some sort of action. He's afraid that if he allows my case to sit idle for too long (and how many years is "too long"?), I may lose some of the considerations that are normally allowed by courts on the grounds that certain motions or briefs must not be too "important", or I would have filed them long ago. He may be right, I don't know. I've never bothered with learning anything about criminal or appellate law. I replied to his letter and told him to do what he thinks best. I'll let you know what happens, but it will probably be several months before the judge responds to anything that is filed in his courtroom on my behalf".

Ted had been busy on his fourth Catholic home study course. He needs to have a purpose each day:

"It's just so very hard to sit and do nothing because all my life I've been taught that only lazy good-for-nothings sit around all day and do nothing at all. So what do I do? Except for the few hours I spend at work in the garment factory, I lie on my bunk all day and read and write, because there's nothing else to do. But it doesn't feel right; I keep thinking that there ought to be something

I can do, something that will make a difference to someone, somewhere."

Ted was now actively thinking about his role in the church:

"I've spent a lot of time lately thinking about what – if anything – I can do for the Church as a Catholic. I don't believe my participation in the life of the Church has to remain passive simply because I'm a prisoner, but I haven't yet figured how to be an active participant. After reading the CLC programme that you sent I thought that perhaps I could adapt them to a prisoner's needs. After all, who knows what needs prisoners may have better than another prisoner? As far as I can tell, Texas prisoners don't have any sort of organised teaching to show how a prisoner can live a truly Catholic Christian life without compromising his beliefs. True, it would probably never be tried here on Death Row but other prison units might be able to use it."

Ted liked the message, learnt through his studies of the book called The Listeners that I had sent to him, that Christ says to the Listeners, "Do not seek to work for me. Never make opportunities. Live with Me and for Me. I do the work and I make the opportunities." Ted clearly understood we have to place all our trust in God.

Ted also disclosed a story that Father Walsh had experienced recently:

"As he was at the airport waiting for his flight down to visit Ted, a young couple with a tiny baby approached him and asked if he would bless their child. He did, of course, and then they all

119

introduced themselves and Father Walsh mentioned he was a volunteer Chaplain on Death Row. The young lady asked him if his work was really worthwhile, and did anyone on Death Row ever repent? He told her that here on Ellis Unit at least, there were three kinds of people involved: condemned men; regular inmates, and people who were free, like the guards and staff who worked there. Of the condemned men some repented and some didn't; of the regular inmates some repented and some didn't, and of the free-world people, some repented and some didn't. The lady began to quietly weep and when Father Walsh asked her what was wrong she said for the first time in her life she understood that the only difference between any of us is that some repent, and some don't. Ted said a lot of inmates felt better about themselves after that".

Cliff Boggess and Ted would often walk round the recreation yard in quiet times, he told me. They would walk round, sometimes for four hours, talking and praying even when the weather was cold and drizzling. They would discuss Church traditions and the presence of God and Heaven. These were precious times. Ted, as a new Catholic, was keen to know as much as possible about the Church and its teachings. They both felt their former anger melt away.

Lesley had also gone through an emotional, transformation. Ted said:

"I was able to watch Lesley's whole attitude change after he started to get deeper into Zen Buddhism and Taoism but especially after we were initiated into Sant Mat. The jokes and pranks began to stop, he became even more generous and never wanted anything in return and he began to speak less and less often of trivial and unimportant things.

"Personally I wish he could have a more joyful anticipation of the prospect of death, but he and I never did see eye to eye on that. I'm not sure what he really expects to find in the "afterlife" – his approach to religion has always been predominately an intellectual one, and without a "spiritual experience" to ponder and examine, spirituality can't really mean much to the intellect. At least that has always been my experience, but perhaps God has blessed Lesley with an inner "knowing" that I don't merit. I don't know."

Someone in the Sant Mat group had said that Ted had "betrayed" them when he became a Catholic. Russell Perkins, one of their members, told Ted when he visited, that his main concern was that Ted did not allow himself to get "caught up" in the rituals so that worship became something done by habit. Ted agreed:

"Already I've found people in our Catholic community who go through the motions as best they're able, but they can't really explain to me the reasons behind what they do. ("Why do we kneel during the Eucharistic prayer?" "Because my missal says to." Or, "Why do we have the "sign of peace"?" "To welcome everyone to church.")

Ted was discovering that he could share his new found knowledge:

"Catholics are in a very small minority in East Texas, so I have a lot of chances, almost every day, to explain why I now wear a crucifix. People come up with some interesting comments to "prove" that the Catholic Church isn't founded on Scripture: idol worship, the use of candles, incense and prayer beads, baptizing babies, confessing sins to men, and on and on. I was taught in the Baptist Church that:

1) God doesn't approve of "repetitious" prayers.

2) We aren't supposed to pray to anyone except God, and we should pray to Him through His Son.

"I am starting to feel comfortable though now with saying my rosary each day. Previously, I just made them, now I pray with them, thanks to my correspondence course lessons and other books. Old ideas and concepts and teachings don't fade away easily. I frequently have to come to my cell and look up an answer to a question someone has asked me, from my Catechism, or one of my text books."

A guard stopped behind Ted's shoulder and said, "Five minutes Cole."

Suddenly, I realised that again it was going to be very hard to say goodbye. After four hours of intense discussion, which had included soul searching and concentration on listening to facts, adjusting to reality was hard. This man was going back to a cell, with all its meaning and restrictions. I was free to vacate the premises with more knowledge and emotions.

All too soon, we were outside the prison and on the road away from Ellis One and from Ted. We stopped for petrol at a garage, only 20 miles or so from Huntsville.

As we paid the lady attendant said, "Gee, I love your accent. What are you doing here?"

We told her and she was very upset. She had no idea that this killing was going on in "her neck of the woods." The very fact that we had come so far to give succour to these unfortunates was a sad reflection on Texans. She was going to find out more about it and try and do something herself. Even if she did not, the intention was there and that cheered us up slightly on that sad day.

Chapter 12

An Interview and an Epitaph

I wanted to bring happiness to the world
But I wasn't happy.

The next morning, after I drove Joy to Ellis One for her last visit with Lesley, I went into Huntsville to buy coloured paper to make a poster for that night's Vigil demonstration. The atmosphere there was no different from usual. As Ted says, "This is prison country – Most people here work or are connected to prison life in one capacity or another."

An execution is nothing unusual. Nothing to get worked up about. Nothing even to mention. How extraordinary that a man's life was worth nothing to these people, who must consider State killings as routine.

Two of Lesley's Sant Mat friends, the Perkins', were witnessing his execution. A lady from Houston, belonging to Sant Mat, who visited him, had asked Lesley if her husband could accompany her to his execution. That let me out as Joy and Cathy Cox, the Salvation Army Officer, Lesley's good friend, made up the six witnesses.

When I picked Joy up from Ellis One, she said that Lesley was prepared to die. He said that one could not rely upon a reprieve. Joy was very upset. We drove to Hospitality House. The day assumed a surreal quality when the prison chaplain came and gave

124

the six witnesses a talk. First, he checked that they still wanted to be witnesses and then explained the official procedure once they were in the observation room. They were not to speak out, talk out loud, or cry out to Lesley through the glass when they saw him lying on the gurney.

For the last half hour, before they went to the viewing window, the six sat around a table and meditated. They remained in silence as they saw Lesley die. He lay on the gurney quietly. He had had no final meal and there were no last words because he too was in deep meditation. They left in silence. He was the 62nd inmate to be executed under Texas Governor George W. Bush.

Rebecca Smith Patton had been shot dead years before, ostensibly by Lesley. Now the media clustered around her daughter, trying to gauge her reaction to the execution. She seemed to find more interest in how the chemistry of the poisons had worked on Lesley's body than anything else.

Joy went in Cathy Cox's car to the funeral parlour where Lesley's warm body was laid out. Cathy and Joy kissed Lesley on the forehead. For Cathy this was the first time in all his years on Death Row that she had touched him. She removed his glass eye and gave it to Joy, who put it carefully in her bag. She was very pleased to have this memento of her pen friend.

I had stayed outside "The Walls", this time with my own banner, which read,

"TEXANS LOVE EACH OTHER,
DON'T KILL EACH OTHER".

The usual demonstrators were there holding banners, candles and praying. There were some new people too. I met a man called Guy who originated from Germany; he looked frail sitting in his wheel chair. His wife, Ursula, told me that their grandson, Anthony, was on Death Row. We promised to keep in touch, which we do by e-mail. As a result of this meeting and conversation with his family, Anthony asked for Joy and I to be put on his visiting list.

At this execution there was only a small media presence. Executions may be headline news in the local paper, but it is usually only a short article with torrid details and an unflattering photograph of the person to be executed. The photo is usually, dredged up from a decade or more before to justify the State killing now taking place.

One TV camera crew arrived to give the feel of the scene and take interviews. A laconic interviewer asked the demonstrators' group whether someone would comment on the execution. Dennis Longmuire, a university lecturer from the College of Criminal Justice of Huntsville, who was anti-death penalty and I, were chosen to speak. It was very brave of him as there were very few people from Huntsville there. Most of the demonstrators came from Houston some way away.

When it was my turn, I was asked my name and where I lived, and what would I say to Rebecca Smith Patton's daughter?

126

I said that this was the "Bible Belt of America", and that Jesus came to tell us to forgive each other. It is the hardest thing imaginable, but we have to try. Otherwise we will not grow spiritually. It will not happen suddenly, but we must persevere. Forgiveness is God given, and don't we expect God to forgive us our sins?

The interviewer said later that I was very vocal. I didn't know whether that was a compliment or not! I decided that it was not.

Although I did not know Lesley very well I was stunned that he had been killed and with such little effect on the watching world. I had admired his artwork and writing and the way in which he had helped other inmates. This system of punishment was morally wrong.

We exchanged addresses and folded up the banners. I gave the one that I had made to Joanne, the organizer of the "Texas Death Penalty Abolition Movement". I had held her banners on other occasions. She came over from Houston for every execution. She is a wonderful woman, who had always fought for justice for all, including supporting the black children's integration into white schools in Mississippi, at a time of great conflict and social change some years before.

Caidiog and Marcus, the Houston cameraman, had an interview for Welsh Television with Joy, who had returned from the funeral parlour. Caidiog had received a call to say that his mother, who was suffering from cancer, had been taken into hospital. It was serious. He was needed back home, so he said goodbye and rushed off to the airport. Life must go on, but death comes in many guises.

Later Ted sent me a cutting from a prison newspaper, which read:

"Texas Clemency Process Criticised By Court Of Criminal Appeal Judges." The article said that,

"Lesley Lee Gosch is dead and cremated, the 149th reminder that capital punishment is alive and well in Texas. But, posthumously, his case lives on and his lawyers hope that it will profoundly affect the State's clemency process"

Ted had written his own epitaph for his friend:

"Lesley was not a cripple who had a bad childhood and died because he made a terrible mistake. He's a winner, a champion who faced challenges most people will never imagine – and he beat them. He wasn't much to look at, at least by society's standards and his entire life may seem a total waste; but he died with a good heart and his soul is beautiful. The man they executed was not the same person they sentenced to die. If he had been sentenced to ten years of love and compassion and mercy, I think he could have made a great impression on the world or, at least, a small part of it. Lesley's story is not rare, though. You might be amazed at the number of truly good people who are on Death Row. But, they never had the opportunity to let that goodness out, and now they probably never will."

The day had been unforgettable - sad, surreal, sun shining, birds singing, and death. Unnatural and violent. By Texan standards justice had been lawfully done - even though "Homicide" is put on the death certificate as the cause of death.

Chapter 13

Carmelites and Cape Town

A man with a dream is a wealthy man,
And a child with a dream has hope;
But a man who has no dream at all,
At his best, can only cope.

It was a relief to leave Texas behind us at Houston the next day and to be going home. The flight back to Charles de Gaulle airport, Paris, was fine apart from a six-hour wait for our Manchester connection. It was 6.00am and Joy had arranged to meet an old friend at 'The Meeting Place'. We waited a long time, then realised that maybe we were at the wrong terminal. We took a bus to Terminal 2 only to find it a 'rugby scrum'. As we fought our way to the centre of the scrum, a bomb, or rather a controlled explosion went off. We decided it would be safer to return to our departure terminal. We sat down in the tranquillity of a deserted café and enjoyed a coffee and croissant, and almost fell asleep, as we had been awake talking through the night on our flight to Paris.

As we strolled towards our departure gates, Joy was delighted to see her French friend, Marciel and his wife ambling towards us. They had also given up hope of seeing us. We had an enjoyable hour with them, which was just as well as they had travelled for a couple of hours in bad traffic just to see us. As Joy and Marciel reminisced, his wife and I compared our children and grandchildren's ages.

They waved us off and we settled down for the last leg of flying. There was a telephone in the back of the seat in front of me. The steward showed me how to use it. Over Paris I rang John. It was strange to be talking to him from the plane. He met us at the airport. We were so glad to return home. No death penalty there. Very comforting.

Soon after this Ted wrote thanking us for our visit, "Thanks for speaking to Deacon Lopez on our behalf. I hope that something good comes from all this mess. Nothing much has changed yet. Father Walsh returned to Boston yesterday, so Deacon McKinney is alone again. We'll just have to wait and see what is going to happen and trust God to provide what's needed".

The build up to a visit is great for him, but he is sad when the guard returns him to the reality of his cell. He doesn't know when he will receive his next visit or a letter. I had posted some cards to him in Huntsville. They were paintings of Indians and of eagles flying over craggy mountains. During our talk he had told me a little bit about his grandfather.

"Thank you for the cards depicting the Indians. My grandfather was a medicine man, or Shaman of the Choctaw Tribe in the State of Oklahoma. He was a really interesting person, but very quiet. If you wanted to learn something from him, you almost had to drag it out of him. Once he got started with his stories, though, he could go on and on for hours and never get boring. He had a very dry sense of humour".

Ted wrote regularly. He also sent me some small tapestries and cross stitch that he had worked on. One was worked in the shape of a cross with 'Hope' worked in another colour. I also enjoy doing tapestry work, but said that I only did pictures. Accordingly, he later sent me a picture of a hobbyhorse on a carousel, exquisitely sewn, far neater than my work. Unconsciously, was this how he saw his life, going round and round, in a confined space going nowhere? Who knows? Now it is framed and hangs in our sitting room.

He also sent me the square flute that Lesley had made and given to him. Another 'house rule' is that a prisoner cannot keep a gift from another prisoner for more than 6 months or it will be trashed, to avoid that he sent it to me for which I was very grateful. Styled in the North American Indian fashion it plays simply but well.

I take these items with me to show people when we give talks. Death Row inmates are not generally associated with art. Audiences are surprised to see such lovely articles. Joy and I find that at least once a fortnight we are off to give talks to groups like the Mothers' Union, Probus and Amnesty International. There are many people from all walks of life, all of whom have different attitudes to capital punishment. Rewarding 'Question Times' show that citizens are beginning to think about what we are saying.

We were asked to give a talk to student Probation Officers at the Community College in Liverpool. These mature students sat raptly. Our story was a very different perspective to their professional training. We had a lively discussion time. Many believed in the death penalty for certain crimes, mainly involving children. But they would not have liked to administer the lethal injection or watch as someone, strapped to a gurney, died.

After one such meeting in Liverpool at the Community College, we were invited to lunch by Mary, a mutual friend from our own college days. She had become a Carmelite nun in Liverpool. She was now the Prioress, and had invited us to address her community. After an appetising lunch, that included home grown vegetables, the Sisters, of varying ages, sat behind a grille and listened intently to our homily.

Carmelites are an enclosed order; their love of God leads them to a life of prayer cut off from the world. This gives them time to devote each waking minute to the work of God. They only speak to each other at particular times. Every undertaking they perform whether it be cooking, cleaning, sewing, gardening is a prayer offered to God. They do not choose their daily tasks but, under the rule of obedience, take the task they are given with love. Walking inside their high-walled garden, they can contemplate in privacy. The Prioress keeps them informed about world news. Once a month she invites a representative from organisations such as The St. Vincent de Paul Society or St. John's Ambulance to address them.

A stimulating "Question Time" after our talk resulted in promises to write and to pray for Ted and Garry, his cellmate.

Ted's stepfather kindly sent me a studio portrait of Ted that he had taken for Ted's mother some years before. Ted also sent me some childhood photos as he said that the guards were coming round more often, and that he didn't want these old family photos to be trashed. They are now safely stored in a photo album at my house in Wales, as are all his Home Study Certificates.

In response to my letter, Ted wrote back about his lawyer/attorney. On April 28th Ted had received a letter from Mr.McLarty telling him the judge was ignoring him and his requests to leave his case. Ted wrote back to him the following day and told him: "I need an "active" attorney – Do something!" McLarty did not reply to him till July 10th. Ted said:

"There's still nothing new concerning my appeal. I still don't have an attorney, but that's nothing new. I haven't had an attorney since July 1993. The Judge handling my case lost the last election, so now on top of everything else my case is in the hands of a Judge, who doesn't know anything about the case or my appeal, and who will have to take some time to get acquainted with what's going on. That was my last Judge's excuse anyway. You know he should have filed my paperwork, and he didn't. They can't execute me if I don't have an attorney, even though I'm not real crazy about spending five or six more years on Death Row. It seems like I've been here forever".

Ted had been unable to speak with Cliff Boggess since he had been moved in to lock-down, in preparation for his execution. Cliff had asked Father Walsh to be his spiritual advisor. Cliff had already started his last painting, which was to be of the Crucifixion.

Ted had begun to learn Spanish for mental stimulation and to enable him to speak to some of the Hispanic inmates. He was also very interested in the Moorish influence on Spanish architecture.

When Ted sent me Garry's name and number to find a correspondent Joy had taken up the offer to write. She found that Garry, 32 years old, was a lively individual. He had been on Death Row for 10 years. He and Ted were good friends. Garry's father visited frequently, and put money into Garry's account. When Ted ran short of stamps, Garry usually had some left to give to Ted who paid him back when the Commissary opened. Garry enjoyed TV and reading.

My eldest son James, his wife Bee and their baby daughter, Francesca, plus John and I went to South Africa. James, a lecturer at the Open University, Milton Keynes, England, had been invited to read a paper that he had written for the Mathematics conference, at the University of Stellenbosch, Cape Town. Although it was their winter, the climate suited us all admirably.

As we were driven from the airport towards the city we were amazed to see a "Shanty Town" on either side of the main road. The dwellings had makeshift roofs of corrugated iron, odd planks of wood and even sackcloth. The difference between these roughly erected, insubstantial homes and the beautiful apartment blocks, the lovely houses and the vast estates that we encountered was overwhelming. Ted was very interested in the descriptions that I sent him. Growing up he had known both physical and emotional poverty.

John and I visited Robben Island, off Cape Town, to see the former prison where Nelson Mandela was held as a political prisoner for 27 years. Brutality had been rife. The guide told us that the corridors would sometimes be awash with blood. The building, set round a large courtyard, was only one storey high. This was a huge contrast from the tier upon tier, cage upon cage, of Death Row, Texas.

Nelson Mandela's room was small. He had a desk and a chair. Ted has neither. Nelson's room had a window with a courtyard view. He also had a real mattress on a wooden bed. Ted's "only piece of furniture is a narrow bed bolted to the concrete floor". Mandela was allowed to go outside and tend a small plot in the grounds. Ted would love to do some gardening in the prison grounds. Nelson Mandela survived. The men on Death Row do not. They are systematically killed. Some though, do find hope, as they wait to die, through God's loving forgiveness. Some anticipate eternal life by spending the precious time left here on earth by praying for forgiveness and finding out as much as they can about their Saviour.

From his cell, Nelson Mandela led the struggle against Apartheid, becoming a figurehead for forgiveness, integrity and hope. His moral outlook has made him loved and admired internationally. The publicity of this in such a short time was quite miraculous. Nelson Mandela became the President of South Africa in 1994 until 1999. Now in his eighties he believes in, and practises, reconciliation and peace.

Ted told me that "one of the guys here" loaned him a book about the selective writings of St. John of the Cross. His own Friars, disliking his new ideas, imprisoned him. Ted wondered what he was missing and intended to learn more about this Saint.

On the 11th June Ted wrote: "My life can be a powerful witness to God's mercy and love. My past is what makes me who I am."

Ted was also interested in another saint: "I did hear back from Father W.J. O'Brien, C.M., who is the Director at Mary's Central Shrine ("The Central Association of the Miraculous Medal" in Philadelphia). I had written asking for further information about the Miraculous Medal, and Father O'Brien sent me two books and several pamphlets and prayer booklets. I've only started the book about St. Catherine Laboure, but I already love her story – her devotion to Mary, her purity and her goodness".

Cliff was to be executed on 11th June. The day before Ted attended a special Mass:

"We had the privilege and pleasure to attend a "special" mass yesterday evening. Cliff had asked Father Walsh to have it approved by the Warden and whoever else was in charge, and believe it or not, permission was given immediately, and with absolutely no reservations. Officers were instructed to make all the necessary arrangements and then to leave us alone.

"Attendance was by Cliff's invitation only. He only invited those of us who had shared his Christian life and helped him live it. There were only five of us [from Death Row], Father Walsh and Cliff. The Mass itself was a very moving and (for me, at least) a very profound experience – there were no distractions, no disruptions, no unbelievers. There was only the seven of us, and Our Lord.

"By noon today he will have given the last of his personal property to a visitor from Houston, and when he leaves his cell a little later he'll carry nothing with him except his rosary, and a scrap of cloth from a habit of Blessed Sister Faustina, and he'll leave nothing behind except a brown paper sack of trash. Did he tell you what he's going to request for a last meal? Two double meat, double cheese hamburgers, an extra large serving of French fries, a quart of milk, and two large slices of "birthday cake". Happy birthday, Clifford!

"Well, it's about 5.15pm now and I'll be going to the Commissary with the rest of the cellblock at 6:00. I'm going to buy ice cream and pastries, and by the time I return to my cell Cliff will be with his Father and Garry and I can celebrate his birthday and his homecoming.

"7:15p.m. – I'm back and it's done. 54 minutes ago, at 6:21 pm Cliff released his last breath and went home. Our loss. His gain. I'm going to eat chocolate ice cream and a cherry sweetroll to celebrate Cliff's birthday and then pray 15 decades to celebrate his death.

"A short time ago Cliff and a another man, Jonathan Nobles, asked Father Walsh about seeking forgiveness from the victim's family and making reparation. Father Walsh spent three days thinking about it, praying about it, getting advice from other priests and praying about it some more. This is what he told us concerning capital punishment and forgiveness. These aren't Father Walsh's words verbatim. It is the essence of what he said though:

"Only God can forgive sin. When we ask a fellow human for forgiveness, maybe we receive it and maybe we don't - we can never be certain because the tongue seldom speaks what the heart truly feels. If one feels the need for human forgiveness, he should ask for it and then get on about his business, no matter how he's answered. We can do no more than ask.

"As for capital punishment, execution and seeing expressions of hatred and detestation on the faces of people who don't know us and who are happy to see us die, we have only to look and see the example of Our Lord. Only two people in the history of the world have been completely without sin – the Blessed Virgin and her son Jesus. The rest of us, without exception, are sinners. I am no more or less a sinner than any other man or woman. But like Our Lord I have been accused publicly by and before sinners. Unlike Our Lord I am guilty. If a world of sinners insisted and still insisted on condemning Our Lord who was, is and always will be innocence itself, then how can I, an admitted murderer, expect (or even desire) less?

"If legitimate authority should decide to forgive my crimes at least partially, and allow me to live, then I should accept that as the Divine Will. However if I am executed by an unforgiving state then I have an opportunity to forgive others and to offer up my life as a sacrifice – joined with Our Lord`s should he deem my intentions acceptable for the conversion of sinners".

"Father Walsh was just here for a short visit and told us of Cliff's last hours. The Good Father says that in spite of what the newspapers here have printed, Cliff's last words were, "Father, into your hands, I commend my spirit."

"He took one long, slow breath, then didn't move again. He died with his Rosary around his neck and the relic of Blessed Faustina in his breast pocket. Father Walsh gave him the body of Christ shortly before he entered the death chamber, and he spent his last two hours praying his rosary. After he was pronounced dead Father Walsh was allowed to enter the death chamber to bless Cliff's body. He wasn't allowed inside during the execution, and so, like Our Lord, Cliff died surrounded by his enemies. Another friend has gone. Heaven's ranks have grown. Our Lord is faithful and just."

Chapter 14

Adieu to Apu

I can't do your work Lord,
While sitting and lying down;
There are many in this sea of sin
Use my hands, lest someone drown.

By June 12th Ted had still not heard from Cathy and Everett: "Paul, my step dad, said in a letter they'd gone to the National Institute of Health in Maryland for some tests on Everett's blood."

A day later Ted's thoughts were on his religious education: "We met again yesterday morning for our weekly Catholic Bible/ Spiritual studies. For the past two weeks, we've been praying the rosary (I think we've all given up hope that McKinney will actually be able to "teach" us anything). Last night, there were only five of us there, plus McKinney.

"I finally finished the 5th and last course offered by the Catholic Home Study Service. What I ended up with (scores) is:

(1) "We Believe A Survey of the Catholic Faith"   99%

(2) "The Privilege of Being Catholic"   98%

(3) "Morning Star…Christ's Mother and Ours"   97%

(4) "A Catholic Guide to the Bible"   97%

(5) "The Catechism Handbook   99%

"Not too bad for someone who never finished High School and who doesn't have a quiet place to study!"

Around the first week in July Ted had an interview with Associated Press reporter Mike Graczyk. It was something Ted had never done before and his attorney, McLarty, was to be less than happy:

"Mike had heard from another prisoner here that I've been waiting five years for an evidentiary hearing and that I had an Attorney who can't touch my case, so he wanted to hear about it from me. Mike and I cooked up the story that I was trying to drop my appeal but couldn't get the judge to pay any attention to me. I explained to him that I needed a story that would "piss off the judge" and cause him to bring me back and appoint another attorney. I think he'll end up writing about it, mainly because he doesn't care much for judges and State Attorneys, and this makes them look very bad. I'm hoping he'll be able to sway public opinion, especially in my hometown, and cause the judge to do something. I found out from the reporter that the State Prosecutor has been pushing the judge to set an execution date for me. We'll just have to see what happens, I guess."

Despite Ted's own problems, he had time to ponder outside events:

"The bombing in Ireland and those near the American Embassies in Africa – I can't understand that sort of hate and rage, and hatred was my constant companion for many years. Now, I only

142

want to pray for the victims and hope it's not too late for their killers. If there's hope for me, I guess there's hope for everyone."

"As I write this, I have the voices of the monks of Santo Domingo de Silas ringing in my ears. About a week ago, McKinney brought a tape player and some tapes (Gregorian Chants), and this morning he brought some more tapes. Besides the chants, there is also a tape of the Pope praying the Rosary (in Latin, of course) that is absolutely beautiful."

"Nothing at all has changed for me in regard to lawyers, and courts, and such. My "Attorney-of-Record", Carlton McClarty, has (for the third time) filed all the proper paperwork with the court clerk to have himself removed from my case and have another Attorney appointed for me. That was over a month ago, though, and everything still remains as before.

"Back in April, I wrote to the Antonian Association, here in the U.S., trying to find a book of St. Anthony's sermons that I'd read about. Well, somehow, my letter ended up in Padua, at the Basilica del Santo. It had been sent to the Director General of the Shrine of St. Anthony. I don't remember now what I'd written, and in fact, I had actually given up on ever getting a reply, but Father Varetto sent me the book of sermons, "Seek First His Kingdom", as well as a smaller book of Anthony's prayers called, "Praise To You, Lord", a beautiful colour book with many prints of the Basilica. I'm really enjoying St. Anthony's sermons. He has a unique way of using scripture to illustrate the points he wants to make. I'm also soon to begin to receive the monthly magazine, "Messenger of St. Anthony", as a gift from the Basilica.

"It seems awfully quiet around here without Cliff. Now all his temptations have been left behind and his faith has been justified. I hope I'll be able to keep the enthusiasm that Cliff and I once shared concerning Christ and his Church, but I don't really expect to. It's so difficult to do what's right to live and for Jesus, when we are constantly surrounded by the things and attitudes that we want to leave behind and we have no control over the sort of people we have to live and work with. If not for scripture reading and prayer each day – especially my Rosary – things would be a lot more difficult in here. Having Garry as my cellmate helps, of course, but for some reason, I can't get him to commit to a monk's life! Why in the world would anyone not want to spend every day reading Scripture and praying and studying?"

"I have a book, He Leadeth Me by Father Walter J. Ciszek, S. J. that I would highly recommend to anyone who is interested in the way prisoners think, and what it's like to for us to literally live one day at a time. Garry's reading it now. I've always felt what he wrote, but could never put it into words. He does an excellent job of it.

"I'm exhausted. I arrived back here this morning from a bench warrant to San Angelo to "drop my appeal" - a six-hour drive in chains and shackles with an electronic "shock box" (electric shock belt) strapped to my back (Can you imagine? They think I'm dangerous!). I'll probably be scarred for life, I was in San Angelo

144

two or three days but I did make the judge agree to arrange for me to get an Attorney! I appeared before Judge John E. Sutton of the 119th District Court (who had already removed McLarty from my case as the "attorney of record"). He asked if I was prepared to drop my appeal at that time – I replied that I was not going to drop my appeal and I merely wanted an active attorney. The judge went through the roof.

"But I don't actually have a new attorney yet. When I went back on bench warrant the judge only signed the documents that make it possible for the court of appeals to appoint one for me. That could take up to six months, and even then I wouldn't know about it unless this attorney decides to inform me of his appointment. Frequently they don't want us to "bother" them while they're "working", so they don't even introduce themselves until time for a court appearance. It doesn't sound proper, but it's all perfectly legal.

"Being bench warranted is usually a major pain. A bench warrant can be for almost anything. It's really nothing, but a common subpoena, with the difference that the person who's wanted is already in prison somewhere. So, the "bench" (the judge) issues a "warrant" for the transfer of a prisoner, for whatever reason: execution date; trial; hearing; as a witness in someone else's trial. It's called a "bench warrant". Actually, the bench warrant itself is the document that carries the judge's signature, but the whole process of being transferred is called that by name. I won't go into all the painful and humiliating details, but it was a 4-day ordeal,

145

and I was in the courtroom – the reason for the bench warrant – for less than 15 minutes.

We had been rather worried about David, as he seemed to be continually tired. He had returned to Exeter University in September but was feeling so bad that John and I decided to visit him. We saw the college doctor and blood tests were taken. It was discovered that David had glandular fever. He returned with us to Wales to recuperate. The situation made me ask Ted what happened when he was ill. He told me that a visit to the doctor costs the inmates $3 per consultation, usually a different doctor each time they visited. They also have to pay for medication, which can be quite expensive. No money means no doctor.

Ted was still finding his spiritual journey fraught with difficulty:

"I'm beginning to feel like a spiritual hermit, and it doesn't feel right. I'm not a good person. I feel myself extremely blessed that our Lord takes me as He does. I'm a perfect example of just how merciful God really is. I know that I displease and anger and sadden Him so much unintentionally, that I can't afford to take anything for granted.

"The Trappists at Holy Spirit Monastery have offered to supply me and Garry with any book we want from their catalogue – all we have to do is ask. They're the ones who were so kind and generous to Cliff and for whom he did his last (unfinished) picture.

146

The monks have sent me several books recently that have been keeping me busy. One of them – the one that is becoming most special to me – is The Complete Collected Works of St. John of the Cross. There were also several other books that dealt with the different types and aspects of prayer. I had written to them asking several questions about prayer, and the books were their answer. I wish there was some way I could repay their generosity, but I'll have to be content with simply remembering them in my prayers.

In prison, life was rather hectic: "The guards have a new captain who seems to feel that it's his "duty" to be extra hard on prisoners (if we're having a "good time" – whatever that is – then the guards aren't doing their jobs right) so they've been coming through on a regular basis, "searching for contraband". I'm still not certain what taking property off a shelf and throwing it on the floor has to do with a "search", but since it's their way I guess they can do it any way they want to.

"I've never been on lock-down for any sort of disciplinary reason – in fact, I don't have a disciplinary record here at all. I go out of my way to do as I'm told by my "superiors" and to stay out of trouble. That's one of the reasons I get so frustrated when one of the idiots who work here (I mean that in the nicest possible way, of course!) comes in and trashes everything I own.

"This last invasion could have been much worse, I suppose. At least I didn't lose anything of real value – a couple of books and some old letters. The missals and photos and the small white devotional are still intact, but maybe next time… I don't want to dwell on it, though. I'll only end up angry and grouchy! We don't want that, now, do we, my friend?

"Garry still hasn't received a reply from Chaplain Groom (concerning who is allowed inside the "death chamber"); or from Bishop Fiorenza (concerning "permission" to be cremated in his diocese); I still haven't seen or heard from my sister or step-dad (the last letters were back in June); the Redemptionists still refuse to send me the "free prayer card and picture of Our Lady of Perpetual Help" which they've been advertising in so many Catholic magazines for so long, and they won't answer my letters asking for an explanation even though I always provide them with a stamped and pre-addressed envelope (I've written them 6 letters to date). I also wrote to the Confraternity of the Most Holy Rosary, back in March, and they haven't replied either. I guess its time to write to them again. Our diocese paper has managed to once again "upset" me with an article that trivialises well meaning Catholic prisoners; and I can't seem to get an answer to my own letters to the Bishop (I wrote asking him to please define for me just exactly what a Catholic prisoner's place is in the Catholic church, and what did he intend to do to make sure that our "right to be educated in the faith" was protected. I don't really expect a reply.); and that's probably more than enough moaning and groaning for now."

In September Ted at last had a visit from his step dad. Ted worried about him, especially when his letters went unanswered for two or three months. On this visit his step dad looked well and was in good spirits and paid to have some photos taken. Ted felt "old and grey" when he saw them.

Ted and Garry had been busy making rosaries. They packaged off about 40 for us to distribute as we wished to people in schools and hospitals and to our friends who would pray for them both. Ted, however, had firm views on the rosary as a fashion accessory: "Most of the "Catholics" round here are more than happy to wear rosaries around their necks as jewellery, a practice I personally don't approve of but there's no way they'll be caught [praying] with "all these beads"; it's just not manly enough for them. It's rather sad really."

Ted, as always, was eager to improve his religious knowledge:

"I've begun to explore Carmelite spirituality. I've written to a couple of Carmelite monasteries and to the Carmelite vocations office, as well as a couple of the secular Carmelite organisations. I've been in touch with a couple of Third Order Carmelites who seem to be supportive, but I won't take instruction from just anyone. We'll see what happens. I will find my place in our Church, one way or another."

Jonathan Nobles, who was to be executed on 7th Oct. 1998, had the Eucharist as his final meal at his last Mass on the Tuesday evening. Ted wrote:

"Everyone had a chance to say their "goodbyes". Cliff's Mass was much more honest and "real", but I guess you can't expect an honest expression of feelings from people who are only Catholic

149

on Sunday for a half hour. It was all rather pathetic. There was one good thing that came from it, though – a man received Confirmation and was accepted into the Church."

In his letter of Oct. 21st Ted showed both self-doubt and dissatisfaction:

"Christ calls us to holiness, not mediocrity, and at my very best I'm a poor excuse for a Christian. I don't see anyway to improve myself and become a more Christ–like person if those who can teach me – and whose duty it is to teach me – refuse to do so!

"Our "Chaplain" was here bright and early this morning, wanting to know if we wanted to go to "Communion". I swear this man passes the host out like it was a cookie, or something! And the priests he's been getting for us lately aren't much better than he is. The priest last Saturday had no idea what he was doing during Mass. ...he kept skipping around so much. He completely omitted the Creed and threw a "Hail Mary" into the middle of the Liturgy. McKinney tells me not to worry about it, but it's my Mass too. It doesn't belong to the Clergy alone, that they can do what they please with it!"

By Nov. 11th Ted had finished a couple of books by Michael Brown:

"They were interesting and managed to keep my attention, but the guy seems to be able to find demons and witches and evil everywhere! Granted Satan exists and he is evil and he has demons to serve him, but I think there are very few things or people in the world who are truly evil or demonic.

"There's a whole lot of praying going on in those books, and that's not something I've ever seen a lot of. Most of the Catholics around here – and that includes our Chaplain – seem totally oblivious to the concept of two or more people praying together! I've frequently heard someone say (usually in a casual or offhand way) "pray for me" but I've never heard anyone say, "pray with me". Even during the Mass, most people are silent during the prayers and responses. How can anyone not want to participate in the greatest prayer of all? I just don't understand it"!

In our life things were also hectic as John's father, Dr. Theadore Aczel, or Apu, as we all called him, which translates as "father" in Hungarian, was ill. John travelled to Stoke Poges, Buckinghamshire, to shop for him, liase with the doctor, and confer with Michael, John's brother.

Apu had lived in the same house for nearly fifty years. Whenever I think of the house, with its diamond shaped leaded light windows and the heavy oak front door, I can see Apu's welcome smile and open arms. He was a generous, highly intelligent, dignified man with a strong will and a determination that overcame many obstacles in his long life.

His delightful, spacious house and garden were up a romantic, winding lane. The houses were on one side of the lane, their frontage looking out through tall trees to flowery yellow grass beyond. Behind his house, Gray's Meadow sprawled beyond his one-acre back garden. The only sounds were of horses swishing their tails as they munched on the tall, lush grass, or the birds whistling and singing in the fruit trees and hedgerows. I have great memories of our children racing round the garden, or riding their bikes there. We always came away in summer, laden with fruit from his trees, or blackberries in the autumn. From the old days I remember Anyu, John's gentle mother, as we sat leisurely enjoying afternoon tea on the lawn and discussing the latest news or the most recent book or play.

It was a great shock when Apu died on November 2nd, just two days before his 96th birthday. He had been a loving, kind, if somewhat autocratic father, to his two sons. He had been so proud of them and their families. What a difference from Ted's experience of his own father. Nevertheless, Ted sent his condolences to John on a card and offered up prayers for the repose of his soul:

"John and his father are in my prayers. I would imagine that John is feeling a bit lost without his twice-weekly visits to London to see the old gentleman. I pray that God will dull John's pain and that he'll always remember the good times he shared with Apu."

Ted was acutely aware of his position, and its shortcomings, in relation to the Church and his own burgeoning spirituality:

"In the past year I have come to love the Church - her teachings and traditions, rituals and prayers, priests and bishops and nuns and laypeople. Most especially, I've come to love the Pope and all he represents, and I've come to cherish the Blessed Mother of our Lord. I now have access to the Sacraments given by

Christ - things I wasn't even aware off a couple of years ago. I know I must appear to be very ungrateful to God at times, because He has given me so much and I'm still not satisfied. There are a lot of things I don't have, of course: a quiet place for prayer and rest and contemplation, a chaplain who understands his "job" and our needs, a supportive and encouraging community of Catholic believers. But I don't suppose those things are all necessary for a person to be a good Catholic. They would certainly be a big help, but they aren't absolutely necessary.

"But there are times – and lately they seem to come more frequently – when it seems as if life itself is against me and Christ appears so far away. I find myself feeling angry and frustrated, and with no way to deal with it. There is no one here to talk to. There is no one to ask for advice or help. These are just things which I'll have to work through myself, with a lot of praying for grace and mercy. I'm told that it's always darkest before the dawn, so I have reason for hope.

"Towards the end of this month I will have been confined on this charge for 11 years. In all that time I have never had a single quiet moment to myself; there is always noise and confusion, though the nights here are relatively quiet. Every saintly and holy person I've ever read or heard of, attained that state of being through long hours of prayer and silence and solitude. Even those who are known for their long hours of social work say that so much has depended on going off by themselves for a while to pray and commune with God.

"The fault lies with me of course. I'm here due to my own actions, so the circumstances are of my own choosing, so to speak. And we have God's assurance that we will never have a burden we can't endure – I just haven't yet figured out yet how to cope with all this, and God hasn't yet seen fit to enlighten me. And I don't suppose it really matters – this is a trial, a test, and I will pass through it in my own time and everything will be as it's supposed to be. I have no idea how any of it will turn out – I can only trust that He's still running the show here.

"Two more days 'til Thanksgiving. Lots of turkey, ham, roast beef, vegetables, salads, pies and cakes. And I'm dreading it. It won't be too much longer before the big "Christian" groups start coming in with all their Christmas cheer. I don't mind them too much, as long as they aren't too determined to "save" me, and I kinda enjoy debating with the anti-Catholics (I used to think like them so I know where they're coming from). Actually 90% of them sincerely believe all the nonsense that comes out of their mouths.

"And then we'll have Christmas close on the heels of everything else. Ordinarily I don't particularly care for Christmas holidays. It's just so depressing. It seems – judging from radio and television and newspapers – that Christmas is all about parties and presents and having fun, and for some reason I generally feel left out of the festivities. This year, though, I'm looking forward to my first Christmas as a Catholic. I can celebrate Christmas by welcoming and worshiping the newborn Christ just as I think he would want. I'll probably be able to find a few people who are in need of something that I can help with, and I can always find more than a few people to pray for. I intend to have a very good Christmas this year.

"I can't help but feel that everything that's going on in my spiritual and religious life – each consecration, every fraternal or societal membership - brings me closer to something God wants me to do, though I haven't a clue as to what it might be. It's only a feeling, though. Pray for me."

Chapter 15

Escape from Death Row

The odds seem insurmountable,
My foes are full of lies.
My fate looks quite predictable,
Though blurry, through these teary eyes.

All Ted's hopes and expectations for the festivities were to be cruelly dashed within days of Thanksgiving 1998, as he explained in his next letter:

"As most of the world is probably aware by now, there has been an "incident" here on death row. Everyone involved had been living on my cellblock and, as you might imagine, the authorities have us locked down tight. I have no idea when we will be allowed to go to Commissary again and I'm rapidly running short of postage stamps."

Six death row inmates attempted to escape from Ellis One Martin Gurule, it was said, managed to clear two perimeter fences, which were topped by razor wire whilst being shot at by a guard in a tower 15 to 20 times. The others surrendered.

"Today is the fifth day since Martin Gurule decided he'd be happier elsewhere and went over the fence. There is a very good chance that the "work-capable" program will be terminated because of it. If it is, I suppose I will be able to find plenty of "free" time to work on the story of my wayward life since we'll all be back in lock-down again. More time for prayers and study as well, I suppose. I

156

can always find a useful way to fill any extra time I might have on my hands."

Opponents of the Death Penalty have said that the attempted escape was a set-up by those who needed an excuse to move the prisoners to Terrell, a maximum-security prison, where the inmates would be isolated. The condemned men would not come into contact with each other and each would be in single man cells. Previously, in 1997 there had been an attempted escape from the same place in the prison but nothing had been done to tighten security. Everyone was punished. The elite Texas Rangers were deployed and interrogation was the order of the day. Life would never be the same again for the inmates of Death Row at Ellis One.

Finally, it was said that the guards had been careless. But for the prisoners who had come to terms with their life on Death Row, and those who had little hold on reality, and who would now be cooped up for 23 hours with nothing to do, it was a nightmare. Many were to drop their appeals, deciding that they would rather be dead. Ted was sure that the move to the Terrell Unit would occur some time in the fairly near future as a direct result of this episode.

Ted had been anticipating his first Christmas as a Catholic with such enthusiasm but again he was doomed to disappointment. Nothing stays the same for long in life, Death Row is no exception. In January 1999 he wrote:

"Christmas was a major disappointment. I was hoping to at least be able to go to Confession and take Communion, but God saw fit to arrange things differently. We had a priest here on Dec. 12th, who celebrated a very short form of the Mass, but from then 'til the 2nd, last Saturday, there was nothing at all – the sheep on Death Row went hungry because McKinney is no shepherd. He was gracious enough to provide us with about a 10 minute Communion service on Saturday though. I didn't bother to go myself, because there were so many "visitors" in attendance that there weren't enough seats for everyone. Harry went, but he ended up so disgusted with McKinney's absent-minded and slipshod performance he told the chaplain not to expect him back again. Personally I'm tired of the whole affair.

"Cathy is a grandmother now – her eldest son, Randall, is a new father. I don't know his girlfriend's name, or the baby's name, and I'm really not sure when the birth took place, or where… (Is the child a boy or girl? I have no idea!) My step dad just happened to mention in his last letter that Randall was a father, and nothing more. I guess he thought that was all I needed to know!

"I don't have her [Cathy's] address now, so I sent a Christmas card to her at my step dad's address. He wrote "Not Here" on the envelope and had the post office return it to me! And – as usual – the only Christmas greeting to me from non-religious people was a card from Garry's Dad. I guess Christmas just sort of slipped up on them again. It's such a sneaky holiday, you know, and so easy to completely overlook!

"It would be nice to get a visit from anyone. My step dad never showed up at Christmas, nor my sister. No letters, no cards. Not even in the widest definition of "close" could we be considered a close family, and it's understandable that they could all forget my birthday – but how can they all forget Christmas?! I'm beginning to feel positively abandoned over here! One would think a person would get used to that eventually, but I suppose not.

"We were actually allowed to attend Mass this morning! It was crowded of course, because everyone seemed to see it as an opportunity to get out of their cells for a while. I can't really blame them. It was standing room only though. That should change next week – McKinney has been instructed to make a list of all baptised and confirmed Catholics (something he should have done a couple of years ago!) and we're the only ones who will be allowed to attend without special permission. I suppose that's good, in a way, because it will cut down on distractions and we might even be able to have more "meaningful" Masses – Catholic Masses – instead of seemingly interdenominational church services – and that's fine with me. Father Joe Nasser, a Jesuit from Houston, celebrated the Mass this morning.

"I don't know where God is leading me through all of this, but I trust that when I get there he'll let me know. I want to be good. I want to be pure and holy, someone our Lord can use in whatever way He sees fit, but being "holy" is all new to me. It's a constant fight with myself – my habits, pride and selfishness – and I was tired even before the fight got started. Last Saturday I was able to go to Confession with Father Walsh, and take Communion – with God's grace and Our Lady's protection – I've gone almost a week without a single mortal sin on my conscience! Do you have any idea what kind of accomplishment that is for someone like me? I begin each day with my morning offering to the Most Holy Trinity, and I end each day with a rosary, with the Divine Mercy Chaplet, and a Chaplet to the Immaculate Conception; everything in between is done simply with hope and prayers. I honestly believe that if it weren't for the wonderful letters of encouragement I receive – I would very quickly go back to my old familiar ways. I daily pray that God will never allow that to happen. Please don't ever forget me in your prayers!

"We were notified today that all our craft making privileges have been suspended. Between the two of us, Garry and I had ordered (and the warden had already approved) nearly $300 worth of rosary supplies, but now that they've been delivered they're locked in the craft shop while our new warden decides whether or not we can have them. If he decides we can't make any crafts at all, then we'll loose all the supplies. What's even worse is that about $130, had been given to Garry by a friend, and he was to repay it with a dozen nice finished rosaries. So, he'll have to come up with the money somewhere to pay that back too.

"In the last month I've written to almost 50 different convents and monasteries and Catholic lay organisations trying to find some sort of correspondence course. The answer is usually the same: Catholic religious education is to be done at the parish level and I should get in touch with my parish priest. My goodness! Why didn't I think of that? In this whole country I can only find one group that has any sort of "program" for Catholic prisoners. I know I should be more grateful for the few crumbs these Catholic "missionaries" throw me. I'm not real sure why I even look for crumbs in the first place – I'll never be satisfied. I'll always want to learn more and more, and that only leads to frustration in here.

"There's really not much happening round here right now. We're still locked down 23 hours out of the day, except for quick showers and to get our meals. Still don't know how long all this is going to go on, though there have been half hearted assurances from some officials that we will continue to have some sort of work program. It will probably be much smaller and have many more restrictions on what we can and can't do. None of that really matters, however, since "They" are going to do with us whatever they want."

Ted spent much of his time reading religious books; among them he had read Silent Music, In Silence with God by Arch-Abbot Baur and The Sanctifier. He and Garry had written away for books, or people like Joy and I send some. Joy is always a wonderful source of new reading material. His reading was some consolation against his increasingly difficult living conditions. A lot of people had begun sleeping during the day and staying up all night so it was never quiet anymore.

"There's not really much news to report – life on the Row is still hell, and things will get worse before they get better. A couple of weeks ago, religious services were discontinued indefinitely and there

161

is a ban on volunteer chaplains. Supposedly for "security" reasons, but no one seems to know for certain. If God tests those he loves, we must surely be his favourites.

"It probably wouldn't be so bad if I had some sort of "life" in here, a job and someone (or even some thing) to take care of, something to fill up so many empty hours. Garry and I had talked about filling the hours of the day with prayer through the celebration of the Liturgy of the Hours. After checking the price in the Trappists' catalogue that idea sort of flew out of the window."

At home events were making life very hard for me. My aunt, Tanya, had decided that she no longer wanted to live in her flat. The house next to her flat had been up for sale for nearly a year. She decided that she would prefer living in a house rather than a flat. It was duly bought and renovations began. By January it was discovered that more work, than had been originally intended, needed to be done to the house.

Ted and Garry were very amused by the antics of our plumber and some of the workmen. The plumber's work was particularly dire. Not only was it untidy, it didn't work. I had to call in another plumber, and buy more materials, as the last one had removed as much as he could to jeopardise the job. It had also been left in a dangerous condition, which had to be rectified.

They told me about the short cuts some builders take and how they can take ages to finish a job. This was from personal experience (I think that Garry had worked in the building trade sometime before his arrest) and from the gossip of builder friends. Ted said that they would like to come and finish the work for us, but he did not think that the warden would understand if he left.

But, by Easter, with the work still in progress, Tanya changed her mind. She said that she wanted to live in our house. It has a sun lounge right on the promenade looking straight out to sea, a view that she loves. As it was, she came to our house every morning about 7a.m. so it therefore made sense for her to live in it. John said that we would move out and go into the renovated house that was not yet finished.

In the meantime, arthritis had set in Tanya's hips quite badly. She found walking difficult. She did not want to have a hip operation, even though the Doctor pointed out, that the Queen Mother had had one at a more advanced age than Tanya.

Tanya was adamant that she was not going to have any more operations. She settled very happily into our house where she only had to walk from the en suite ground floor bedroom to the sun lounge. There she is entertained all day long by passers by and the sea. Most of the regular walkers wave or blow kisses to her as she sits watching the world go by. She is taken out in the car for little trips, even sometimes with the car roof down. She loves the house and sits in the sun lounge, and raises her glass to the beautiful sea view each day and thanks God. Her ready wit and fortitude is an inspiration to all who meet her.

Time was passing quickly on Death Row and with four imminent executions Ted was thoughtful:

"Well, Ash Wednesday is fast approaching. It occurred to me the other day while praying my rosary, that's it's a bit ironic that ashes will be brought to us on Death Row to "remind" us that we are mortal and will someday die. As if we need to be reminded!"

His favourite picture A studio portrait taken in the 1980s.
Ted was in his 20s.

Chapter 16
Anthony

Are you not a God of mercy and grace?
Didn't you say that we've only to call?
Then give me a reason to continue
As I sit and wait for the axe to fall.

My second grandchild was due at the beginning of June 1999. I did not want to be away when that happy event occurred. I hoped to look after Francesca, my first grandchild. It was decided that Joy and I would go to Texas in early May. We flew from Manchester, but this time direct to Dallas.

Nearing Dallas the Captain said that there was a particularly bad thunderstorm just above the city. He told us not to worry and to fasten our seatbelts. The plane began to shake. The thunder and lightning rolled around us. We were extremely glad to land safely through this raging storm. The bad weather continued as we drove carefully through the city centre. We were surprised by the enormity of the metropolis. We both remembered Dallas, the soap opera, and had thought that Dallas was a modest Texan town. With more time we would have liked to visit Miss Ellie's ranch.

We crawled out of the city in a traffic jam. The surrounding countryside was flat. Thunder and lightning still encircled us. Then we noticed a tornado approaching. We thought that it would be wise to leave the road and spend the night in a motel. All the cars were parked out of the wind in a corner of the motel courtyard. We parked likewise, after unloading our cases.

We originally intended to meet Cathy Cox, the white haired Salvation Army Major, and also a visiting prison chaplain. She travelled from Dallas every week to see her 'boys' on Death Row. She would drive to McDonald's in Huntsville for six o'clock every Friday morning. This was the only diner open at that hour. She would be at the Ellis Unit by 8.00am opening time, and have a full day visiting those inmates who wanted to see her. As we were late going to bed, and had had little sleep due to the time difference, we were still asleep at that hour. We would catch up with her later on Death Row.

Somehow this whole visit had a much happier feeling to it. One reason was that there was to be no execution. What a difference this made to our attitude towards Huntsville. We had thought of it previously as "Horrible Huntsville!"

On our travels in Texas Joy always made a point of asking people if they believed in the death penalty. On our first visit only one person to whom she spoke was anti-death penalty. The mood had changed on our second visit. Half the people we spoke to thought that the death penalty was wrong. We talked to a good cross-section of the community. By this, our third visit, nearly everyone was openly against the death penalty. I say openly, because when we originally talked about it, people had been reticent and quiet. This time research started at Customs and

Immigration at Dallas airport. We put holiday for our "purpose" to visit the States on our arrival form. At the desk the officer asked,

"What is the purpose of your visit?" Joy replied, "We are here to visit friends on Death Row." I expected to be sent back home immediately.

"Good, I don't believe in the death penalty either," the officer responded. We were amazed.

We discovered that there were several reasons for this change of heart. Apart from the killing of Karla Faye Tucker, there had been media controversy about the then Governor, George W. Bush, taking just a few minutes to decide a Death Row man's fate. He reportedly signed death warrants for mentally handicapped people on Death Row without pausing for breath. Some people make one mistake and that is the end for them. It was getting through to the population that Death Row had no wealthy inmates. Having money enables one to procure the services of the best legal minds, then the very worst that one can expect is a long-term imprisonment that precludes Death Row. There was also a frightening issue being bandied about that pre-teenage children should be put to death if they continually committed serious crimes. The media was full of this mad talk. So the unmentionable was being discussed at last, and not before time.

Another alarming phenomenon occurring there is the peer shooting by American school children. The Gun Lobby claimed firearms were not the issue. Maybe when there are enough youngsters killed someone will connect the two. Guns are dangerous. They kill. I know how easy it is for any person to buy a gun in an American Wall Mart store. A video on the counter shows the most suitable gun to use on wildlife. I watched as a white haired lady bought a gun and ammunition for "protection".

With my two-day 'special' visit I was allowed 4 hours daily to see Ted. Having gone through the usual formalities at the gate, we were subjected to tighter security. Guards passed a handheld machine over our bodies and we were lightly searched before being allowed onto the Unit. Nevertheless, we put all the bad things behind us and concentrated on visits. Joy was going to meet Garry for the first time.

I was very pleased to see Ted. He had put on a little weight, and was as interested and interesting as ever. I told him about my granddaughter, Francesca, and how John and I had looked after her in our home. Had he had any children?

"No, I blew that one, didn't I? he replied.

He enjoyed partying, which is fine for a while, but he said it didn't last, and the day of reckoning comes too soon. "Was a retrial possible?" I asked him. His reply was both honest and sobering:

"I have no case. My appeal can never win another trial for me unless I have substantial proof of my innocence. And I'm not innocent. So the most or least I could hope for is to have my sentence commuted to life in prison and as you know that's the last thing in the world I want. It's easy for those on the outside to wish that for me - life at any price - but they're not the ones who

168

have to live with constant humiliation, abuse and harassment. My entire physical circumstances are in the hands of crude and sadistic guards who think they have a legal and moral obligation to make us miserable in payment for our crimes. I've put up with it for ten continuous years and the situation has steadily gotten worse, not better, and I'm tired of it. I won't drop or abandon my appeals, though. I have every legal right to do so, but I also won't actively fight my sentence, either.

"I intend to let my appeals continue through the courts, and if God chooses to have a good attorney appointed to my case who will get me a life sentence I will accept that grudgingly, and I will try to praise God for the opportunity to be miserable for many more years. If on the other hand, he causes a mediocre attorney who does sloppy work to be appointed and if I'm finally given an execution date that is carried out, then I will truly praise God for setting me free and I will gladly embrace death as my ticket to an eternal holy day. How could another ten or fifteen years in prison possibly compare to that?

"Of course, there are many who don't agree with me on that subject both in here and out there, but I think it's safe to say that they haven't spent most of their lives behind bars. I think most people are simply afraid of dying, and I always thought it rather strange that people who profess to believe in an afterlife, not just Christians, but of many religions, but are afraid of the process that leads to it. Others simply don't want to "turn loose" what they have here on earth, even their own folks here, though why they would want to cling to this is beyond me!"

I am continually amazed that Ted can speak so openly about himself and his actions, but I take it as further proof of his impressive personal development. He was not being facetious, just honest. He has become a very good man, but the penal system for Death Row inmates makes no allowances for remorse, or good behaviour. There is only provision for bad behaviour, where the punishments are becoming harsher for lesser reasons. His situation, without an attorney and with no hope of reprieve, is desperate. Only death confronts him, yet he manages to get through each day with his reading, writing, prayer and contemplation.

We spoke about the power of the Holy Spirit. My motto has always been, "I place all my trust in You Lord." We all have God given gifts, which we use at different times in our lives. I was fortunate to be born to a devoted, happy, caring couple. They gave me demonstrative loving security, rules to obey, a good education, and the knowledge and love of God. Everyone has problems. I try to solve mine to the best of my ability and place all my trust in God, remembering that it is God's will that is important, not my own.

Ted was born into a home that practised: "Do as I say, don't do as I do." He said that this attitude did not help a young boy to construct worthwhile habits. He began to stray and "party". Children copy bad habits easily, and it is hard to change without constructive, loving guidance. Ted took the easy path early on in life.

He had been physically abused when imprisoned at 16, by inmates and guards alike.

Now Ted told me he had learnt so much recently by reading the inspired and the memorable lives of Saint Theresa of Avila, Saint Anthony of Padua and Saint John of the Cross. Ted felt uplifted with courage and began to think and hope that he might be allowed to join the Third Order of Carmelites:

"I have also been in touch with the Lay Carmelites. I haven't had a reply from them yet but Father Harry, the priest I write to in Houston, has talked to the head of the Order about me so maybe they'll be able to find a place for me somewhere on the slopes of Mount Carmel. Figuratively speaking, I really feel that would give my life more of a "focus", or purpose."

Father Harry and Father Walsh gave Ted a great deal of encouragement for him to begin a series of studies about becoming a member of the Third Order of Carmelites. It would take some time, but by December or January, he would be eligible for reception into the Order. Then he would begin a two-year novitiate. Three years afterwards he would be able to take vows and join the Third Order Regular. It sounded formidable, but he was looking forward to the journey, assuming that he truly had a calling, he said. But he added it all depended on him surviving another five years on Death Row. A sobering thought amidst his evident enlightened enthusiasm.

The four-hour visit passed quickly. I was sad to leave, but I would see Ted the next day. I told him we were going to meet

Anthony Fuentes that afternoon. I had previously met Anthony's grandparents on the evening of Lesley's execution. He was very pleased. He knew Anthony slightly, but would say, "Hi!" the next time he saw him, usually on the way to the showers accompanied by a guard.

When Ted was escorted back to his cell, I went to find Joy. We asked the receptionist for the number of our chairs for the afternoon visit with Anthony. As we waited for him we snacked on crisps and soft drinks from the dispenser at the numbered seats allotted to our next visit. Soon a very handsome young man appeared with a guard.

Anthony, 22 years old, is of medium height with very dark hair, and pale brown skin. He shares a cell with an older man. At first they did not get on well. It is very hard to live with a stranger in a tiny cell, especially as they had to share an open toilet and a small sink. The problem was that the older man hardly ever spoke and Anthony loved to talk. But, after a couple of years together, bit by bit, they began looking after each other.

His grandparents, parents and family, horrified at his predicament, visit regularly. According to Anthony, his court -appointed solicitor at the time of the trial did not do his best. Apparently he and the police withheld vital evidence. Being young and angry that someone had plea-bargained his name Anthony was sulky and did not cooperate; he volunteered nothing in his defence. Now he says he has woken up and finds himself in this dreadful situation. He assured us that he did not kill anyone.

Anthony is full of vitality. He has always been keen on sport. He keeps fit by playing football. He talked so much and so enthusiastically. He discussed sport, TV cartoons, his love of cars, and martial arts films. I find it very difficult to believe that he is a dangerous criminal. He talked about what he would do when he is released from prison. The thought that this might not happen did not enter into the conversation.

I felt so sad visiting Anthony. It was very exhausting talking and concentrating for four hours, almost non-stop. It was emotionally draining to listen to this young boy retelling his story as well as he could in broken English. We can try to escape from the present through our communication, laughter and reminiscence, but we are brought back to reality with a sudden jolt. This is no joke. We are not on an outing. This is deadly serious.

Anthony had given up some of his precious visiting time with his grandparents to talk to us. His grandfather, Guy, had been ill, and Anthony was very worried about him. Guy was originally from Germany, where Anthony had been on visits several times. He liked what he had seen there. He talked about his family continually. They had all gone their own way until Anthony had ended up on Death Row. Now they were united, so he was pleased that he had achieved something good.

Joy and I spoke of our sadness for Anthony as we left the prison. He was very optimistic that he would be off the Row soon. We hoped and prayed that this would happen. His grandparents e-mailed us in England to thank us for our visit. It was heartening for them to have interest from friends from abroad. They were glad that someone else cared, because he was so young, and they were working so hard to obtain his release in the near future.

His grandparents reiterated that the authorities wanted to move Death Row prisoners to The Terrell Unit, a maximum-security prison at Livingston. Here, the prisoners would be in solitary confinement. They would have their meals alone, and the work programme would be stopped. They would be in their cells all day. Hobbies such as cross-stitch, rosary making, painting or woodwork would be forbidden. They would also not have any religious services. They did not think that Anthony could cope with this. He loved to be with people. It sounded horrific. The group of 'friends', Amnesty International, Texas Death Penalty Abolition Movement and other organisations, were totally opposed to the move. But, the authorities were adamant. The attempted escape was "proof" that this was the right thing to do.

Joy and I decided to view The Terrell Unit that evening. On the way we passed a wonderfully happy scene – a beautiful tree-lined lake, people sailing boats and splashing at the water's edge. Terrell was found with difficulty, hidden away down a small, dusty road. The tall trees had been felled and a sparse landscape surrounded the bleak, grey building. We took photos from a distance. We couldn't get closer because of the security fences. I felt very threatened and wanted to get away as fast as possible back to Hospitality House. It had been an eventful day. We were both pleased to have met Anthony and wished him well on his long journey, although hopefully not to "The Terrell Unit"!

Chapter 17
Baby William

Miracles are taking place around me;
The magical power of life is everywhere.
Mother Earth no longer lies sleeping,
And her love songs are filling the air.

The next day, May 19th, was a Red Letter day. John rang Hospitality House to say that James, our eldest son and his wife, Bee, had had their second child, a boy called William. The birth was slightly premature as it was discovered on an antenatal visit that the baby, who should have been quite active, was hardly moving. An immediate caesarean operation thankfully saved his life. A few hours later Bee underwent another operation, and was given 6 units of blood due to complications. John went to see if he could help to look after their daughter, Francesca, for a couple of days. But first, he telephoned me with the wonderful news, just before Joy and I went to Ellis One Unit to visit Ted and Garry.

Joy had wanted to speak to Ted, whilst I spoke to Garry. We needed the warden's permission to do this. He agreed. Joy spoke to Ted for an hour, whilst I met Garry and enjoyed a lively discussion with him. I hadn't corresponded with Garry, but knew that Ted shared my letters with him.

On Death Row for ten years, Garry shared Ted's cell. Fortunately they were good friends. Garry's father and his third stepmother visited him whenever possible. His own mother had

176

written but had not spoken to him since he came to Death Row. Garry's dad also sent him money whenever he could. In fact, he kept the family together as much as possible.

Garry, tall and large, was now thirty-two years old. He had a sad, but ready smile. His shaved head was due to the heat and an ineffectual barber. At some time he had had a job as a prison porter. He enjoyed reading novels and writing letters. The time went quickly and we said farewell. I moved to the chair in front of Ted as Joy sat in the one that I had just vacated in front of Garry.

It was good to be back with Ted. He was sitting opposite a window. Through it I could see a small, enclosed patio with a few stunted trees. Water dribbled over some rocks and a pair of tortoises meandered slowly around some marigolds in the flowerbeds. The sun shone through the glass. It was a lovely view for Ted. Sadly for me, it was difficult to see his face because of the sun's reflection on the glass between us.

A prisoner from "population", with a guard standing by, was noisily repairing a nearby wall. There was no consideration for anyone trying to converse. It is hard enough trying to talk through glass. What it must be like for a mother to visit her son like that for twenty-three years! We met one such lady at Hospitality House. She had not been allowed to hug, kiss, or touch her son in all those years. She watched him die by lethal injection, which takes from seven to eleven minutes, until he was pronounced dead.

This injection consists of a lethal dose of Sodium Thiopental, which sedates the prisoner, even if he wanted to move

177

slightly whilst strapped on the gurney, Pancuronium Bromide, a muscle relaxant, which collapses the diaphragm and lungs and Potassium Chloride, which stops the heart. The State of Texas adopted lethal injection, a process costing around $75, in 1977. Hanging was used from 1819-1923 and the electric chair from 1924-1977.

His body was immediately taken to the funeral parlour, where for the first time, she was able to touch and kiss his still warm body. I did not voice these macabre thoughts to Ted obviously, as he was telling me about the youngsters coming onto Death Row. They were of all races and beliefs. Some had been somehow caught up in drugs. Youngsters from broken homes, with parents in prison or unemployed, were at particular risk from drug abuse. Ted said that any guidance had to start with the very young as this was where he had first gone wrong.

I told him about an American pilot programme, where pregnant teenagers from deprived backgrounds are singled out for preventative action, while their offspring are in the womb. Michael Clarke, a Home Affairs Correspondent for a local newspaper, was quoted as saying, "They are given five years help with childcare and training in raising their children, and finding work for themselves. Researchers say that the youngsters have been shown to be far less likely to end up as criminals than others from similar backgrounds not helped by the scheme."

Ted was sure that a similar nationwide scheme would help to reduce the number of young offenders ending up on Death Row.

But he thought that much more positive assistance was needed to be done at the start of a child's life. More help should be given to those parents who request a helping hand early on with children who have learning difficulties. This was the case with Joe Cannon, whose mother's pleas for help were ignored.

Too much is spent on punishment, instead of crime prevention. Ted was adamant that more and more finance was being spent on increasing prison and public prosecution officials, and building more high security units, than trying to provide funds for nurturing family life from an early age. He felt that good, loving family life would succour worthy citizens. Parenthood was one of the most important aspects of life for which we are all mostly ill prepared, he thought.

I was delighted to be able to tell Ted that our new grandson, William, had been born the previous night. Ted was sorry that I hadn't been there, but was glad that all was now well.

Ted had mixed views about an uncertain future:

"The only thing I'm absolutely certain of is that this move to Terrell is going to push a lot of these men right over the edge. A lot of them (us) don't have a real firm grasp on reality as it is, but the solitary condition of that place will be just more than many can handle.

"Personally I think it will be a great opportunity to finally start living a truly monastic and truly contemplative life (or relatively so, anyway) and for the first time in 11 years I will be able to spend some time alone – just me and my thoughts. Plenty of time for prayer, scripture and study. I might even be able to get some writing done."

Prayer was proving to have very real spiritual benefits for Ted and Garry:

"We have started praying the Liturgy of the Hours every day. It gives us something to organise our day around, and brings a rhythm to the day that helps to compensate for the disordered and chaotic sort of life we usually have. I really enjoy it. I've also noticed how it keeps my mind focused on God, because I'm constantly aware of the passing time and what it is that I'm waiting for. Every three hours, from 6:00am 'til midnight – that makes for a pretty full day. We have the one volume Liturgy, though, so we only have a limited number of prayers and readings to choose from. I might be able to get the complete four-volume set from the Carmelite nuns at New Caney.

"I suppose that theoretically at least, it should be enough that I'm able to pray and worship in communion with the whole church - no matter where I happen to be - but it's no secret to you that I have a hard time feeling like I'm truly a part of the Catholic Church (it's sort of like being adopted by the head of a large family, but all my foster siblings refuse to recognise the adoption because I don't quite "fit in" with their idea of what a family member should be!)

"The first group of men from Death Row [Ellis One] should be getting transferred to Terrell sometime within the next three or four days. Supposedly, they won't get all of us moved over there until the end of October or first part of November. I expect everything to get steadily worse around here for us until then.

"McKinney has informed us that he will soon be transferred down south in order to take over a program that helps inmates on parole to find jobs and housing. No one knows yet who (if anyone at all) will take over his spot in the Chaplaincy. I guess we just need to pray for a really huge miracle, because that's what it will take in order to find a Catholic priest who cares about prisoners and who is also employed by the Texas Department of Criminal Justice! It's been my experience that those who truly care don't work for the state."

The guard came round again, and gave Ted five more minutes. I felt very deprived we could have gone on talking for much longer. It is very difficult to say something sensible when one knows that the time is so limited. It certainly cramps one's style.

"Well, goodbye son, God bless. I will write, Goodbye, Ted." I had come a long way. Now I was going to make the formidable journey back. I didn't know when I would be able to return.

The guard returned. Ted rose quickly from his chair and waved. "Goodbye, thank you," he mouthed and was gone. He has to obey immediately. I am sure that there are repercussions if he tarries. I was left feeling very empty and unhappy. I had enjoyed the meeting very much, but the end had been too unsettling. What a place in which to live! However, in there, but for the grace of God, could be any of us.

It was with relief that we eventually boarded the plane home. Joy said that as it is such a long journey, she was unsure that she would do it again. I took little notice as she had said that before when she was tired. Probably her back was hurting her. I hope that she did not mean it.

All was well when we arrived home in England. John and I went to Banbury the next day to help the family and meet baby William.

Ted in prison issue white. Death Row, Ellis 1, Huntsville, Texas. 2000.

Chapter 18

Sea Mist

I thought happiness was something
you got from other people,
never understanding that
true happiness comes from within.

Ted had told me during our meeting that he had never seen the sea or an ocean. I was amazed, I had grown up by the sea it was the first thing that I saw when I opened my bedroom curtains in the morning. We had lived half way up a mountain and had a grandstand view of the Menai Straits. Now, with John I was back living in Wales so we decided to enjoy the pleasures of sailing there. I had told Ted all about our boat and how we had fared in our new sport. He was very interested.

John and I had been sailing off the coast of North Wales for the weekend. We had taken part in our first race in Sea Mist. We were fourth out of about 12 boats. Most of them had experienced crew aboard and had sailed in Pwllelli before with the organisers, Dickies of Bangor. This was my first race as Captain. My crew consisted of John as navigator and a friend from the Conwy Yacht Club with his wife. The sea was rough. We were pipped for third place at the finishing line by members of Dickies' boat company, in one of the company boats. They cheered when they just beat us.

Racing seamen might appear calm and relaxed on land but they are deadly serious about winning.

It was extremely exhilarating holding the wheel in that strong wind. It filled the sails and made the waves dance and thrash about, tossing up foaming white waves in our path. Sometimes, when some of the larger boats hurtled through the water close by, it was quite scary. We followed the organisers' route, racing round buoys out in the open sea. In the hazy distance, below a wide blue sky spattered with racing clouds, were the hills of the Lleyn Peninsula.

Our sail home the next day was tranquil. There was a pleasant breeze and the sun shone. Seals swam or lounged across craggy rocks. We kept a sharp watch for lobster pot identifiers, strategically placed by local fishermen. Had we snarled a line, we would have damaged the boat's rudder and the lobster pots and their occupants.

We sailed for the Straights, and sat at the table in the boat's cockpit eating egg and bacon. We slid past Caernarfon Castle where Prince Charles had been invested as Prince of Wales by his mother Queen Elizabeth II. We glided smoothly past the velvet green lawns of Plas Newydd, the fine stately home of the Marquis of Anglesey, which now belongs to The National Trust. We reached the "Swellies" with just enough incoming tide to take us through this notoriously treacherous stretch of the Menai Straights and under Stephenson's iron bridge that connects Anglesey with the mainland at Bangor. The evening was glorious. Ahead were the

Snowdonia Mountains on which were reflected the rays of the rosy, setting sun.

In a letter dated June 24th Ted was also excited about imminent changes:

"The first group of 55 inmates was transferred a few days ago. Father Walsh was supposed to have been here for confessions, but a few of the guys seem to be of the opinion that they didn't have to go if they didn't want to. So, Father Walsh was turned away as the tear gas was flying, and those few inmates quickly learned what they should have known from the very beginning: the State of Texas and its prison administration are going to do what they want to do, and there's not a single solitary thing that we can do about it from in here. We can either accept what comes and make the most of it, or we can end up bruised and broken and made to go along with the program, but – either way – they will do what they want."

"I try to not let it bother me any more, since being bothered doesn't seem to help. I just tend to ignore the guards and most of the inmates, unless they're speaking directly to me. They have their own agenda, and I have mine, and they seem to be at opposite ends of the spectrum."

Ted and Garry sent me a very attractive card for my birthday in June 1999. Ted wrote about his life:

"If I get bored living it, I'm fairly certain that you would get bored reading it! For the first time since last Friday I have a couple of hours to myself while Garry is at recreation. There was an escape at the Estelle Unit, another centre of correction, last Sunday, so we were back on "lock-down" status until yesterday while the guards were out hunting him down. The gentleman managed to slip lease from the so-called "super-max" unit! But that's the only new item of mild interest in the last several weeks."

Their punishment surprised me, as the Estelle Unit is a completely separate house of corrections a few miles away from Ellis One. Ted continued:

"Father Walsh has been around for a while. This is his third week in a row. He and Richard Lopez are supposed to be meeting with the warden from the Terrell unit to discuss the difference between – as far as religion and ministering are concerned what should be and what will be. I personally don't hold out much hope though. Judging from the television interviews given by the Directors and Wardens, they seem to be determined to show how tough they can be towards all us hardened criminals. But as long as they will allow me to have my books and lessons I don't really care what they do.

"Everything is about the same as last time as it's been since last Feb., when our last Mass was celebrated. The Mass was the only thing that divided one week from the next, and now we just have a long string of Mondays. We have frequent lock-downs and shakedowns, but they seem to be random so they don't really count for much except for major annoyances.

"Another surprise! The mail was just delivered and I have a letter here from Father Bill in Houston. He has spoken with the Director of the Lay Carmelites and together they have decided that since I've been studying Carmelite literature with Father Bill for the last seven months or so, they will waive the six month formations and I can be officially received into the Lay Carmelite Order and invested with the Carmelite scapular on July 10th when Father Bill comes in to celebrate Mass for the general population inmates. So in about 10 more days, God willing, I will be able to sign my letters: "Ted Cole, T.O. Carm."! (Not that I would even do that! It would seem so pretentious. But I could). Anyway, remember me in your prayers especially on that day."

Sadly misfortune was to follow Ted again. He was not to be received into the Carmelite Order until October as Father Walsh for some reason had delayed it. Ted was still adhering to a strict spiritual timetable:

"I'm really enjoying the Liturgy of the Hours. Between praying in union with the Church seven times a day and being able to study the Carmelite formation material, I'm finally beginning to feel that maybe there's still some sort of purpose to my life. We all need to feel useful, I think.

"The Divine Office is still very much part of my life. Members of Third Orders aren't required to pray the Hours like priests or Religious are, but we are very strongly "encouraged" to pray at least Morning, Evening and Night Prayers. I just do all of them, unless the time gets away from me and the Hour passes unnoticed.

That doesn't happen very often though. I'm also able to include all the Carmelite celebrations as well.

"This place has been a madhouse for the last couple of weeks, and I really don't think it will get any better until we've been moved to Terrell. The total lack of privacy is really starting to get to me. Of course, there has never been any real privacy in prison, but with the lock-down still continuing, there's no longer even the semblance of privacy. And the noise! As each day passes everyone gets a little more bored and restless. The only time it's quiet is after midnight when I can steal a couple of hours for meditation and my rosary. But as they've changed our recreation time to 6:00am I have to drag myself out of bed just so Garry can have some time to himself. He usually sleeps through it but at least he has two hours available if he wants to take advantage of it.

"The guards have started complaining about their "poor working conditions" and have begun taking sick leave to protest. What are they complaining about? If I can live in these conditions for 24 hours of each day, they can certainly bear to work in them for eight hours. And of course, as always they take their frustration out on us, but they've always done so. You'd think we'd be used to it by now, but I guess some things one just doesn't get used to.

"I got to go to Confession this morning – first time in three months. It feels good to be "clean" again. I've a suspicion that once we get to Terrell, confession will be a lot harder to get to. Then again, once I'm by myself and don't have to listen to all the

189

garbage that seems to pass for conversation around here, I'll have a lot less on my conscience."

His Carmelite formation studies continued to be fun and interesting. He also wanted to get started on the St John of the Cross studies. He was unsure of the reason for the delay, as he could not get a straight answer from the Carmelite institute.

The weather in Texas was up in the mid 90s during the day, a little more bearable than the 105 degrees previously experienced. Meanwhile the weather in Wales was much cooler, as we moved into our newly refurbished house.

Ted wrote to tell me that he had also moved:

"Garry and I have both been moved to single man cells and I'm still trying to get everything unpacked and put away. I really dislike the bother of having to move. Garry's only a couple of cells down from me, so we can still share news and books and magazines and such. This cellblock has half as many people as the other one so it's quieter than what I'm used to. Not that I'm complaining, mind you – quiet is definitely a good thing! Fortunately I have plenty to keep me busy. I have all my correspondence courses as well as my Carmelite formation studies."

Ted was having problems was his electric typewriter: "Everything they sell us is a factory reject that they picked up dirt cheap somewhere, because it can't be sold to the public. Not long ago I had to buy a new fan – my old one was about six years old – and when they brought it to me from commissary they also brought the instructions for cleaning and oiling it. There's only one problem:

190

a couple of the screw heads are stripped, so I can't take the thing apart! Since all the paperwork is done and the money is taken off our accounts before they bring our purchases, they don't care if we want it or not, they've already got the money! We're also not allowed to send anything out for repairs."

Fr. Stephen Walsh, OFM and Deacon Richard Lopez.
Santiago de Compostela, Spain. Summer 2000.

Chapter 19

Changed Lives

For I've only the company of my own mind
And I can only converse with my soul.

Joy and I were invited to address the October 1999 Life Lines Conference in London. As the main speaker was Sister Helen Prejean (Author of Dead Man Walking, the book which inspired the Academy Award Winning film starring Susan Sarandon) it was widely publicised. She gave a moving account of Dobbie, a Death Row inmate with advanced arthritis. He could barely walk. He was taken to the killing room some ten times before he was finally murdered. The question of his innocence was quite immaterial to the authorities by then but many observers were sure of his innocence. His wife and family were the heroes. They unequivocally forgave the authorities and were not bitter. Amazing grace.

When it was our turn to speak Joy gave a moving account of our Death Row experiences. She had the audience in tears. I, on the other hand, gave an account as a novice with a touch of self-deprecating humour and had the audience smiling. Some people said later that I had given them the courage to go to Texas. A year later, at the 2000 conference I met a lady who recognised me and who said that she had visited death row and had thought of my words as she drove to the prison.

Ted's work was once again in print: "The Carmelite newsmagazine printed one of my poems, "I Will Build an Altar" in their last issue. It still feels strange to see my name in print, someplace other than newspaper headlines."

He also managed to get a few pages scribbled for an article (John of the Cross on Death Row) for The Spanish Carmelite Provincial about what it's like to try and live a contemplative life while on Death Row. His American Provincial also wanted a copy for the Christmas issue.

By this time more than 140 people had died since Ted had been on Death Row. There was no immediate prospect that things would change:

"There was another execution a couple of days ago, Domingo Cantu. There are another 13 scheduled between now and 26 January. I'm sure some of these will receive stays of execution, but many of them won't. From my cell I can see the back door of the clinic, through which they come out to the vans that take them to the Walls Unit and the death chamber. It's rather depressing and a far cry from my previous view. I would much rather watch the visitors' children play on the front lawn. I can also see the cross atop the chapel steeple. I've heard that they wrap it in coloured lights at Christmas – a little something to look forward to I guess.

"This is McKinney's last day here at Ellis One. He came round this morning with communion and had the Chaplain from the Estelle Unit with him, a Chaplain who still wears the Roman collar. That's unusual here in prison. His name is Adams. I hope he gets over his paranoia soon, though. I swear you can almost see his body shaking with fear when he's here. The Estelle Unit has solid walls and doors, so he never actually has any physical contact with the men over there and he can't seem to adapt to the open bars over here. When McKinney introduced him and I put out my hand to shake his and the man looked at me as if I'd lost my mind, and then backed up against the railing and refused to move. He's supposed to come round with Communion next Saturday. That should be interesting.

"There's no sign that the administration is even remotely considering giving us religious services again. And I've almost decided that I don't really care. I have my Divine Office, my Bible, my courses and (hopefully) someone to bring me Communion each week. That's more than a lot of people have, so I'll try not to be so dissatisfied because things aren't better. This may be the very best of days for a long time so I might as well enjoy it".

Ted had had little contact from his family. His stepfather had visited around 1st August. But Ted had not heard from him since then:

"Still nothing from my sister. I should have known better than to get my hopes up when she wrote in July. I honestly believe that all her years of drug abuse have affected her brain, because she just doesn't think like a normal person does (whatever normal is!). I know she has a life of her own to get on with, and the HIV/ AIDS that she and Everett have is a major problem for her. My step dad even agrees that when she talks to someone, she says whatever she thinks that person wants to hear, but then she will immediately forget what she said. She will even claim later that she didn't even say it all. So when she writes saying she'll visit and write more often, I should have known better than to believe her.

"My step dad doesn't write any more either. He says that there's nothing happening out there and he doesn't know what to write about, yet he's constantly going places and visiting people. I sort of expected it from him, though. I knew when Mom died he would gradually disappear from my life. And it is not as if he owed me anything.

"I'm having a hard time saving money. Seems like every time I turn around I'm having to spend a "little bit" on this, that, and something else. I get $40 a month from my step-dad, except when I want a book or magazine subscription and then it's less than $40. Every trip to the clinic, whatever the reason, costs $3. And we have to buy our own medication. One would think it would be in their best interests to make sure we stay healthy, because cold and flu and such are spread so easily in such crowded conditions, But it seems they are only interested in making money.

"All of our over the counter medications and vitamins we have to buy ourselves. My allergy medication and nasal spray cost me about $4 a month, writing supplies for a month (20 stamps ($6.60), paper ($3), envelopes ($1.50)) are a little over $11; soap, shampoo, toothpaste, etc. are about $6.00; and I don't probably need it, but I usually end up getting something to eat (an "evening" meal is served at 3:00pm, so I'm always hungry at 8 or 9:00) for the month – 15 soups (25cents each) and four or five bags of Tortilla Chips (crisps to you, I suppose) (80 cents each), so that's another $7.00 or so. That's about $30.00 altogether.

"I try to save as much of the remaining $10 as I can, but I have a hard time resisting the urge to send donations to the monasteries and shrines for Masses or birthdays or when someone is sick. I probably spend more on Masses and Mass novenas than I should, but they're the only "gifts" I can give people any more".

On November 30th Ted was able to say he had a visitor: "Father Harry was here for a "formation" visit yesterday morning. I think he was a bit disappointed about the way our visiting room is set up. He was expecting to visit us in a big room, sitting at a table with nothing but air between us, so he wasn't real thrilled about me showing up in handcuffs and being locked in a cage, and with so much glass and wire-mesh between us. Personally I find this treatment demeaning and insulting since I've never given anyone reason to use restraints on me, but Father Bill took it much worse than I did. Well, I guess learning a little humility won't hurt me much. He'll like it even less when I'm sent to Terrell, because we'll have to visit over the telephone there. He seems to have the idea that, since he was able to visit with me that first time in front of my cell, he should be able to visit that way every time he shows up.

"I can't make him understand that he was able to do that only because he'd come in with McKinney and had celebrated Mass

196

in the chapel [for population inmates only]. But he's not a chaplain here so he can't come like that all the time. I reckon he'll figure it out sooner or later. We had a good visit, though, and managed to cover just about every topic imaginable in the two hours he was here.

"Father Walsh is supposed to be here sometime this week He was here a couple of weeks ago for John Lamb's execution, then he went to Florida to spend Thanksgiving with some of his family. James Beathard has a date set for December 9th, I believe, and Father Walsh will be here 'til James is gone. James was Cliff Boggess' cellmate, and he also wrote some of the material featured in the book, Welcome to Hell, so you may have heard of him before. He also had a visit yesterday, and was in the cage next to me so I had a chance to talk to him a bit. That was the first time I'd seen him since we were taken off the work program. He seems to be in pretty good spirits though (like many of us) he wears his mask well and always has.

Two days later Ted had another visit:

"Father Walsh was just here for a few minutes. He's supposed to be here for a couple of weeks so I'll probably see him again before he leaves. I hope so anyway – I wanted to take advantage of his visit to go to confession, but he was in a hurry this morning. The administration is giving him a hard time because he requested that the warden allow several of us to attend a last Mass for James Beathard. They told the padre this morning that he can't visit us anymore unless he keeps a plexiglass "shield" between himself and us. We already have bars and steel mesh

197

between us, but this is simply harassment. It's not really all that surprising, though, since the officer in charge of building security has stated for the record that religion is wasted on people like us. He feels the only time we should have access to a priest or a minister is just before we're executed! "

As Ted recorded on December 4th conditions were more than difficult:

"As you know, we've been moved around again. I feel like I've died and gone to hell! What this cellblock needs is an old fashioned exorcism, because if these folks aren't possessed they're at least not far from it. This is the first time I've been in this end of the building in almost twelve years, and I'd forgotten just how crude and vulgar we convicts can be! But I don't want to write about my new living conditions. Hopefully they're only temporary and I'll be on my way to Terrell before long (it would be more pleasant and much less stressful to share a desert cave with scorpions and rattlesnakes! At least they're quiet!!).

"I've been able to see and talk to Anthony a couple of times since I've moved. They decided he could remain in the new work programme, so he hasn't been moved and he gets four hours recreation every day rather than two. I'm glad he wasn't moved. He's a good kid but he tries too hard to be "grown up". The older Mexicans have almost got him convinced that "real men" are hard and tough and cold and Tony just hasn't got it in him. I don't know how he's going to survive if he's ever removed from the work programme. I expect to thrive on the solitude and silence but kids like Tony just can't handle that. Let's just pray about it instead, shall we?

"I would love to read the chapters as you progress with your writing. Have you started writing yet, or is everything still in the planning stage? You wrote that you might call it Changed Lives, because both our lives have been changed, but especially yours. I think you told me during our first visit that when Joy asked you to come over with her, you'd never even considered visiting or writing to a prisoner. And just look at you now! You've certainly made an impact on my life, and before you're through you will affect the lives of many others as well.

"I haven't been able to do much of anything at all since being moved to this end of the building. Thank God for the Divine Office! I believe being able to pray the Hours each day is the only thing holding my little world together! I force myself to concentrate long enough to study a little each day for my correspondence course, but then I put on my headphones and turn up the volume on the radio just to get away from the noise. About the only thing I can do while listening to the radio is write letters, so I'm not getting much reading done. I'm reading a book, Celtic Spirituality, that's pretty good. When I finish it I'll start on one of the books Sr. Joy sent. St., John of the Cross has most of my attention though.

"My formation studies for the Lay Carmelites are coming along well. I'm enjoying it, but I think it would be more interesting and fulfilling if I was able to be a member of an actual community. As an "isolated member" all I have are my own thoughts and

199

opinions about what I read in the formation texts. I don't get any sort of "feedback" from other Lay Carmelites. Father Bill tries to help as best he's able, but he's just too busy to read and really respond to my letters. I don't suppose it matters too much, though, because since I'm alone here it will mainly be up to me as to what "shape" my prayer life takes.

Mary has had an important place in my life from the very beginning of my conversion, and the rosary is one of my favourite forms of prayer, so as a "Lay Brother of Our Lady of Mount Carmel" my prayer life won't be too much different than before. I hope it will progress, of course, as I continue my studies of John of the Cross, but it will just be a matter of persevering. I guess ultimately it doesn't matter if you're a priest or a nun or a layperson – either you have an active relationship with the Lord, or you don't. And if you don't, then all the Orders and communities in the world won't do you much good

"One of the things I love about the Church is the doctrine of our communion with the saints. So, even when it "feels" like I'm all alone, I know that there's a spiritual aspect of our existence that transcends both time and distance – we're always together: you and me and all the saints, living and dead, all the time and in all places! I guess that you could say that eternity is all around us.

"Our cells all have three concrete walls and one of bars (in front). There are three tiers of these, and each tier has 21 cells side by side. I wish we were allowed to decorate our cells, but this new warden seems determined to make sure that our cells stay plain and austere. I guess he just doesn't want us to forget where we're at. Not that there's much chance of that happening! I've heard things are more lax at Terrell – the warden isn't totally heartless over there – so maybe next Christmas will be better."

"I got a letter from Garry yesterday evening. He's not handling things at all well. I wrote him a week ago and asked how he's doing with the Liturgy of the Hours and his correspondence course and he said that he's all but stopped praying and he hasn't done much at all with his course. He spends his time reading cheap spy novels and exchanging harsh words with the guards. It sounds to me as if he just doesn't care about much anymore. The people on his cellblock are just as bad as the ones around me he says, but if he just doesn't at least try to keep God in his life and stay active with prayer and study this place will drive him crazy. It's mainly the incredible noise and the constant harassment by the guards that gets under his skin. But he has the idea that when he gets angry and loses his temper and tells off a guard or two it "proves" he's not a good person and God's not going to hear his prayers so why bother praying and religion is wasted on him so he stops trying.

"It's easy to understand his problem though. We can only relate to spiritual things, love and compassion and forgiveness by what we learn from our families and Church while growing up. In Garry's case he's learned that when you screw up, people turn their backs to you. That's how he sees God. Garry's Dad is the only person who hasn't deserted him. All the other members of his

201

family and all his so-called friends cannot forgive him and I don't think he has ever really forgiven himself and he has a hard time believing that God will forgive him. I'm not there to encourage him anymore and we don't have a Chaplain (Deacon Adams is assigned to the Estelle Unit) so Garry is on his own. Maybe things will improve for him at Terrell if he can manage for that long."

Ted sent me some photographs of his home territory: "It's probably hard to believe that a person could really be homesick for places like that, but it truly is beautiful country. Especially after a spring rain shower when the cactus blooms and everything is fresh and green for a few hours. Otherwise it's mostly snakes and spiders, with an occasional coyote or bobcat. But it's home! A far cry from the green hills and valleys of Wales, though isn't it?

"Well, it's Monday now. The 13th. I took a break from your letter last night so I could get all my Christmas cards sent out in this morning's mail. I got a letter this morning from an attorney. Not my attorney – the court still hasn't assigned me one yet. This guy apparently knows that I haven't got an attorney, so he wrote to let me know that the Court of Criminal Appeals has turned down my request for an evidentiary hearing. So that ends my appeals in the State Courts, and I'll be going into the Federal Courts now. Since my case is pretty much "open and shut", they'll probably just rubber stamp it so I can be given an execution date. I'm not sure how long that will take, but they seem to be hurrying things along as quickly as they can. Anyway – he wrote in his letter that he or his law partner would be here sometime to "discuss my options", though

I'm not sure why he would come all the way out here at his own expense, just to give me advice."

By the closing days of the 20th Century Ted had spent twelve years on Death Row. In his letters there was neither mention of Christmas 1999 or the New Millennium. Perhaps it was not surprising. Maybe his mind was on other things. Just a few days earlier, on 9th Dec. 1999 James Beathard, 42, Cliff Boggess' cellmate, had been executed and another 13 executions were scheduled before 26th January 2000.

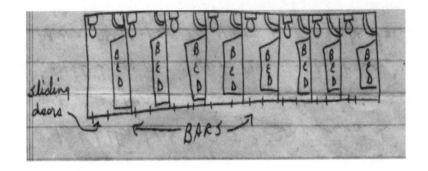

A diagram of Ted's cell taken from one of his letters.

Chapter 20

Millennium

Love doesn't recognise the past,
And the future may never be;
Love lives only for the moment,
And today is all it can see.

Christmas in Wales was lovely. Richard and David came home to stay, which is always fun. On the 25th Tanya and Joy joined us for the celebration lunch. James, Bee, Francesca and William joined us for the Millennium New Year.

Richard and Carrie became engaged at our New Year Millennium party. It was most exciting. Our friends came. We had champagne, a buffet supper, dancing, games and fireworks on the beach. Now they represented another more personal celebration. What a wonderful start to the New Millennium! Richard and Carrie planned to marry on the 21st July 2001, which seemed ages away.

Meanwhile things were very different for Ted: "Christmas, I'm sorry to say, was a big disappointment for me mainly because the chaplains seem to have deserted us. Father Walsh was here for James Beathard's execution, and he came by with Eucharist the following Sat., but then he had to return to Boston and we haven't seen anyone since then. I don't really expect anyone to show up until Father Walsh returns. I had so wanted to go to confession and have Communion before Christmas, but it just wasn't to be. Oh, I know a lot of people don't really approve of frequent confession or Communion, but both sacraments bring me a great deal of comfort. But our Lord knows my heart, and I thank God that Christ is not confined or restricted to a small wafer of bread. He isn't obligated to come to me by means of a priest or deacon, and bars and cement walls can't keep Him from me.

"I've been down with the flu for the last four days. Not much to do for it except to stay in bed all day and try and sleep. There have been so many people ill during the last couple of weeks. They've even run out of aspirin on the cellblock (which is the only thing available). We can always ask to see the doctor, but it can take anywhere from six to ten days to get an appointment, and by then it's too late.

"Rumour has it that we'll all be moved to the Terrell Unit either the last week of this month or the first week of February.

"I got a letter from Garry tonight. He's on a rampage about the way our local church (and especially our Bishop – Garry calls him "Bishop Pilate") treated James Beathard before, during, and after his execution. James was one of the few people here who was really innocent of what he was accused of. He was a good Catholic and kept the faith all the way to the end, but he wrote to our local pastor and to our Bishop several times before his death, and never got any sort of reply. James could not find a single person or group who would speak out for him, even though the man who actually did the killings admitted that James was innocent.

"Garry thinks that since James was a Catholic in good standing with the Church, and since the Church wants to pretend that justice is important in the Christian community, that the Bishop had an obligation to speak out against James' execution. It may not have done any good, but he should have tried.

"Garry has written a very scathing letter to our Bishop, and apparently didn't like the reply he got back. (The Bishop assured Garry of his on-going ministry to Death Row, and said he would always do what he could to help abolish the death penalty — totally missing the whole point of Garry's complaint!).

"He seems to be coping with his situation a bit better. He's once again praying the Hours and his rosary, anyway, and that at least will help to keep his mind on God. Bro. Gabriel, the Benedictine monk that he writes to, has offered to send him information on the Benedictine Third Order, and Father Bill promised me that he would find me a Cistercian who will take time to actually be a friend to him. I think he'll be okay once we're at Terrell. He reacts to stress in a way exactly opposite of how I do — he gets loud and argumentative, and tends to want to strike out at whatever is causing the stress; I, on the other hand, tend to withdraw into my own little world so I don't have to deal with the stress, and I get quiet and moody.

"I have an advantage over Garry, though, because the "world" I withdraw into is a world of prayer and study (or else I listen to my radio and write letters); but when Garry gets loud and abusive (verbally) toward the people who "cause" his stress, he only invites retaliation which increase the stress, which increases… And so it goes. But I think he'll find his way after he's spent some time alone, and has a chance to "chill out".

"I have all four volumes of the Liturgy of the Hours now. The Carmelite Sisters of New Caney sent me a set that had belonged to a nun who had recently died. I rather like the idea of having and using a set of breviaries that have been used by a nun. It sort of makes them special, you know?

"I just finished a correspondence course on the Catechism from the Sisters of Saint Joseph. This was my second one from them. I'll be able to start another one dealing with scripture in a couple of weeks. If the rumours are true and we are moving to Terrell in a couple of weeks, it will help me to stay busy. My Carmelite Formation Studies are coming along well, as is my course on St. John of the Cross. Now if I can get a little peace and quiet!!! Soon, God willing. Very soon.

"I'm afraid I don't know enough yet about what's going on in my case to be able to tell you anything. All I know for certain right now is that the Court of Criminal Appeals has refused to grant me any relief in my state appeal and have moved it to the Federal level, and I still don't have any attorney. I'm not going to push them about it, though, because I want to see how far they'll try to go before they allow me proper representation. I think if they screw up my case badly enough it can be used by Death Penalty abolishment groups as "proof" that the whole system is screwed up.

We'll see. But it really won't do much good to speculate on any of it until we know what's going on.

"On 13th December, I got a letter from Rob Owen (a partner in a law firm with Raoul Schonemann) who had "heard through the grapevine" that my state appeal had been denied, and that either he or Raoul would like to meet with me to discuss my "options". Not long after that I received a visit from Maurie Levin. She was actually here to visit with another of her clients. She just wanted to give me a brief explanation of what was going on.

"On January 14th I first met with Rob Owen and he expressed a desire to take my case. He seems a decent enough sort (for a lawyer). He'd heard that I was trying to drop my appeal and wanted a chance to see if he could "make something happen" with my case. I told him he could take my case if he wanted it. He was about to begin a new trial, but as soon as it was over he's to send me the necessary papers to fill out and sign, and then he'll request the judge to make his appointment official."

Gary's father had to read a newspaper to learn important developments concerning his son's fate. I heard about it in Ted's letter of Jan. 27th 2000:

"By now you probably know that Garry's appeal has been turned down by the Federal Court. All he has left is the Supreme Court, and we all know that the chance of them seeing things in a positive light is very slim. He expects to have an execution date in six to nine months, maybe a year. It's just a matter of more sitting and waiting. We seem to be doing a lot of that around here."

208

The following day Ted signed papers during a legal visit with attorney Meredith Rountree, Robert and Raoul's partner. This gave Robert and Raoul permission to begin work on his case.

Ted was very positive about the progress of his spiritual journey: "The course on St. John of the Cross is really great. My instructor, Father Culligan, has been very patient with me, but I'm sure he must be irritated by my many questions sometimes. Most of his students, if not all of them, take his course as part of a wider study or in able to get some sort of degree; I, on the other hand, am trying to actually live what I'm learning, so sometimes his stock answers aren't quite enough to satisfy my "need to know"".

For people living in North Wales the name of Clatterbridge on the Cheshire Wirral brings a feeling of trepidation. When the skin specialist told John that he should go there I was very nervous. As soon as we opened the doors to enter the hospital the friendly, hopeful atmosphere engulfed me. People talked to each other in the reception area, in the refreshment centre and outside the different radiation treatment facilities. It was enlightening and helpful to know that there were others with similar problems, to meet them, to see and hear their positive attitude.

As this treatment had to be performed on three consecutive days, with a weekend break then two more days, we would stay near Liverpool and visit the city. We booked into a pleasant, old hotel in one of the leafy villages on the Wirral across the river from Liverpool. After resting, we motored through the Mersey tunnel straight into the city centre. It had changed a great deal from my student days there. Deep thoroughfares had been sliced across the city. I drove along them trying to identify my position.

The rotund, beige stone library building was still recognisable. That special smell of books that hits one on entry was also there, as was the hushed silence and the myriad, multi-coloured tomes that lined the walls to the glass-domed ceiling. The gallery, the oak stepladders, the rolled up, faded, well used cream navigation charts that tingled the imagination with hints of sea, sailing schooners and far off lands, were all as I remembered.

The huge edifice next door, the museum, was also recognisable. Inside we enjoyed the new and interesting display of peoples and their culture. One of the best was of a replica of a pharaoh's tomb with hieroglyphics and their translations.

The new Catholic Cathedral sits fittingly on Mount Pleasant, Liverpool's highest viewpoint. With its crown-like dome, vast concrete structure and many steps the new Cathedral is a revelation. The spacious interior is a colourful sanctuary. The centre altar is the main focus with seating for hundreds in the round. Small, peaceful side altars nestle in open alcoves off the concave walls. My lasting impression of this truly wonderful Cathedral is of light and hues of yellow, orange, red and green from the magnificent stained glass windows and the incandescent gold of the candlesticks and brilliant white of the altar cloths.

Again I am struck by the necessity for a place of worship. In this large, thriving, trading city there has always been the sanctuary of many churches. Today the city's architectural legacy includes a new Cathedral for the praise and love of God. But where is the one for Death Row, Texas?

In Texas Ted was once again experiencing a clampdown by the prison authorities:

"By now I'm sure you've heard about the "armed standoff" that took place on the Terrell Unit on the 21st Feb. Like every prison in the whole state we were also immediately placed on lock-down status. For the last nine or ten days it has been the usual: no TV, no showers, no recreation, no visits, no hot meals, or commissary privileges so I'm out of stamps. At 6:00a.m. they showed up to start tearing things apart while they look for weapons and other contraband. I still say that Hitler's Gestapo could take lessons from the "gentlemen" who work in this place! Supposedly they were looking for evidence of a "conspiracy" between the inmates at Terrell and us. But the truth is they were just lashing out at us because we're available. Not that the reason is really important: the results are the same regardless. I did not lose much but I can tell that my books have taken a beating. I just keep telling myself that Lent started early and that it will be alright."

During this time in the United Kingdom, we had an intensely public period as Lethal Justice, Joy's book, was published. We took every opportunity to tell the public about Death Row in Texas. It resulted in many radio and television interviews. We spoke on Woman's Hour with Ann Widdecombe MP. She had just become a

211

Catholic, but interestingly she was pro-death penalty. There are divergent views and opinions in the community, but the Catholic Church has recently stood firm on this point. The Pope has asked President Bush on many occasions to spare the life of a Death Row inmate only to be ignored. Ann Widdecombe would not comment on the American legal system.

We went to Norwich for a six-minute Sunday appearance on a live programme for Anglia TV. Our aim was to spread the word about Death Row and to tell as many people as we can what is going on in that Texas prison. Is it not punishment enough that they are to be killed at some specified time without having to be treated inhumanely on the way? They bear the results of their many mistakes and their violent life-styles and so, too, do the authorities. Both sides carry the millstone in their different ways during their daily contacts with each other. Do the prisoners who do something positive; show remorse and repentance find redemption? Many who live with hope and die with courage counter the fear that is making the State of Texas lash out blindly with its policy of Death Row extermination.

Chapter 21

Moving home

Just fill me with your love and joy,
Let me live each day without fear;
Fill me with Your peace O Lord,
Let me live in Your presence here.

On Friday March 3rd 2000 I spoke about Ted at the Women's World Day of Prayer at our Church in Conwy. The theme was Jairus's dying daughter. Jairus put his trust in the word of Jesus and his daughter was brought back to life. Ted heard the Word of God, put his trust in Him and found life and hope where there had only been hate and despair. Pam Baguley, the wife of one of the ministers, spoke to me afterwards and later gave me a testament of her story, which I sent to Ted. She has had many health problems and is an asthmatic like myself. Ted was impressed by her testimony. He thought she was truly blessed and he would add her and her husband to his prayer list.

Despite the "armed standoff" that Ted had reported, all Death Row prisoners at the Ellis One were transported to the Terrell Unit at Livingston, Texas:

"As you can see from our new address we've all finally moved to the Terrell Unit. Personally, I'm glad it's all over and done with. I prefer this place over the Ellis Unit, but I was dreading the actual move itself. To be honest the move was just as bad as I thought it would be.

213

"Father Walsh had just sat down in front of my cell yesterday when they told us to pack our belongings up. Seems like every time he visits, we get interrupted with something. They moved us this morning – all of us, except for about 35-40 inmates who will be coming tomorrow or Monday. I am so glad that's over with.

"I'm used to the fact that the guards at Ellis have always gone out of their way to humiliate us in any and every way possible. It's almost second nature with them. I would almost say they can't help themselves. So I was prepared for being stripped and poked and prodded by both men and women alike. It was unpleasant, but not unexpected.

What I wasn't prepared for was being handcuffed and having chains padlocked around my ankles, of having that chain – about 8 inches long – connected by another padlock to my handcuffs, and then having to walk like some sort of duck – all bent over and taking tiny steps so as not to fall – all the way to the bus. It's rather difficult to hold one's head high when in that sort of position, don't you know? They also took everyone's eyeglasses, for some silly reason, and I didn't get mine back until about 10:30 or 11:00 that night, by which time I didn't really care as I had a blinding head-ache.

"All of my papers, letters, course papers and legal papers were taken out of their individual folders and mixed together in a large bag. It almost looks as if someone had shuffled them together as you would a deck of playing cards. A lot of stuff is wrecked and many papers have what seems to be honey, or syrup, on them. I guess someone had a jar of it in his belongings that leaked, or perhaps was cracked or broken, during the transfer to Terrell. I still haven't sorted through the stuff. It's just lying here in a pile, looking depressed and unhappy. It's much better for the papers to be depressed than for me to be!

"My typewriter has a few dents and scuffmarks and the casing is cracked, but it seems to still work just fine. My radio came through OK. I think that my headphones have several shorts in the cord now. They don't provide us in any way to repair things like that, so I'll just have to replace them. Fortunately, I wasn't planning to listen to the radio much anyway during Lent. This way I wasn't tempted, because it's just too much trouble.

"The only real complaint I have besides the condition of my papers is that someone at Ellis stole my coffee and hot chocolate from out of my belongings! I've got addicted to hot chocolate in the last few months and enjoy having a cup before going to bed.

"My cell is great! I was fortunate in getting on a 'pod' [line of cells] that doesn't have any of the noisier folks (which means Garry probably got stuck with them, though, I hope not!). As you might expect, most of the guys were pretty loud today – the excitement of the move, and then each guy wanting to find out where his friends are (not to mention the noise due to the sheer boredom – it took almost 14 hours to get our belongings "searched" and returned to us!). But, even with all the yelling back and forth, it was still quieter than my old cell was.

My noisy neighbours' yelling and banging and crashing has been reduced to a distant and muffled roar. I can think again! It sure makes reading and studying so much easier. My new cell is almost twice as large as my last cell – and it's clean and has been freshly painted. It's also much brighter, because I have a large florescent light now instead of a glaring bare bulb. And, for the first time in 12 years, I have both cold water and hot! I think I'm going to like this a lot!"

"Father Walsh was here Tuesday afternoon. He was looking very confused, as he wandered around trying to find all his "flock". I don't think he's very happy with this move since "his" Death Row is over here, but his Secular Franciscans are all at Ellis. But, as he puts it, "I don't presume to advise the Lord. I just go where I'm sent".

"Anthony was moved over here on my tank [cell block] yesterday, so I don't have to wonder how he's doing now. I also saw him last Friday (I had an interview with Rob and Raoul that lasted a little more than an hour) in the visiting room. He was visiting with his grandfather, and didn't look the least bit happy with his circumstances. I guess that's to be expected, though. Hopefully, he'll find a routine for his days that will provide some sort of structure for him and will preserve his sanity.

"Rob and Raoul had asked to see me, just as a courtesy, I guess. They were actually here to visit a couple of other people, but since they were "in the neighbourhood"... But, Rob made the mistake of asking me how I was passing the time. Big mistake!

Rob was raised in the Baptist Church and has no idea what the Catholic faith is all about, so I got started with the Liturgy of the Hours; John of the Cross; Carmelite formation; praying the rosary, and so on and on.

"He surprised me, though, because after about 10 or 15 minutes, he was asking questions and wanting further details. They stayed more than an hour, but not quite an hour and half. Then, they still had to go to interview the people they'd originally come to interview! Our "Interview" was much more like a visit, but then I don't do interviews anymore; I only visit with friends."

Ted's first legal visit with Robert and Raoul together was on March 10th. As he rather succinctly put it, "they wanted to "plan Strategy" – I wanted to sleep."

"I still haven't heard from Garry, though he did send me a couple of books via Father Walsh, and then last Friday evening about 7.00pm he sent a priest around to my cell to tell me 'Hello', and that he was doing OK. The priest was Father Manion (or Bannion, or even Manning!). We heard McKinney call him all three names when he would come to Ellis to celebrate Mass for us way back then. I even asked him once what the proper pronunciation of his name was, but his brogue is so thick, I couldn't understand him!! He said he comes to the Unit about every 3-6 weeks depending on his schedule. He's the pastor of a church in San Antonio, and one of his parishioners is here. You have to admire a priest who will follow one of his own all the way to Death Row just to make sure he has access to all the Sacraments. Too many priests would say that he's no longer their concern.

"You may remember me and Garry commenting in a past letter, about a priest who insists on throwing a "Hail Mary" into the Mass at odd moments? Well, this is the same priest. He has a beautiful Irish accent, and I could listen to him for hours. And sometimes, he would forget his teeth at home, and then he sounded as if he were speaking a completely foreign language! Anyway, I was able to take Communion - complete with a "Hail Mary" - and he actually stayed a few minutes asking how I was doing and if I needed anything. He also asked me if a priest had been around the previous day, so evidently, there was someone else here too, though that may have been Father Walsh finishing up his rounds. I'd hoped to see Father Walsh again before he left, but since he was staying until the 13th, I suppose I've missed him.

"I don't know if I would go so far as to say that the guards here are more respectful, but they are more professional; and though the general attitude of most of the guards is somewhat disdainful of us, I haven't heard a rude or obscene remark yet from any of them. What struck me most, though, is that there is no hostile atmosphere towards us here like there was at Ellis. If anything, the atmosphere here is indifference, which can be just as bad on a person's sense of self-worth.

"Calvin Burdine is over here with us now, right next door to Tony, I think. Calvin was my cellmate several years ago – but only for a few months. Calvin and I were born in the same hospital at

Goodfellow Air Force Base in San Angelo, Texas, and only a few weeks apart. Our mothers had a mutual friend, also, though I don't think our mothers ever actually met each other. Calvin and I also know quite a few of the same people from San Angelo, though we never met till we came here."

Calvin Burdine is currently out of Death Row awaiting a re-trial. His attorney was asleep during some of his original trial.

Despite the move to Terrell the food was still unappealing to Ted:

"I'm getting really tired of this stuff they're trying to pass off as food. For lunch today we had two pancakes with a mixture of peanut butter and jelly between them (and we have that at every meal!) and we also had a slice of salami between two corn tortillas. So, it's filling, but everything is cold – some of these "sandwiches" are actually still frozen – and it's getting rather monotonous. But, it does make fasting on Wednesdays and Fridays much easier, since I'm not giving up much!

With some friends from Llandudno, John and I went to Manchester to see the Lowry exhibition. The pictures, done in the naive style, of life in a pre-war factory town, are full of purposeful "matchstick" men and endearing cats, dogs and children. Lowry, a rent collector, would walk the streets with his pencil and sketchbook in his pocket, capturing the moment and later transferring his sketches to canvas.

219

In my next letter to Ted I asked him if he had tried his hand at drawing:

"While I was at Ellis, I bought watercolours and coloured pencils and paper, and was just waiting to get over here where it's nice and quiet before I got started in my attempts at drawing and/ or painting. But, when I got over here, I found out that I have to have something called an "Art Card". This card will enable me to gain the "privilege" of drawing and painting, and will allow me to purchase art supplies from the Commissary. However – without said "Art Card", anything I draw or paint becomes "contraband" as soon as I try to send it out, and all "contraband" will be confiscated. So, I have paints and pencils and receipts proving I bought them at the Ellis Commissary – but I can't use them until someone is gracious enough to provide me with an Art Card.

Chapter 22

Light of the World

Give me access to your strength,
For I have none of my own.
Lend me courage also, Lord,
On this path of thorn and stone.

Garry was once again on Ted's mind: "I really hope Garry will take advantage of Abbot Kelly's gesture of reaching out to him through correspondence. I'd told Garry that I was going to write to the Abbey on his behalf and he seemed to be okay with that, but sometimes he tends to lose all confidence in himself and in what he believes and thinks, and then he'll withdraw from the offered help so that he won't make a "fool" of himself in the eyes of someone who appears holy and wise to him. I suppose there are times when I have an advantage in that titles and positions just don't impress me much. Except when it comes to the Pope! Anyway Garry is a bit of a fan of Thomas Merton (which is one of the reasons I wrote to Merton's former monastery), and as fate would have it, the present Abbot was Assistant to Merton during Merton's last year as Novice Master at the Abbey. That alone should impress Garry at least a little, and give him reason to reply to the Abbot's letter.

"I saw Garry for a few minutes yesterday, and was able to talk to him for a little while. The shower on our section of the pod wasn't working right for some reason, and they took me to the shower in Garry's section – which just happens to be right next door to his cell! I took a very quick shower and then we got to talk for a few minutes before they came back to get me. The very first thing he said was, "Hey, I got a letter from the Abbot! And he actually knew Merton!!" I think it's safe to say that the letter from Abbot Kelly brought a small ray of sunshine into Garry's life. I'm really glad.

"They have three executions scheduled for this week, two for next week (seven total – so far – are scheduled for June). I just heard that on the radio. It's hard to keep up with all the executions since we moved to Terrell. I hardly ever see anyone or get a chance to talk to anyone. I see Father Walsh once a month and get news from him, and Garry writes with what little bits and pieces of news that he hears. I seldom know what's really going on around here!

Ted had definite thoughts about my proposed book:
"If you can get people to understand the circumstances that lead kids to prison and Death Row, and if you can make people understand that society is responsible for making kids who and what they become, then maybe you can effect a change. Telling people how terrible this place is won't help, though – most people who care already know what it is like here, and those who support capital punishment will only see a situation as nothing more than what we deserve.

"Your book is in God's hands, every bit as much as my life – and all lives – are. He gives us free rein to do as we please, of course, if that's what we think we want, but when we place even the "everyday" things in His hands then he'll take care of everything. When you've finished your writing, you'll probably re-read some finely worded and inspiring phrases and have to ask yourself, "Well, where in the world did that come from?" God still inspires if we let him."

His enthusiasm for his favourite saint was far from waning: "If you want to know more about John, I would suggest that you read his works now. Take your time with it and I've no doubt he'll speak to your soul the same way he spoke to mine. I would recommend The Collected Works of St. John of the Cross, translated by Kieran Kavanaugh, O.C.D. and Otilio Rodriguez, O.C.D. (1991 revised edition). I don't believe you'll find any better authorities on John of the Cross, and you can depend on the accuracy of their translation.

"I finished the course I was taking on John. I sent my last paper in to Father Culligan a couple of weeks ago and will probably get it back from him in another week or so. I'm sure he'll be relieved to be rid of me – I'm not the best of students for a professor who's trying to concentrate on writing a book, as I tend to ask lots of questions if I'm not sure of something or if I want more details! I don't know what I'll try my mind at next possibly a course on Br. Titus Brandsma.

"I've written a few times to the lady who teaches that course, and she's also on the board of the Committee for the Canonization Cause of Brandsma. Titus was a Dutch Carmelite who died by lethal injection at Dachau. He was a journalist, a professor of philosophy and of the history of Catholic mysticism, and an outspoken defender of Catholic education and of the freedom of the Catholic press. I find his life and teachings interesting.

"I have one more paper to write on John of the Cross, and I should be finished with the course on the Bible in three or four weeks, and then I think I'm going to try and do some writing before I start another course. You know, when I finish these two courses I will have completed twelve different courses in the last two and a half years! I think it's time for a break. I'll still have the Carmelite formation studies to do, of course, but I'll probably be doing those the rest of my life.

"Well we've been here for three weeks now, and I still haven't seen or heard from our chaplain. Father Walsh had said that Chaplain Stanley was pretty active with the prisoners here, but you couldn't prove it by me. I've written to him twice asking that my name be added to the list of people to receive Communion, and also asking him to please come get all the books I've finished with. Garry and I have gotten a couple of large shipments of books from Liguori Publishers, but the way it usually ends up is that – out of maybe twenty books – there will only be four or five that we might be interested in. We only have to pay the shipping costs, so the books themselves (which are usually slightly damaged or out of print) are free. I think it's a pretty good bargain."

Easter at Deganwy was lovely with most of the family at home. We went to the Puppet theatre in Rhos on Sea with the grandchildren and had ice cream on the seafront afterwards. We also enjoyed some sailing, including a passage to Holyhead on Sea Mist. The sight of small islands like Little Mouse and Middle Mouse from the sea makes for an interesting voyage as they are rarely seen from the mainland. They are tucked out of sight of the main roads on Anglesey. These Islets are only visible to walkers rambling in the fields that roll down to the water's edge. It was rewarding to sleep on board after a hearty meal in the cabin and with thoughts of what the next day's sailing might bring.

Things however were far from easy for Ted: "Last Monday night about 11:00pm, they showed up at my door and informed me that I needed to get ready to go on bench-warrant to Lubbock and that they'd be back to get me in a couple of hours. I tried to explain that the date for my hearing had been moved to August, but they had the teletype from the court saying that I was supposed to be there on May 10th, so all the talking in the world wasn't going to do me any good. About 1:30am, they came and got me, loaded me down with handcuffs, leg shackles, and lots and lots of chains, and they put me in the back of a van.

At about 7.30pm, Terrell called the van – we were almost to Dallas – and told them to bring me back. We got back here a little after 12 – noon, so I spent almost eleven hours in 'cuffs and chains bouncing around in the back of that transport van.

And to add insult to injury – they gave me two sack lunches, each of which contained three pancakes with packets of syrup, a small box of dry cereal, and a half pint of milk, none of which I could eat the way I was 'cuffed and shackled! And you know what? Those eleven hours were even more miserable than I thought they'd be!! No fun at all, I can assure you."

I had previously enquired if Ted was interested in writing his own book. His reply was emphatic: "I don't think so. I've never cared much for publicity and if I write a book it would only be an excuse for opponents of the anti-Death Penalty crowd to smear what little reputation I have left. (Actually, that's what I expect to happen when your book is published, though maybe I'll be dead by then and it won't matter.)

"I even got a couple of nasty letters from Carmelites who were offended by my last published poem, Blessed Art Thou! One was a priest and the other was a seminary student (though neither had the courage to actually sign their name!) from Chicago. I'm thinking of using a pseudonym if I ever submit anything else for publication, and leaving out all the references to me being a prisoner.

"Things aren't really that bad here, except being unable to sleep. I seldom go to bed before three or four in the morning, and then I get woke up by the noise about seven or eight o'clock. I don't guess I really need much sleep, though, since I never really do anything. The main problem at the moment is boredom. I'm tired of reading and studying and I don't want to get so tired of it that I can't stand it, so I've started limiting the amount of time I spend at them. Even Religious in convents and monasteries have times of recreation when they can walk and talk of more mundane and worldly things.

I had previously written to Ted enquiring about access to computers. He wrote: "The only electrical items we are allowed to have are the ones that are sold by the Commissary and I'm afraid computers just aren't on the list of available items. It's the same with clothing and food items and toiletries – nothing can be sent in from the outside, and we can only buy the few items stocked by our Commissary."

On Sat. 6th May John and I went to Dublin for the day to see the world famous Lipizzaner horses from Vienna. I told Ted about them. He recounted how he and his friend Dwayne had seen some of those beautiful stallions from the Florida School:

"Anyone with any appreciation at all for beauty and grace would easily fall under the spell of the Lipizzaner horses. Even standing still in their stalls they seemed so full of energy and power and intelligence. If the security guard hadn't been there with us, I would never have dared to go up close to them. One of the riders had a camera and took some photos of me and Dwayne with the horses, we gave him our name and addresses. They arrived a couple of months later. After having got over her initial anger at our having defied her orders to stay away from the arena, Mom was proud of the photos and just had to show them to everyone! The pictures disappeared along with a lot of other tangible "memories" when I came to prison at the age of 16. But no one can steal the memories in my head."

The Catholic UK Prison Chaplains had a conference week in Oxford and Joy and I were asked to give a talk. The weather was beautiful, the listeners attentive and the Mass afterwards made one feel the strength of the Holy Spirit. These kind, gentle, sincere men were fulfilling a difficult task with God's help.

On our way to the station we went to see the original painting of Holman Hunt's "Light of the World" that is permanently displayed in a side chapel at Keble College. The image is familiar, the handsome, expectant Shepherd with a luminous halo round his head and a lantern in his hand, knocking at a door that looks as though it has been shut for ages with overgrown weeds and rotting timbers. The artistic symbolism represents Jesus knocking at the door of a sinner. There is no handle to the door so it is we who have to open it to let in the One who will save us and lead us to safety.

We were not alone. Three American ladies were carefully examining it. Joy and I waited until they had finished. They thanked us for waiting and said how beautiful it was. We agreed and recognising the accent, asked if they were from Texas. They were from Dallas they told us and they did believe in the Death Penalty. We discussed the situation but I suspect that we made little impact.

As a result of the talk in Oxford we were asked to address the inmates by the Chaplaincy at Brixton prison, London. We went on Monday May 22nd. What a difference from Death Row. The inmates and staff were saddened due to the suicide of a young man with family problems there that morning. However, even with that tragedy, there was a different aura in there.

The men had specified relaxation periods, indulging in table tennis, talks, radio, group T.V. educational programmes, skills and hobbies. They had meals in a canteen. They were free to walk there unencumbered by handcuffs or shackles. Neither were they strip-searched by the staff every time they left their cell. They are paid a small allowance in order to buy necessities for themselves. There are always problems, but if punishment is necessary it is dispensed, for example, by depriving that culprit of his tobacco for a week. Dignity is kept and dignity is given

We were able to have Mass in the Chapel/meeting hall. Afterwards about fifty men were allowed to attend and listen to our story. They sat in a semicircle around us. Afterwards the men were allowed to walk around the room freely. They could shake hands or hug us, eat a biscuit, and have a hot drink. They could talk to us, if they wanted, and we heard some sad stories. Even "lifers" are given a much better existence in Britain.

Ted later wrote of my encounter: "The prisons in Britain are more humanely managed than my own humble home; harshness towards people doesn't make them better citizens, though it appears that the State of Texas will never learn that.

"Still nothing new from my attorneys. I talk with one or the other of them – sometimes both of them – every three weeks or so.

There are times when talking to them is a bigger trial than everyday life on Death Row. They're continually trying to dig up the past and I'm constantly trying to bury it. Needless to say, they don't get much cooperation from me. I just don't have any interest in what they're doing. For me it only means Bench Warrants and having my life story splashed across the front page of the newspapers, and all I want is to be left alone! I really wish they would do all this without me – they can tell me all about it in a letter after everything has been said and done!

Ted elaborated on how his attorney's gathered their information from their clients:

"Robert and/or Raoul would generally bring at least four or five students with them so they could interview several prisoners at the same time. Most of the research of the cases is done by the law students - Robert and Raoul tell the students the generalised things they'll need to find out from us, the students ask us more specific questions, and Robert and Raoul go from interview to interview checking on progress and making suggestions or asking questions. But they come here to the Unit about every two-and-a-half or three months or whenever they just happen to be "in the neighbourhood". I don't really remember most of the students, though. Several of them have visited and then promised to write, but of course they're busy with their studies and don't have time for correspondence.

"I'll tell you a bit now about why I find John of the Cross so special. First of all it's because he was a tremendously charismatic person and that shows in his writings. He was a little man, just four feet eleven inches tall; frequently he was described as "small and delicate" but he commanded great respect from everyone. Well, everyone except his superiors, but that was because he'd joined with Teresa of Avila in bringing reform to the Order.

"John always thought of himself as a priest and servant of the poor, even though he had a great intellect and managerial skills. He often went door to door begging food and alms for the nuns so they would be spared the humiliation of begging for themselves, and he would frequently do the nuns' chores – washing, cooking, scrubbing floors, and tending the garden – so they would have more time for praying and recreation.

"John was a priest, of course, with all that goes along with that: preaching, counselling, hearing Confessions and celebrating Mass. But he was also a poet, writer, artist, architect, bricklayer, schoolteacher, house painter, tailor, and on, and on. He did his own work, and then he did all the things that other religious people couldn't do or didn't have time to do, or just simply didn't want to do.

"I think all those things make him an ideal person to take as an example of how to live a Christian life of service to others, but most important to me is the fact that he was a mystic who knew God very intimately and who was blessed with the knowledge of Divine Union and was given the ability to write books of "instruction" concerning the spiritual journey. Now, I know that there's a fairly large number of saints – both "official" and unofficial – who have written about their mystic experiences and visions, and an even larger number of Catholic authors who wrote about their theories concerning Divine Union. But John's works provide - for me at least - a tried and true spiritual path that can prepare a person to live in "perfect love", should God see fit to grace a person with Union.

"It's difficult to put into words why John is "special", but his writings speak to my heart in a way that no one else's works ever had. I'm also impressed by the fact that some of his best poetry was composed during the nine months he was held in prison in Toledo, when he was repeatedly beaten and humiliated by his fellow friars! I guess the best way to understand how I feel is to read his works for yourself if you ever have the time and inclination.

Ted had time to think about his relationship with his lawyers: "I know my lawyers job is to "get me off", and I don't mind if he does his job. But, I don't have anyone to talk to, so if my lawyers make the mistake of coming to see me, they'll just have to put up with me before I put up with them! "Go with the flow?" – That's what I've been doing for 12 years, just drifting on the current. You know how I feel – I refuse to "fight" for my life, but I won't drop my appeal and God knows I've wanted to at times!) – so, all I can do is just "go with the flow".

Despite being in a highly "protected" environment health was still a major issue for Ted. I thought that ear plugs might subdue the noise level somewhat for him:

"They do sell earplugs in our Commissary, and I got a couple of pairs of them a while back, but I've always been prone to terrible ear aches and inner-ear infections, so I can only wear them for a couple of hours a day. I can't even listen to the radio with headphones for very long without risking earache! Health care in here is a joke, so I have to be extra careful not to take too many chances with my hearing. And the noise isn't so terribly bad all the time. It could always be worse, you know?"

"My allergies are acting up again and driving me nuts. They've been working on the ventilation system for the last three days, and I think I've got about 10 year's worth of accumulated dust and pollen in my cell. They'll shut the system down for an hour or so, and bang around in the air ducts dislodging all the dust, then they'll turn the air back on for a while just to see how it's "working". After a couple of hours they'll shut the system down and do it all over again! I haven't been able to breath properly since they started all this three days ago. And I can't see that they've accomplished anything at all besides making a lot of us miserable (more miserable?)."

As the month of June came to a close it was sobering for us on the "outside" to learn via Amnesty International that Texas was still leading American states in the number of executions.

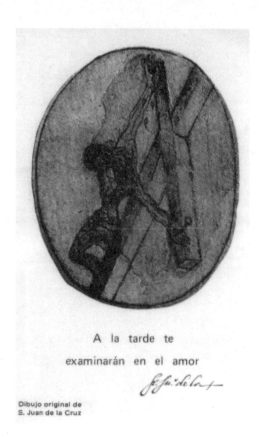

A la tarde te

examinarán en el amor

Dibujo original de
S. Juan de la Cruz

The Crucifixion. From an original drawing by St. John of the Cross.

Chapter 23
Bench Warrant

Thank You for my enemies –
By loving them I grow;
Thank You for my many friends –
Through them my blessings flow.

John and I had met at Roehampton Tennis Club. We were introduced on the grass courts there. When we married we bought a house amongst the green pines of Cobham, a small Surrey village. We kept up our tennis by joining the Oxshott Tennis Club and made many friends there. With some of them we also played bridge. John and I often played in Club tennis matches, but not usually for the 1st team.

My parents had always lived in North Wales, my father alone since my mother had died. When he became ill, I travelled up to Wales every fortnight to spend time with him. I did this journey for two years. It was a very hectic time as I still had David at home to be looked after, fed and schooled. He was studying for his important "A" levels. Nevertheless, he and John managed as my father had further strokes. He needed constant supervision with a carer as he was unable to do anything for himself.

Witnessing my six foot, energetic, sports - loving father reduced to such incapacity was very stressful. We had always had an extremely good relationship. I could talk to him about anything.

John decided that it would be better if we moved up to Deganwy to live near my father as the journey was becoming very hard for me. Our social life also suffered and John missed me. We already had a house there on the promenade. David finished his schooling and we moved to Wales, leaving our home of nearly thirty years.

We kept in touch with our friends and John with his business associates, so we often went to London and Surrey. On one such weekend we decided to visit the new Dome and the Eye in London, erected in honour of the Millennium. John decided the best way would be to go down the Thames on a special boat. It left from the Embankment where we could ride on the Eye first. When we arrived there the queue for the Eye was very long and the queue to get tickets to actually ride on the Eye was even longer.

The ticket office was housed in one of the magnificent buildings that line that part of the Thames. It was crowded. The noise was deafening. In the hustle and bustle it was difficult to understand which line was for today, tomorrow or even next week. We decided to telephone and make a booking that way.

Instead we went to the adjacent building that housed the Dali Exhibition. The peace and tranquillity that comes from looking at fine art was a welcome relief. We wandered from room to room where the paintings, jewellery and sculptures were thoughtfully displayed. Dali had been a man of eclectic taste.

I chose some postcards to send to Ted. I especially liked the sculpture of the green girl with the wiry hair with her arms up holding a hoop in her hands. It could have many interpretations, fine food for thought apart from being well executed. When Ted replied to my letter in which I had outlined my visit, he told me that the Dali crucifixion had been inspired by a sketch drawn by St. John of the Cross. It is angled in such a way as though one is looking down on the Cross from above. It is an unusual view as we usually look up to Jesus on the Cross.

We continued on our journey to the Dome by a Thames River tourist boat. We stepped from the noisy, busy, solid Embankment into a world that lurched and swayed to the whim of every passing swell. The engine came to life, the lines were cast off and the boat smoothly edged its way into the mainstream of the River Thames.

It was an interesting ride downriver, past all the important landmarks that flank the Thames; the Needle, the New Tate Gallery, the Tower of London, past the OXO building, warehouses, and beautiful new apartment blocks. The boat pushed through the murky water under many famous bridges. Police launches sped past us with particular urgency. Loaded barges chugged by. Even rowers in small skiffs were glimpsed.

Rounding a bend in the river we had our first view of the Dome. It was a captivating sight. I assumed that it would be as interesting inside as it looked from the outside. Having visited places like the Epcott Centre and Disney World with my father when he was 80, I was expecting something similar. However, this was not to be. Most of the sites were amateurish and disappointing.

The only truly exciting and noteworthy item was the show. The vast height and space in the dome's centre was used by daring performers, who swung and danced their way in the air suspended by wires allowing them complete freedom of movement. After climbing ropes to a small balcony encircling the top of The Dome, they launched themselves off.

Three themes were explored on the ground as well as in the air. There was a huge central edifice on the floor that opened and closed according to the scene. Performers clothed in strange shapes moved about on stilts or bounded about, ran, and somersaulted, all in time to the music.

The first theme was happy, sunny and peaceful - the beginning of a world or of life. The sky dancers twisted and floated up and down, round and round, throwing long, wide coloured streamers. There was so much to see. It was a visual feast. The second scene was war. The cacophony of sound accompanied by the sombre colours of the "baddies" and the bright brilliance of the "goodies". It was vibrant, kaleidoscopic and spectacular.

It was a challenge to look and see everything as it all happened in the round, in the air, and on the ground. Of course, the "goodies" won... The third and final scene encapsulated forgiveness, reconciliation, harmony and peace. The young people sitting near us said that they had enjoyed the show and I certainly agreed.

Ted had once told me that he had never played tennis so as we had tickets for Wimbledon I thought about how I would explain to him the way it is played and the strength and skill needed to be exact and prepared. It is also a psychological game in that you push yourself to get the best results possible. It is about rising above depression when loosing a game. Sometimes losing can be beneficial if it is thought about and used to improve one's tactics another time. It can be exhilarating to see a loser winning in the end. It is about mind over matter, disappointment, hope and practice. Many people enjoy playing this game, as there are skills to be learnt at all levels.

I also told Ted that the visit was a trip down Memory Lane for me as I used to teach in the town of Wimbledon and would go to the All England Club after school during Wimbledon fortnight.

Ted also left home for a few days. He went to see the Judge: "On August 1st I was Bench Warranted to Lubbock. I was placed in the transport van. A female sergeant put handcuffs on me as tightly as she was able after being made fun of by the male officers – it was her way of proving she was just as tough as the men were. I was not impressed by her toughness. After being placed in the back of the van, I was given in to the custody of a male sergeant and another male officer for the drive to Lubbock; after almost ten hours we arrived in Lubbock and I was placed in a jail cell where the handcuffs were finally taken off my now numb and blue hands; the sergeant apologised for the "lady's" actions and promised that it wouldn't happen to anyone else.

"The trip to Lubbock was bad enough, but the trip back was sheer hell! When I got here, I found that they'd packed up everything I owned and carried it all off to the "Property Room" for safekeeping. That was Wednesday night; today is Saturday, and I only got my property back this afternoon! I only thought I was bored before! After spending about 64 hours in this cage with absolutely nothing, I have a new appreciation for the situation guys who are "level-3" are in. But they even had more than I did!

"When I say there was nothing here, I mean that quite literally – no cup (I slurped water out of my hand), no toothbrush or toothpaste, no comb, nothing to read or write with, there was just nothing here but me and a whole lot of nothing! When I tried to find someone who could get my property for me, the only responses I could get were: a) "it's not my job" b) "I haven't got time for that crap" c) "You need to get that done on the next shift." And my favourite, d) "You better leave me the hell alone! I didn't take you to raise!!"

"To make matters worse, someone forget to reactivate my Commissary card/ I.D. card when I came back (our cards are deactivated when we leave the prison so no one else can possibly use our cards while we're gone) so my card was rejected when I sent my Commissary order in yesterday. Due to lockdowns and rearranged schedules, I haven't been able to buy anything since July 14th.

"There's still no news as to when Father Walsh and the other priests will be allowed back in. And after this past week, I definitely need to go to Confession before I receive Communion again! Or maybe I just need to have my mouth washed out with soap? I'm glad you weren't here to listen to me because I might have hurt your ears!"

Ted was also pleased to relay something he had seen in a newspaper article. Apparently Mr. Charles Terrell was unhappy having his name associated with Death Row. He no longer supported capital punishment and had asked that they rename the unit. So, ideas really were changing!

Mr. Polunsky, a member of the Board of Pardons and Paroles, had no problem with the Unit taking his name. He seemed to be proud that this dreadful, archaic, department be named after him.

Fr. William J. Harry, O.Carm. August 2000.

Chapter 24

Barney

I woke up this morning complaining –
And missed a whole handful of miracles!

Garry had an execution date. It was to be on the 5th December 2000. We could not believe it was real. But life kept on moving.

Barney, our collie, had become ill whilst we were at David's graduation at Exeter in October. We had gone down by train for the weekend. That Sunday night there had been a torrential storm. On Monday morning the railway lines in, and around Exeter were flooded and remained closed. Our vet in Llandudno had taken Barney into their hospital in Craig-y-Don, They rang to say that Barney was very ill. We hired a car and drove home. The roads were empty. Fields on either side of the motorway were flooded and in parts water had spilled out on to the tarmac.

We went straight to the surgery. Barney, sad and tired, was asleep in a cage. His fur had lost its shine. I opened the cage and stroked him all over, talking to him in the way that I always did. I stroked around his ears and reached out to hold him in my arms. He rallied round after a while and tried to sit up. He stretched, recognised me and I managed to get him out of the cage, half of his body resting on my legs and arms. We sat there on the floor for a long time. I rested my head in the space between two cages. I held Barney's head. He fell asleep again. He seemed more peaceful.

Barney had been a wonderful friend, always with me, sitting beside me in the car as I did the school run or shopped. When I left him to do an errand he sat behind the wheel and looked out through the windscreen. He always knew what I was doing and where I was in the house or the garden. When we went for walks he would keep everybody in sight. He almost tried to round us up as if he felt he was in charge of us, his family. Whenever I had been out without him I would receive a tumultuous "welcome home" from him on my return. He would jump up high, almost to my chest, and turn round and round on the spot, delirious with delight.

We sat there on the floor for a long time. John went home. I rested my head against the wood in between two of the hutches above Barney's cage. I held Barney's head. He fell asleep again. He seemed more peaceful.

During a pause in my crying, I was aware of something close to my head. I moved my eyes warily and looked into the face of a sympathetic, all-knowing little black cat. There was a strong empathy between us as we studied each other closely. Then I realised that I was in close proximity to two other cats who it seemed, were giving me tremendous silent support. They looked at me with grave consternation and dedication. I silently thanked them and they seemed to relax. The cat owners came for their little friends and left us alone.

He knew that he was with me when he died in my arms, his eyes looked with love into mine. He slowly sank into oblivion. He will never be forgotten.

On our drive back home I could not help but contrast Barney's death, surrounded by those who cared for him, with the probable way in which Garry would spend his last hours on earth.

Having read the Death Row statistics for the following month they made depressing reading. There was still no let up in the carnage. There were 440 men and seven women currently on Death Row, Texas, with the average age of executed offenders being 39. State Governor Bush had so far overseen 149 executions.

In October 2000 John, Richard and I went to Spain to relax for a week in some sunshine. We had a look at a few marinas there to see if it was feasible for us to moor our boat. We decided that we would not be comfortable in the hot weather. Instead we found a flat to rent, and booked it for January 2001 for six months. I wrote some typical picture postcards to send to Ted, of sandy beaches and the white, narrow, streets of sun soaked Andalucia.

In Ted's letter of November 20th he thanked me for the cards and said that he would love to wander through those white villages with the cobbled streets. He enjoyed seeing the trailing red geraniums and the orange and lemon trees. His own living conditions showed a small improvement:

"They turned the heat on here about a week ago, so I'm comfortable. At Ellis, there were always so many broken windows that they refused to replace and it was always cold, even with the heat turned up high.

"I have just finished what is probably the last letter Garry will receive from me. It generally takes anywhere from 12 to 16 days for letters to get to each other, and he has exactly 16 days. I'll probably continue to write to him up until a week before his date, but I don't think he will get any of them. The bad part of it is that he'll keep writing to me right up to the day of his execution, which means I could still be getting letters from him for as long as two weeks after he's gone!

"I got a letter from him Saturday, and he seems to be in good spirits. His only worry is his Dad – he [Garry's father] hasn't taken things well at all, and his health isn't that good to begin with. Keep him and Garry both in your prayers. Garry's Mom, too – he hasn't seen or heard from her since he got his date."

Brother Curda, a monk at a New Mexico monastery, had been in correspondence with Ted. The New Mexico community had agreed to enrol Garry as an Oblate and wanted to provide him with whatever he needed in the way of books, and instruction in the spiritual life, as Ted was happy to relate:

"One of the reasons Garry is in such good spirits because on the morning of Oct. 24th, he was enrolled as an Oblate novice by the Benedictines at Our Lady of Guadalupe Abbey in Pecos, New Mexico, and then on Oct. 30th Father Walsh performed the required ceremony and got all the necessary papers signed and sent back to the abbey, so it's all official.

"Garry and I hunted for more than a year, writing letters to dozens of monasteries trying to find a Benedictine community that would accept him as an Oblate (a lay person who lives his life following the Benedictine Rule), and it looked like we were going to run out of time. But it's all worked out okay and Garry has found his "niche" in the church at last.

"Father Walsh will be back here on Decembe 3rd in time to celebrate a last Mass with Garry. At least the administration here allows us that much."

Chapter 25
Alone To Texas

The people are cold and brittle here –
The air is even crisper –
And if there's any warmth at all,
It comes sealed in a written whisper.

It had been a big shock in August, to hear that Garry had an execution date for 5th December. Ted suggested that I should make another visit. It was difficult to plan one before December for various reasons. First and foremost, Joy was incapacitated with Sciatica affecting her back and her legs. She was ill for over six months.

John was unhappy about my making the journey alone, but he was unable to leave his work for a week to accompany me. I knew that I could manage it alone. It was not a problem. The other main factor was that John was not on Ted's visitors' list. Therefore, he would not be able to go inside the prison. A new rule meant an additional name had to be documented for six months at that prison.

Feeling guilty that I was leaving Joy, John and Tanya behind, I flew by BA down to Gatwick early in the morning of December 1st. John had driven me to Manchester airport where we had parted sadly, both wishing different things. I, that John was accompanying me, John that I was not going. The 6.30 a.m. flight was comforting. My luxurious, wide leather seat offered plenty of legroom. I had an appetising breakfast and even had time to glance at my free morning paper.

My luggage was automatically transferred to my next plane. The airport was busy, but I found a phone and rang John to see if he had arrived home safely. The flight to Texas was uneventful. As the plane was only half full I was able to lie down and rest. It was early afternoon when I arrived in Houston. Having left cold and rain behind me I was happy to see the early afternoon sun shining through the coach windows on the way to the car hire centre.

I had been undecided where to stay. We usually stayed at Hospitality House in Huntsville, but Ted had now been moved to the Terrell Unit, Livingston, which was forty minutes away from Huntsville in another direction. Both were at least an hour away from where I picked up the car. As I had a cold coming, I decided to go to the nearest bed that I could remember - the Holiday Inn at Woodlands, en route to both Huntsville and Livingston. It was a good choice, convenient and comfortable. Friday had been a long day as Houston is six hours behind UK time. I was glad to sleep well and long.

The next day I left early to find Livingstone. Although I had seen the Terrell Unit from the outside, with Joy on our third visit, we had approached it from Huntsville. Woodlands, however, is situated on the north-western outskirts of Houston. I had the choice of going up to Huntsville and then turning right to Livingston, or going straight to Livingston from this location. I opted for the latter.

The map that I bought showed a link road, but I missed it. The journey consequently took that much longer.

Feeling rotten, with a heavy head and aching limbs, I drank lots of water. It was dark at 5 p.m. when I drove slowly in through the prison gates and along the drive. I joined a queue of cars that were being searched by security guards with flashlights. I took out my driving licence, but had no idea where the button was to open the bonnet and the boot. The guards heard my accent and decided that they would help me. Of course they found nothing. It was really cold as I parked the car and hurried over to the prison entrance.

It was a much larger reception area than at Huntsville. At least we were inside a building, and not standing outside a small wooden hut as in Ellis One. But as I opened the door, to my horror, I saw it was full with people standing in line. It was not even half past five yet. The man in front of me only had his driving licence and his I.D. card. I asked him if I needed my airline ticket. He looked at me as though I was mad. "No." I dashed back to the car and left the airline ticket safely locked up. Different Unit. Different rules.

I had missed my turn in the queue as someone else had arrived and taken my place. Gradually the line shortened. Before people were allowed in the guard ran the security machine over them. Winter coats had to come off. It took ages, especially when sometimes buckles and buttons made the dreaded ping. Then the process had to be repeated. There must have been previous security lapses as they were so careful.

There were three people in front of me when the reception officer said that we would have to wait now until 7.30 p.m. as the cubicles were full. They did not have enough cubicles here to accommodate visitors. With nearly 450 men on Death Row more should have been built. A Mexican lady in front of me, and her daughter, decided to go to Wall Mart for a meal. Would I like to accompany them? Thanking them, I said that I would probably follow them later.

As I went out towards my car, a tall black lady, who had been standing in the queue behind me, opened her Cadillac door and asked me if I would like to join her. The suggestion appealed. The interior of her car looked warm and comfortable. I was tired. I thought of my now cold, basic, hire car, driving again, the busy, noisy Wall Mart and feeling out of sorts. I took the line of least resistance and got in.

Her name was Marion. She lived in Houston. It was also her first visit to Terrell. Her daughter had asked her to visit her friend who was on Death Row. Marion, had an infectious ready laugh, and was good company. When we talked about the death penalty she stunned me by saying that she looked after her three grandchildren, as her daughter, Erika, was on Death Row.

Erika had been on Death Row for seven years, since the age of nineteen, when her third baby was only ten months old. Marion told me proudly about her grandchildren, how well adjusted they were, and how ably they coped with the situation. She had had a great deal of help all through these troubled times from her

251

own mother and had many good, supportive friends. She had a very positive attitude towards her problems.

That cold, Saturday evening Marion would have preferred to stay at home. But Erika had asked her to visit her friend who was unwell. She felt like going home and coming back another day. However we stayed in the car chatting.

She has a very good job as a computer analyst for a Houston firm, which she enjoys. She uses her home computer to e-mail people about developments in the world of prisons. Marion was very interested when I told her about our friend and Texas co-ordinator, Sue Lusk. With some friends Sue has set up Human Writes, a British magazine sent to Death Row inmates by their pen friends. If they are interested, or able to write, they can ask for a pen pal to write letters to them from England. This offers them a view of the outside world. In some cases, this is the only contact that prisoners have with people, other than inmates, outside the prison.

I went to my car to find the copy of Human Writes that I had brought with me to post to Ted from America. He would receive it much quicker than if I had posted it in England. Marion was very impressed with it. She thought that it would be a good idea to start one in America. A magazine would reach people who did not have good communications such as Internet access. Naturally no one on Death Row was allowed a computer. Some could afford to buy a typewriter from the Commissary, even though the ribbons were quite expensive and the typewriters were poor quality.

Marion and Erika had known Karla Fay Tucker well. She had been a good influence in prison. The other women liked her. She had had many friends. Marion thought that it had been wicked to kill her. What had it achieved? It was another murder.

From the warm, cosy Cadillac we stepped into the black night and hurried into the prison waiting room. We stood behind a couple already in line. More came, including a kindly looking black lady who sat down on one of the few chairs. She recognised Marion and called over quietly,

"Are you Erika's mama?" So she was well known. Marion nodded and walked over to talk to her.

The Mexican lady and her daughter were the couple in front of us. They had come back early from their meal at Wall Mart. I explained that I had not felt very hungry and had stayed in the car park chatting. She explained she and her daughter had come 500 miles to visit her son. They come as often as they can. He is only 20 and he is innocent, she told me in a low voice. Just then two people came out of the door leading to the prison. The lady and her daughter said a quick goodbye and stepped close to the cubicle where the reception officer sat. They gave her some papers. Some time was spent looking at them, a short phone call, and then they were given permission to proceed. They were searched, and allowed to pass through the door out of my view.

In the car Marion had told me that if I had mentioned to the receptionist that I had come from England, I would have been allowed inside to visit earlier, as I had travelled more than 500 miles.

253

She also said that not all the visiting room cubicles were opened on a Saturday night, hence the delay. We had to wait until someone came out. It was not a staff shortage problem, she thought, rather, just that the administration tried to discourage visitors by making difficulties for relatives.

Then it was my turn to be allowed in. I handed my passport over. The officer wrote down my name and passport number. As she returned it she asked, her mouth working away at a wad of gum, who was it that I wished to visit? I said, "Ted Cole, No. 000906." Although I know his number off by heart, I almost forgot it. She wrote that on the form and then rang the main building to say that one person was coming through, and repeated Ted's name and number so that he could be collected from his cell. I was searched before I could enter.

Through two doors, a long walk up a wide pathway, and in front of me was a huge glassed-in area. Where was the entrance? I would have to guess. Lights were on inside. As I got closer I could see the door handle recessed into the glass. Once inside I was in a large reception area. A corridor led off it and at the end was a screen of ceiling to wall vertical bars. Voices came from that direction. With nowhere else to go I walked along the corridor. As I neared the bars they slid slowly open and two guards emerged chatting. They had coats on and carried small bags. They called "goodnight" to an unseen woman who replied, and immediately told me where I should go next. As I walked through the door of sliding bars I saw her sitting in a guard box pointing to another set of sliding bar doors at right angles to the ones I had just come through. As I waited for them to open I could see down the corridor to another set and beyond that more guards.

It was all very different from the Ellis Unit, much cleaner and bigger, and freshly painted. Through the next set of doors and I was in the visiting rooms. Only one room was in use. This was illuminated. It was hot and noisy. Some of the visitors walked about the area doing various things, especially the children. Many were feeding money into well-stocked vending machines. One asked the lady guard, who sat at an open table, to take her photograph with a prisoner. The guard just had time to tell me to sit at No. 5 before she went down the row to take the photo with a Polaroid camera.

I looked about me and saw prisoners in small cages. They could only see directly in front of them as the wooden sides holding the telephones jutted outwards. Directly in front of the cage were one or two chairs. I recognised the man who had stood in front of me in the line a couple of hours earlier. He was sitting with another man looking into a cage. He held a telephone and was talking earnestly in to it.

I walked forward to find No.5. It was on the left, half way down the row, but when I arrived another man was seated inside, not Ted. I did not like to stare but I was quite startled. I had been expecting to see a familiar face.

I hurried back to the desk. The guard was just coming back from the photo session. I told her what had happened. She took her time as she looked at her list. Just then I heard "Margôt! Margôt!" I looked around and saw Dawn and her friend Shelley, both from Human Writes. They were visiting a prisoner they had been writing to for some time. We were very pleased to see each other. The guard told me that Ted was waiting in No. 5 so I hurried back. It was the same man who looked out at me when I reached No. 5.

Back at the desk of the harried guard I waited nervously. I tried not to look around at the private huddles of people sharing precious moments. It was difficult. My brain said that this was not the place to catch anyone's eyes. But where was I supposed to look as I stood at the desk that was placed so that the officer could see all of the visitors. A familiar face glided past - Betty Matthews with her long blond hair. She was one of the chaplains I had met at Ellis.

The lady guard was flustered. She assured me that Ted was now in No. 5. I dreaded going back through the middle of all those people again. I told myself that no one would take any notice of me and I walked back again to No. 5 cubicle. No, this was definitely not Ted. The man spoke urgently to me. I could not hear a thing apart from the noise in the small visiting hall. He gestured wildly. He picked up his phone and mimicked that I did the same. I lifted the phone and put it to my ear, I could hear him plainly as he asked, "Where's Chris?" I said that I did not know, that there was no one waiting at the desk but me. He kept repeating the question as he sat on his stool in the little cage. I was very hot, bothered and confused. I assured him that I would go and check with the lady guard.

No, there was no one of that name around. Several of the prisoners in their different cages waved and smiled as I walked past again. I took little notice, just smiled vaguely as I did not recognise them. I thought that they might just be being friendly. I carried on trying to make some sense out of this awkward situation. The young, harassed officer gave me a different number and I sat down gratefully at an unoccupied cell to wait for Ted.

Eventually Ted was brought handcuffed, escorted by an officer. There was hardly room for the two of them in the corridor behind the cage. I realised that there were cages and visitors' spaces on the other side but that was all in darkness. Ted came into the cage with his hands behind his back.

He had to bend backwards, after the guard closed and locked the door with a resounding bang. He put his cuffed hands through a small hole in the door and the handcuffs were unlocked and removed. He stood up straight. He is a tall man. I expect that the authorities have to cater for small men and so put the hole low down on the iron grill-like door. He rubbed his wrists, sat down on the stool and greeted me all in one moment.

It was great to see him. We commiserated on the short time that we had left that evening, probably made shorter by the muddle. I decided that when I visited on a Saturday night again I would arrive early and be in the front of the line. As it was, it was a bonus meeting anyway. We talked about Garry who was due to

257

die the following week. In his latest letter to Ted, Garry seemed to be in good spirits. Ted thought Garry was ready to go to God. He would much rather have lived. Garry was only worried about his father who had poor health.

"The whole thing is probably rougher for him than for Garry!" thought Ted. He asked me to "Keep Garry's Dad in your prayers. Garry's Mom too – he hasn't seen or heard from her since he got his date."

Ted had already told me that Garry did not want any visitors, so I had not arranged, via the prison administration, to visit him. I appreciated that Garry was saving all his visiting time for his Dad. I was one of the last people left in the visitors' room, I realised, as the guard came down the corridor behind Ted jangling keys. Ted stood up immediately and I said, "See you on Monday." Ted nodded as he put his hands behind his back, lent backwards to try and find the hole to put them through.

The guard put on the handcuffs, locked them and unlocked the cage door. Ted stepped towards me to allow the door to open properly. He turned round. He went out without looking at me. He was led away as dignified as one could possibly be in that situation. He is not a troublesome prisoner. You would think that he would be given some allowances for good behaviour.

I walked out of the now empty room. The guard switched off the lights. I followed the sound of voices and caught up with some visitors standing at the closed doors. The guards on the other side were talking loudly. The doors opened noisily and we trooped through.

There were already people waiting there for the next door to be opened. Only when one is closed does the next one open. I recognised the Mexican lady and her teenage daughter. The mother was carrying a large plastic bag of books that she had collected from her son after he had read and shared them round with his neighbours.

As they were staying at Hospitality House, they would be driving in the opposite direction to me. It was nearly 10 o'clock. We said a hurried goodbye in the cold car park and I set off to join the queue to get out of this inhospitable place. With flashlights dancing in my face, the officer asked me to step outside while he had a quick look inside my car. When he had also looked in the boot I was allowed to proceed down the drive and out of the gates. I felt relieved to be free, and I was not even a prisoner.

With my mind full of all that I had experienced that evening, I drove towards Houston. Maybe I was not concentrating or I missed the sign because I ended up on the toll road that led to Austin, miles away from where I wanted to be. As soon as I realised I came off at the next exit. Feeling very tired and hungry I stopped at a fast food bar to have something to eat and look at the map. I did not dare stop on the roadside in case I was mugged. I had not been out so late alone before in America.

A smart looking young lady sat in a corner of the empty restaurant. The waiter asked her to help me find my way back to the Woodlands area of Houston. He told me, in a conspiratorial undertone, that she was a policewoman on duty. I sat at the table adjacent to her. This was a self-service restaurant. When I came in I did not know what I wanted to eat. Maybe I was overwrought. The easiest and most nutritious thing was a chicken salad. The assistant suggested that I sit down and he would bring it to me when he had made it. I must have looked tired.

When he brought it over it looked appetising. I did not think that I would eat it, but as the policewoman was telling me where I had gone wrong on the expressway I managed to eat without tasting anything, but my hunger was assuaged. I realised that I had not eaten all day.

I was most impressed that this attractive young lady, with brown shoulder length hair tied back off her face, was sitting here as a possible target. There must be a patrol car and officers watching nearby. Her gun holster on her waist was out of sight under the table. She did not lean over to look at my map on my table. She took the map from me and examined it at her table, which was empty except for a glass of half drunk cola. Neither did she come near me. She always kept her distance.

We did not discuss any of the possible scenarios that she could be in, except the absurdity that I should have come all this way to Austin. The place was empty so she and the waiter had a good laugh at my expense. The waiter then returned to the bar to serve a new customer. I finished my coffee and listened as she explained where I had gone wrong. It was an unlit highway sign. One wrong turning and I had ended up nowhere near where I wanted to go; a little bit like life.

Chapter 26

Garry

O Lord, when I am weary
And think I need to rest,
Remind me, Sweet Beloved,
That I've promised you my best.

The following morning I decided, after the nocturnal wanderings of the previous night, that it would be much more convenient and time saving if I moved to an hotel closer to the prison in Livingston. Also, I did not want to travel far because of my bad cold. After asking the hotel receptionist to book me in at the Livingston branch of the chain I checked out and went for brunch at the nearby Woodlands shopping mall.

It was Christmas and sale time. The atmosphere in the mall exuded seasonal spirit. People looked happy in their red and white festive colours as they sauntered arm in arm, or rushed about with too much to do and no time to do it all. Children had a look of anticipation on their faces and ran about trying to decide what they wanted from this glut of choices. Every shop looked enticing, silver and gold coloured wares displayed to the best advantage. One wanted to meander everywhere.

Glittering white or emerald green Christmas trees sparkled on every crossway. Some had boxes tied with broad red ribbons lying scattered around the floor at their base, almost shouting "presents, buy presents". Some had animated creatures singing rhymes round the tree. Others had Father Christmas in his sleigh, drawn by papier-mâché red-nosed reindeers. Yellow, blue and red parcels peeped out temptingly from the open neck of his bulging sack. Dwarves, with long white beards and red shoes, scampered around a beautiful Snow White. It was all meticulously arranged. Glossy green boughs of artificial holly and fir decorated the mall. They were laden with luscious looking artificial fruit and flowers of every hue.

At the food area I found a site that crushed fresh fruit with ice - "smoothies" - just what I needed to keep my temperature down. I kept returning to the "smoothy" stall after each purchase to cool down. The two festively attired assistants were quite amused as I tried a different fruit combination each time, banana with mango, strawberries with pear, pineapple with peach. I delighted in the thought of so many wonderful tastes with such exotic aromas. But my cold mainly obscured both the taste and the smell!

For Francesca, I bought a doll's pottery tea set in white with little pink flowers on it. I saw some beautiful party dresses, bottle green, apricot, all at reduced prices. For William, some lovely Texan denim dungarees with pale blue and white check shirts. Also I found some excellent educational jigsaws for both grandchildren. The Christmas spirit, helped by the endless Carols, was in full swing. Once or twice a window would display the true meaning of Christmas with a Nativity scene. Holy Night and Away in a Manger made a tranquil change.

I sat and sipped a "smoothy" and thought about the men on Death Row. They were a world away from this. Yet, some of the many hundreds of citizens here must have experience of prison, one way or another, either from one being confined or having a family member in prison. How sad some of these humans walking past me here must be. I thought about Garry, his parents. How were they spending this last Sunday of Garry's life? What must they be feeling? It seems there are so many victims.

My energy levels were running low. I left the brilliant, artificial, retail world to find the car. I must drive on to Livingston. The heat, smell and noise of the mall changed immediately as soon as I opened the door and stepped into the grey afternoon. It was wet. Rain was still in the air. The many cars merged into neutral beige-grey across the crowded car park. Cars prowled past me looking for a space to rest. What a contrast. Here was the real world. Puddles, petrol fumes and damp clothes. Now different discordant sounds: engines rumbling, doors banging, people shouting, background music.

An enormous police horse was near my car. The rain soaked police rider was having a very heated conversation with a motorist sitting in his car and a gesticulating pedestrian. The problem was an empty space that they both felt it was their right to occupy. The pedestrian was keeping it whilst his partner brought their car round. The motorist however, felt that it could not be "held" and that he had a right to it.

There was an ambulance parked on the grass kerb behind the police horseman. Its doors were wide open. A young skater was being carefully lifted inside. I had not noticed the dirty, cream-coloured skating rink alongside the car park but now I could see the shadows of the skaters moving inside to the music. Someone was receiving medical attention in the ambulance. I added to the mayhem as my car space was fought over. Life on the outside has its problems too.

Within two hours I was installed at the Holiday Inn, Livingston. I was so glad to be in a comfortable bed away from all the crowds. I had a sandwich and some tea in my room. Although it was still only early evening I was ready to sleep. I felt happier knowing that I was near to the prison and would thus avoid a great deal of driving.

Ted had said that there was no need to get up at 6.00 a.m. as I had done previously to be at Ellis by 8.00 a.m. Ted had his breakfast from 3.00 a.m. till 3.30 a.m. then slept until 9.00 a.m., when he usually got up and made himself a coffee. I arrived about 10.00 a.m. There was no queue in front of me this time. I walked through the two gates, into the building along a corridor to a set of electric doors. I showed the paper that I had been given at the front reception to a lady who operated the gates to allow me in.

What a difference. There were few people about that Monday morning, although, I had passed a couple going out on my way inside. The guard gave me a number. I sat down to wait for Ted when I remembered the "snacks". When I stood up and walked past a cage a young man waved at me. Was it Garry? He had changed so. His hair had grown. He now wore thick-rimmed glasses and he had put on more weight since I had last seen him. I picked up the telephone in the cubicle on my side of the cage. He said that he and his Dad had seen me on Saturday and he had waved. I was very upset that I had not recognised him.

His dad and stepmother had also been in this morning. Had I seen them as I came in, he asked. I could just about recall a couple walking past me with their heads bowed low, however, I had been concentrating on finding my way and hadn't taken much notice of anyone. Garry asked me to try and get a meeting with him when I had finished visiting Ted. I was still on his visitors' list. This was a man who was going to die the next day.

"Do you want anything?" I asked.

"I'm fine, give my love to Ted. See you later," he replied.

As I replaced the phone a lady sitting at the next cubicle said that I had just committed a very serious offence. I had talked to a prisoner other than the one I was visiting. How can you punish or ignore a man due to die the next day! I did not say anything to her, I felt like crying. If only I had stopped and looked on Saturday at the person who was waving at me. I had been too wrapped up in my own problems to think straight. There had been so much going on that I had chosen to think only of myself instead of trying to find out why that young man had waved at me. Obviously he did not want his Dad to have to come and speak to me. But I could have gone over. I knew that I would not have intruded. At least I could have said, "Hi!" He must have wanted me to see him otherwise he would not have waved to me. I felt really bad about it all.

I went to the food and drinks dispenser, choosing crisps and a drink at random. I thought of Garry and felt very sad that the State of Texas had taken revenge such a long way. It had taken justice completely out of context. Where was mercy and forgiveness shown in this State? Certainly it was not here in this room, for these people. Where was compassion and love, the two most important messages given to us from Jesus Himself? Absolutely not shown here, except by some of the inmates, the ones whom I had met. I put the crisps and drink in the bag provided, wrote down the number of Ted's cage and left them, still feeling angry, on the guard's desk.

She was busy taking a photo of a prisoner and his visitors. I decided to have another quick word with Garry, despite the nosy lady. Garry had his face to the wall in the corner of his small cage. It took me a minute to realise that he was overcome with emotion. He was so brave. He had kept himself occupied talking to his Dad and stepmother. He had sent them on their way. They would not be allowed back into prison as their allotted time had been used up this morning. They would not go in to "The Walls" the next evening to watch him die as Garry had thought the ordeal would be too much for his father. Garry wanted to face death on his own with no family around. He was emotionally and spiritually prepared, Father Walsh had told Ted.

Now here was this good-looking young man who had been on Death Row for 11 years. He had come to terms with himself for the crime that he had committed whilst out of his mind with drink. Garry had taken his punishment daily. He knew that he was going to pay the ultimate penalty. There had been no let-ups on Death Row. The inmates are never allowed to forget just why they are there.

I walked past Garry's cage again but he was still facing the corner. His shoulders were moving very slightly. I felt so sorry that I had not recognised him on Saturday. It will haunt me forever.

I went and sat down again to wait for Ted. I remember him telling me that not so long ago it was the practice that the day before a man was to be killed, if they were Catholics, they were able to have a Mass with their friends present. Now, since the escape attempt, there is no gathering of friends. Garry will be able to hear Mass with Father Walsh in one of the dayrooms with Deacon Lopez and Deacon O'Brien only. No friends present, no one there to say a prayer with or to say "goodbye" to him.

Hopefully, in the corridor, with Garry returning to his cell and Ted coming to the visitor's room, the two old friends might meet for the last time. They would not be able to touch one another, as each would be handcuffed. They would only be able to speak in passing, if the guards were amenable. I expect that it would be a heartfelt, "Goodbye Ted."

"Goodbye Garry, God bless."

"God bless you too Ted."

I thought about all the privations that these people endure daily and felt desperately sad. I knew that I must compose myself and greet Ted with a smile. He was going to be happy for Garry as he was going to God the next day.

When Ted arrived I explained that I had seen Garry and he had asked me to visit him when we had finished our visit. The wait for Ted had been considerable today, so I had to ensure that there was enough time at the end to see Garry. He was pleased that Garry would have a chance to get out of that holding cell again for a little while.

We talked about Spain and my proposed stay where I would start the book about Ted. The climate was so much better for my health than Wales. I told him that John and I would be there for two weeks every month.

I bought sandwiches and an apple for our lunch from the new, well stocked, vending machine. Somehow the time galloped away. There was little time to see Garry. I said that I would see Ted in the morning. He waved as I left first this time. The guard had been late bringing him to meet me. Now he was late collecting him. Maybe, if I hurried, the two friends would see each other again.

I had to go back all the way out to give the guard at the gate Garry's name and number and also to get permission to visit. Speed was my main concern.

The guard on the first electric doors had just let some male guards in and as the doors rolled slowly they had a chat with some emerging female guards. When the chat was over the doors were closed and the doors to let me out were drawn open. I had to wait until they had closed before the outer gates could be operated. I dashed down the corridor out on to the path. Due to asthma, I'm always breathless when I run, so by the time I reached the guard through two more sets of gates I could hardly get my words out. "I wish to visit Garry D. Miller Number 000947." She was agonisingly slow. After consultation via the telephone with someone in authority she handed me a written pass.

The dash back was just as agonisingly slow, waiting for the gates to be opened and closed. The visiting room was empty save for the lady guard who indicated where I should sit and wait next to the prisoners' entrance. I caught my breath and tried to relax even though I anxiously knew that every passing minute was wasted visiting time. The grey, steel room, although now empty of people, reeked of the sadness and despair that people endured every day there.

The pleasant, relaxed lady guard on duty also realised that time was pulsating away and rang to see why Garry was so late arriving. Apparently a guard forgot to notify Garry's guard that he had a visitor. Eventually, with very little time left he was brought, handcuffed and very pleased to see me.

Garry; tall, pale round face, ready smile, sad brown eyes, dark brown hair standing upright, jutting out around his head short and stubby. In just over 25 hours he would be dead.

He told me that although he was prepared, he did not want to die. As it was inevitable, he was ready and calm about it. He was going to a happier place to be with God. He had spent the last months in deep prayer, contrition and contemplation. In honour of the Blessed Virgin he wanted to be dressed in her colours, a light blue shirt, white pants and no shoes. For the last two years he had lived according to the Rule of St. Benedict. He did this on his own without instruction. He was wearing the medal of the Order and hoped he would be able to keep it on for the execution the next day. He was putting his trust in God and felt very peaceful.

Garry was gentle, polite and courteous. He thanked me for my books and letters and for giving his name to Sister Joy, whose letters had been so kind and instructive. Through her he had received comforting letters from other people. He told me that his father had been so good to him and Ted all through the years on Death Row. He had visited, sent money and had supported him all the time. Both he and Ted appreciated everything. They knew it was not easy to love and forgive someone who was guilty. Then the guards came.

"Goodbye, God Bless," I said. The handcuffs were locked into place and Garry walked away looking backwards at me.

"God Bless," he mouthed and disappeared round the corner. The lady guard, who had been hovering, said again gently, but firmly, that my time was up. I replaced the telephone on its rest. "God bless." It was the saddest thing, and yet one had to admire the dignity and courage of this healthy young man. But for the grace of God he could have been one of my own sons. I could not take the place of his mother but I tried. She would have been proud of his bravery.

Father Walsh would be with Garry for two hours the next day, when he arrived at "The Walls" on his last day on earth. He would give Garry Communion. It would be the official chaplain who would be with Garry as he died, a man whom Garry did not want to be there. Arguably, Garry's victim did not have anyone there at the time of her death. This is now and Garry knows that he is going to die. Denying him his confessor at his death smacks of revenge. Eleven years on the nature of the man has changed. Garry had never been a criminal before.

He had taken a long time to come to terms with himself and his crime, and had spent a great deal of that time in both spiritual penance and physical suffering. Forgiveness is the message that we are trying to give to the authorities, politicians and people. Just as we expect our sins to be forgiven, let us forgive those who sin against us. This is the hardest thing to do but God has said to do exactly that. Ted once told me that if God can forgive him, Ted then there is hope for everyone.

Separated by wire reinforced glass - Margôt and Ted. Note the cramped cage Ted is confined to for a four-hour visit – hardly the most comfortable conditions for a six-foot man. Cameras are not allowed. All photos are taken by prison staff – for a fee. Livingstone maximum security prison. December, 2001.

Chapter 27

Vigil for Garry

But then, no matter where you are
In all this wondrous Earth
It's love – and love alone
That gives your life its worth.

The next morning was sunny but cold. The prison looked different from the first time that Joy and I had seen it. Then it was being refurbished into a maximum-security prison. Now pale green grass had spread over the wasteland up to the grey - white concrete walls and over to the dark trees around the far perimeter of the land. If I closed my eyes to the high wire fence, the arc lights, the tall gates, the barbed wire and the watchtowers, it would not seem so frightening.

The reception area and the visible parts of the building were glass. Not glass that you could see in through, even with the lights on at night, only glass that one could see out through. I had passed them and now watched soldiers walking about holding rifles. I realised that they were extra security in case Garry tried to make a run for it when he was led out in handcuffs and leg irons with a waist chain on his way to be killed.

I told Ted about it as we sat in the visiting hall. He said that Garry did not need the "royal" treatment with a guard of honour. He would have gone like a lamb to the slaughter, had they but known.

273

As midday arrived, the time for Garry to leave his "home", life around us continued normally. Yet everyone knew exactly what was happening. The atmosphere heightened as a result. Everyone seemed tense.

When John, Richard and I went to Spain I sent Ted some leaflets and cards in Spanish, knowing that he was learning the language. I also sent a weekly church pamphlet about the saints of the week and what was going on in Malaga. He told me,

"I make certain that I spend at least two to three hours each day with my Spanish lessons. Sometimes I skip a day (to let my brain rest), especially if I'm going to be starting a new verb conjugation. Then I'll just review past lessons or I'll read something in Spanish. I "discovered" a great Spanish author, Gabriel García Marquéz, whose works are surprisingly easy for me to read. I have to keep my dictionary close to hand, naturally, because I'm constantly running across words I've never seen before, but I'm getting better. I really think the key to improvement is to use what I learn each day in several different contexts, both reading and writing.

"My instructor for the course on Titus Brandsma has offered to find some books of Spanish fairytales for me. She is fluent in Dutch and Portuguese, as well as English, and she said that was how she learned to write and read those languages fluently. I think it's because fairytales use simple words but have fairly complex plots. And it's been a few years since I read any fairytales, so they almost seem "new" to me, especially in Spanish. The Diocesis papers you've been sending from Spain have also been a big help, as they've been teaching the words and phrases that are unique to the Catholic Church and are seldom heard or seen in ordinary conversation or correspondence. That will help a lot when I start reading John of the Cross and St Teresa of Avila."

I asked the lady guard to photograph Ted and I. The prison authorities have to charge for this photo as it is taken with their Polaroid camera. She told me to sit on the shelf in front of the window to Ted's cage. She told Ted to do the same. It looked as though we were sitting next to each other, the glass between us being invisible on the photo. The guard took one then said that on the second one Ted should smile! We both acknowledged that we are not photogenic, but looking at them now I am pleased with them. That was how we were.

Afterwards, when we were seated, Ted said, "Still nothing from my attorneys, either. I think they've filed everything they can for now, so we're just waiting to hear from the judge. I'm just praying that, whatever he decides, it won't involve another bench warrant! The Carmelites in Seville, Spain have given me a subscription to their newsmagazine "Escapulario del Carmen". So I've got plenty of good reading materials to practise with. I'm enjoying it a lot and I think I'm even learning a bit.

Ted had asked if John would like to be on his visitors' list. The night before, when John rang, he had seemed pleased to be asked and said that he would like to be on Ted's list. So we made tentative arrangements for the next visit to include John. It would be possible, but difficult in the spring, because Richard, our second son was to be married in July. I decided that as usual I could not make positive arrangements until nearer the time. With a family "things" tend to come out of the blue.

The guard came to say that there were only five more minutes. These flashed by. I said that I hoped that I would see him before too long. He was very pleased that I was going to write about him and gave me permission to use his letters in the book. He hoped that he would read it before he died.

When the burly guard came Ted stood up straight away but you could see that it was difficult to stand up. The stool was low and he had been sitting there for four hours. He must have been stiff. I had stood up and walked about to and fro from the vending machines. He had to bend backwards, put his two wrists together behind his back to be handcuffed through the tiny, low, letterbox of a gap in the cage door. It was not easy. He did not look at me as this was going on, I tried to look away but found that impossible to maintain. I needed to see. He gave me a smile as he was led away. I felt quite empty, and sat for a few minutes trying to come to terms with the fact that I could get up and walk out of this prison.

It was time to make the journey to Huntsville for Garry's execution vigil. I would be going on the same road that he had been driven down that morning. It was usually a picturesque ride of about 40 minutes through some beautiful countryside, driving past the lake, with boats nestled by the banks. Probably in the summer it would be busy. On our last foray Joy and I had passed this way and had stopped to take a photo from the bridge. The water had lapped at the stones of the causeway and I had slipped, almost falling into the water. At the time it had seemed funny. Now the setting sun made the trees where I was heading look dark and sinister.

My thoughts were with Garry, how had he felt this morning seeing this countryside, with its verdant trees and clear sky for the last time, knowing that he was on his way to be killed? Soon the lights of passing cars came on. The evening had begun. Garry would shuffle to the gurney still in shackles and hand cuffed behind his back. Then his guards would unlock the manacles to allow his hands and arms to be stretched out and bound to the deathbed. His shackles would be dropped so that his feet could be secured by the leather thongs to the cross structured table covered in a white cloth.

He was ready and prepared, lying there helpless whilst the poison was poised behind a screen to be administered at the right time. A vein would be found in his arm and a needle inserted connected by tube to the three drugs that would stop his muscles from moving. Eventually, when the witnesses were all in their respective places, behind glass, he would be asked to say his last words.

Dawn and Shelley, the two English girls, were waiting for me as I pulled up in to the large car park at "The Walls" for the vigil. They had visited their friend for the last time early that morning at Terrell Unit. They would try to save enough money to visit some time again in the future. They felt that the visits had gone well. They had enjoyed meeting their pen friend and they said that he had been over the moon with delight to meet them.

There were a great many young people, standing in groups near the tape across the road. I did not know any of them. As we wandered near a couple I asked them if they were local. They, very seriously, answered that they were from the University of Houston, studying law. I left them talking to Dawn and Shelley, and approached a young group who said that they had come from Denmark and Germany. They were on a cultural mission to see the "other side" of America. They had not known that the Death Penalty was in operation in Texas, let alone America. They felt shocked, angry and upset about what they had learnt.

A young man came up to me in the dark. He said that he was from Canada and his name was Julian Elie. He was with a film crew making a documentary about the Death Penalty. Would I give them an interview on Thursday? I explained that I was going home on that day otherwise I would have done. I introduced him to Dennis Longmuire, the Huntsville University professor. He held a lighted candle and was always at the vigils. He says that he is there with his candle to represent all the thousands of Texans who are opposed to the death penalty but are unable to attend the vigil.

I left them to go and speak to an attractive Afro-American lady who was wearing a beautiful turquoise and silver turban. She had been standing praying but now she looked about her. She was part of the Texas Death Penalty Abolition Movement. I had already met some of their members. When she asked if I would like to join I readily agreed and enrolled that evening.

She had been campaigning for years against the death penalty. She used to attend the vigils when the killing took place at midnight. It had been really bad then as she and her fellow campaigners were in a tiny minority. There were usually a huge crowd outside these same walls shouting, screaming, chanting and drinking. It took a lot of courage to come in those days, I thought. Now, she said, the mood of the people seemed to be changing for the better.

People were thinking about the moral issue of "legally" taking a life. People were starting to think and reason. They now understood that killing someone was revenge. It did not solve problems. It created them. It was not a deterrent. It costs far more to kill someone than to keep them in prison for the rest of their lives. People can change, both those in prison and those outside - those who are guilty and have been caught, those who are guilty and have not been caught. She said that it was important that Texans should realise that there is an alternative to the death sentence.

In the wind the candles kept blowing out. It was cold, not as cold as in England but cold for Texas. The temperature matched my feelings as I listened to this attractive lady. We fell silent and prayed as the time passed, my thoughts on Garry. Out of the darkness, unobtrusively, came Father Walsh walking briskly. He carried a transparent plastic bag in his hand. In the yellow-orange streetlights I could see ribbons in the bag. Garry was dead! Those ribbons were attached to his medals, the ones that he had worn to his death. I hesitated to speak to Father Walsh as Ted had said he would be upset about Garry's death.

Father Walsh was fast disappearing. I ran to catch up with him. I thought that I would just say "hello". He had reached his car and had put the plastic bag inside when I tentatively said, "Hello, it's Margôt."

In fact, he was pleased to see me. He said that Garry had been peaceful, penitent and prayerful. We had quite a long talk in the chill air. Then Father Walsh told me to bow my head, as he would give me a blessing. It was one of the most beautiful moments of my life. I felt very close to God. A man's soul had just gone to Him. I was blessed by a very good, spiritual person. The cold, "The Walls", the people all faded into nothing as the words were said over my head.

"I bless you in the name of the Father and of the Son and of the Holy Spirit. Amen. Go in peace."

The crowd had begun to disperse as Father Walsh drove away. I walked slowly towards them and saw Dawn and Shelley. They had decided to return to their hotel. They would have preferred to stay in Huntsville, as there was not much to do at night in Livingston. They had found one club, which they had enjoyed, but they were due to go home the next day and thought that they would have an early night.

Two ladies from the Texas Death Penalty Abolition Movement had asked me to join them for supper. I was delighted. This was the first time that I had been out at night since arriving in Texas. I did not feel like being alone. I slowly followed them in their car. The roads were white with frost. We went to a relaxed Chinese restaurant, one that Joy and I had often visited.

Our meal was interesting. We each brought to the table our choice of menu, something that the others had not tasted before. And we shared. We found out a little about each other. We promised to keep in touch by e-mail. One of the ladies, Elaine, was a retired lecturer. She was intensely interested in learning about everything. Her sense of injustice had started in the mid fifties during the time of segregation in the colleges and schools in the Deep South. She had been an ardent advocate even then. She had marched in Mississippi and Waco and was now protesting about injustice and the death penalty here in Huntsville every time that there was an execution.

We did not linger over coffee once we had finished our meal. They had to travel back to Houston and the cold weather might make conditions on the roads more hazardous. I had to find my Hotel, which was fortuitously nearby.

After such an eventful day I was tired but I did not sleep too well. I kept thinking about Ted and all the other inmates. They too would be affected by the news of Garry's death. They would then think, with dread, how they and their families, if any, would cope when the time came for them to die. Some sooner, some later, but they would all somehow relate to today's events. How would they feel and act as they climbed and lay on the gurney to die? Not all had the sense of peace and hope that Garry had shown and felt. I had heard that some were dragged, wrestling into the chamber to be killed.

The next day, Wednesday 6th December, I had a leisurely breakfast in the foyer of the Holiday Inn. All over town people were turning to their copies of The Huntsville Item, the local paper. On the front page they reported that Garry Dean Miller, with a Bible resting on his chest, as he lay strapped to the gurney, had been pronounced dead at 6:23 p.m. the previous evening. As the 38th execution in Texas, it had broken the record of the most executions carried out by a state in a single year. The previous record had been 37 (Texas, 1997).

I sorted out my suitcase, the clothes that I needed for the journey and the ones that could be relegated to the bottom of the bag. I paid the bill and set off for Houston. It was still cold. The roads were quiet. I managed to find the Alamo Rental easily. That by itself was a major miracle, as we usually spent half a day looking for the right rental road near the International Airport.

Consequently I was early. I was given a good seat again and managed to sleep through the night. It was the first time that I have ever missed a meal or a film on a plane. However, I made up for it at Gatwick by enjoying a welcome home egg and bacon breakfast at 6 a.m. I still had another journey, from London Gatwick on to Manchester airport, where John met me and we drove home happily to Deganwy.

It was great to be home. John was as pleased to see me safely back, as I was to be back. There was a lot of talking to be done with Joy. John was quite happy to come with me next time (Well, we'll see!). The really sad moment of homecoming was no Barney, to greet me.

Chapter 28

"A bad case of the blacks"

And while I slept aboard my ship
A nightmare crew came on;
They cast off lines and spread the sails.
When I awoke, safe port was gone.

Life in Wales revolved round the Christmas preparations. Cards to be written and sent, cards received with all the news from friends. Presents to buy for Tanya, her friends and neighbours, as well as ours. The food had to be bought, menus to compile then cook during the holiday. Richard and David would be with us over Christmas then James, Bee, Francesca and William would arrive for the New Year.

It was very rewarding on Christmas Day to sit round the dining room table in Tanya's house and see happy smiling faces. The house had been beautifully decorated for Christmas. The staircase was wreathed in green foliage with lights twinkling all the way up. In the hall stood an enormous green tree sheathed in white lights, gold angels and bells.

The table was arranged with a red tablecloth, matching red berries and green holly napkins. Silver candelabra took pride of place with bright red candles. It all looked very festive. Tanya was happy.

Tanya's arthritic hips were not improving and she did not want to have an operation. She is able to do little for herself but she has wonderful help from her carers. Without these fantastic people Tanya and I would not be able to cope.

Joy joined us for Christmas lunch. Her sciatica had improved and she was able to drive her car again. We talked about the kind of Christmas spirit that would prevail at the Terrell Unit. We prayed that the inmates would have some peace. Ted had written to say that he had received a letter and a Christmas card from Garry!

New Year was delightfully exciting with the arrival of Carrie and then James and his family. We experienced Christmas all over again, watching the little ones open their presents from under our white tree. Christmas and New Year had been a welcome relief from George W. Bush's Texas, a state that had killed 40 by now in the year 2000.

We had prayed, played and rejoiced. Richard and Carrie's wedding was scheduled for July. We planned to discuss this as it would be the last time that we would all be together before the wedding.

For Ted, the Christmas Spirit was lost except inside his mind. There were no services at all. No Mass on Christmas day. Nor did he receive the Sacraments of Confession or Communion to give him spiritual strength. Ted had a Christmas lunch. Although cold it was a change of diet. Ted also missed receiving Garry's long, funny letters, and he had not been gone a full month yet. Ted was alone. There were yet more inconveniences for Ted as he relayed in his letter of January 3rd 2001:

"We are in the second day of another state-wide lock-down. This is their semi-annual "lets tear everything apart and see what we can find" lock-down, and it usually lasts about two weeks. Fortunately this one was expected since they do it every year, and I was able to stock up on stamps and food items from the Commissary. It's bad enough that we won't be getting any hot meals during this time – just two cold sandwiches three times a day – but to make matters worse, the heating system has stopped working so now we're all freezing. The temperature dropped down into the upper 20's last night and I could sure tell it!

"I also had a letter from Father Bill the other day and I think I'll be able to make my Profession in July on my birthday – or on Titus Brandsma's feast day, depending on how you look at it. I will take the name "John-Titus of the Cross". I'll still have six months of Formation left to complete, since in July I will have only finished two years, but the difficult part is already done. Time passes so quickly – it's already been a year and a half since I was accepted and invested in the Lay Carmelites, and it's been almost three years since you sent me the cards from Huntsville for my Confirmation and First Communion! It doesn't really seem so long though, does it?

"I haven't heard anything from my attorneys lately. The deadline for filing briefs and motions with the court was December

15th, and the judge can hand down a decision any time after that. All they were really arguing about was whether or not new evidence should be allowed into the official record after the deadline for it has passed. The State's attorney says it should not be allowed because of the deadline; my attorney says it should be allowed because it's not my fault that the trial judge waited so long to appoint another attorney for me. The outcome will just depend on which side out-talked the other – just like all politics, I guess. I'll be sure and let you know when I hear something.

"My course on Titus isn't coming along well at all. I am in the middle of what my mother used to call "a bad case of the blacks", but which the medical world calls manic depression. I was diagnosed as a 'Manic Depressive' when I was 12 years old, and re-diagnosed when I was 16. When I was 12, they said it was serious enough for 'treatment', and when I was 16, (and waiting trial for murder), they then decided it was "too late" for treatment.

I'm not saying that my depression was the cause of my actions, because I don't get violent or delusional, I simply get very quiet and withdrawn with no interest – or very little interest – in anything or anyone. I don't know what sort of effect the solitary conditions here have on me, but I'm sure they do have an effect of some sort. For the most part, I enjoy being alone with my books and letters and prayers, but I know very little about mental health – my own or anyone else's – so I don't know how much of my thinking and behaviour is normal (for me) and how much is a result of the last year in this place. You could probably tell better than I could, anyway, as you can compare my latest letters, with those written more than a year ago".

"I can't manage to concentrate on anything, so even though I have almost twelve pages of notes and opinions concerning Titus' form of spirituality, I can't put them together in any sort of coherent form. Trying to force myself to make sense out of it only makes it worse and the frustration is maddening, so all I can do is wait it out. I know there are medications available that would help, but I just don't trust the "doctors" here to do their jobs right. I've seen too many instances of prisoners getting the wrong medication or the wrong dosages, so I think I'll just put up with my mood swings when they come about.

"Usually I can make allowances and compensate in such a way that my depression isn't really noticeable except to people who know me well, but it's been continuing for almost three weeks this time. I'm usually able to pull out of it after a week or so, but not this time. I'll be all right eventually though."

Ted's enthusiasm for St. John of the Cross, was as strong as always, as he wrote in his letter of February 11th:

"Do you remember me telling you in one of my letters about the sketch by St. John of the Cross that served as the inspiration for the painting by Dali of the Crucifixion? Well, I've managed to get a card of John's sketch that I will enclose for you. The quote beneath the sketch is in Spanish (which I'm sure your John can easily translate by now), and the card is from Ubeda, Spain where John of the Cross is buried. I hope you will like the card.

288

"You asked me about our beds here. Well, the mattress is a long plastic sack that is filled with loose cotton (it would be more honest to say that it's actually half-filled, if that). Being plastic, it's uncomfortable, and since the cotton is loose, it tends to bunch up at the ends and become lumpy (the concrete floor is actually more comfortable in the summer). And the mattresses are placed on a steel table that stretches along the back wall from wall to wall, and it stands about one and half feet tall. It's secured onto the floor, so it can't be moved (which is nice, since it makes deciding on how to arrange the furniture much simpler!). And yes, they gave us new mattresses when we got over here – I suppose because they couldn't be certain what might be hidden in the old mattresses!"

"I know you won't believe me, but I really don't "miss" Garry. I miss his letters, but I can't miss him, because I saw him so seldom. I talked to him for an hour back in January or February of last year; I talked to him for about thirty minutes in July of last year; and I saw him just in passing when you were here and I was on my way into the visiting room. So, when I only saw him for about an hour and half during the 16 or 17 month period, there's really nothing to miss, except his letters, which usually came every two or three weeks.

"I was very irritated. After flying down from Tucson, Arizona, Father Bill was not allowed in to see me. He called the Warden's secretary the day before but when he arrived on the Friday they could not find it anywhere on the appointments page and the secretary swears she never spoke to him. Chaplain Stanley refused to help at all. Father Bill finally got in to see the Warden and Chaplain Stanley was there trying to cast doubt on whether Father Bill was an ordained priest much less a Carmelite Provincial even though the visiting record shows that he was here to visit me and Garry last August. Fortunately Father Bill had an official document from the Tucson diocese to prove that he really is a priest. Father Bill finally left in disgust."

On March 24th 2001 Joy and I travelled by train to Crewe to participate in a workshop as a part of the local Justice and Peace movement there. The same day that we were in Crewe, Ted was writing to me:

"Life goes on as usual here. We are locked down again from March 13th to the 21st. – someone on the maintenance crew somehow managed to lose a crowbar that couldn't be found! – but now we're back to our usual routine of having the guards screaming at us at 6:00 a.m. each morning, asking if we want to go to recreation or showers.

"On the 21st February my friend, Sr. Michael of Jesus, passed away. She was at the Liverpool Carmel."

Sister Mary, the Prioress, mentioned Ted in the Obituary notice that was sent to the other Carmels: "Even in the last months of her life, Sr. Michael's gifts for friendship came to the fore. She was introduced to Ted Cole on Death Row, Texas and wrote to him now and again. Ted, now a Carmelite himself, wrote the most beautiful spiritual letters. This contact enlarged her horizons in a number of ways and greatly enriched her own spirituality. Between the elderly nun and the convicted murderer/mystic/poet was a special bond."

I was curious to know how Ted had met Father Bill: "Back in October of 1998, I wrote to the Carmelite Vocational Office about whether or not a prisoner could join the Lay Carmelites, and I asked them to please put me in contact with someone who could tell me more about the Third Order. A couple of months later I got a letter from Father Bill, who was in Houston at that time running their vocational office in the south. We started corresponding and about eight months later I was invested with the Lay Carmelite Scapular. He's been my friend and formation director ever since. Oh – I bet in my previous letters I referred to him as Father Harry! His name is William Harry, but I (usually) call him Father Bill. But, anyway, that's the story of how I met him.

"It was right after I'd finished reading the works of St. John of the Cross, and I found the address of the Vocations Office in the back of the book. I was so impressed with John of the Cross, I decided I needed to be a Carmelite too!"

The skeleton of my book was progressing. The weather began to warm up in Malaga and it was increasingly difficult to work in the little glass bedroom. John needed the dining room table to work on with his computer. The apartment was beginning to feel crowded. We began to think of a larger apartment. I loved the sea view, unfortunately there was not a bigger apartment with one available to rent, only to buy. We had been adamant that we would only rent, but we both began to dislike the uncomfortable bed and chairs. Most of all the heat in the summer was unbearable without air conditioning.

We looked at one flat. Although beautiful it was too expensive. Suddenly, we began to notice many apartments, "se vende," to sell. The one I loved was far too expensive. The pharmacist who owned it would not lower his price. We left the idea and battled on with our work.

Normally Death Row inmates are buried in a twenty-two acre prison cemetery outside Huntsville, near Ellis One called Peckerwood Hill Cemetery. The graves were marked by a simple, white, wooden cross with their prison number painted in black. There are over nine hundred prisoners buried there unclaimed or unwanted.

When Ted had asked his mother if she would bury him she had replied, "The State killed you, the State can bury you, son."

Joy and I suggested to Ted and Garry that their ashes could be brought over to Britain for burial here. They were both relieved and happy with this idea.

Garry's ashes arrived in Wales; Father Gordon in Pantasaph had previously agreed to have him interred there. We held Garry's Requiem Mass on 18th April. His funeral was well attended by his pen friends (including Charlotte Dugdale and her parents Maureen and Eric) and supporters. They included some who had actually visited him, plus members of the Rhyl Justice and Peace group. Pauline Vickers from Deganwy, who was going to play the organ, came with her husband John. Garry had loved Ave Maria, having heard it on the tape given to him by Deacon Lopez whilst still at Ellis One, so taped music of Gounod's version was provided. The eulogy was about forgiveness, love and Divine mercy, all of which, with the Holy Spirit's help, brings us peace. Ted's moving tribute to his friend Garry was also read out:

"Garry Dean Miller is my friend. During the last 12 years of his life, I had the pleasure and privilege of watching him grow up and mature both emotionally and spiritually.

"When I met Garry, my own search for God's love and forgiveness had just begun and Garry fascinated me because - although he said he didn't believe in heaven or hell and hadn't made up his mind about the existence of God - he still felt he was eternally damned and without hope. He considered himself to be unworthy of love and beyond the reach of forgiveness. Garry needed a friend and I needed a "devil's advocate", and our friendship began.

"It's difficult to speak of Garry without bringing God into the conversation. Because of my search for Truth and Garry's denial of heaven and hell, religion and spirituality became the points where our lives and interests met. The Lord alone knows how many miles we walked, round and round the confines of the exercise yard; talking, arguing, debating. But somewhere along the way, while I was involved with yoga and Eastern meditation, Garry developed an interest in God.

"Maybe He really did exist; maybe heaven and hell were real. He turned to the Catholic Church for answers, and through the ministrations of Father Stephen Walsh, our very own Franciscan friar (and Garry once told me that he had no choice but to be impressed by the courage of a man who would dare to wear a dress into a prison!), he found his answers in the writings and teachings of St. Francis and St. Anthony. Garry embraced the Church and her teachings, was baptised — taking St. Anthony as his patron — and confirmed and, even though it's not easy being a practicing Catholic in a Texas prison, his only regret was that he felt the Church he loved never embraced him in return.

"When I grew disillusioned with Eastern religion and philosophy, it was partly due to Garry's encouragement that I began to study the teachings of the Church. He had listened to me babble about God and religion for so long that he knew my arguments against Christianity, and while he didn't trust himself to explain the faith, he always knew where I could find the answers I needed, who to talk to, which books to read.

"And when I finally decided that I could do worse than to join the Catholic Church and serve God as he wanted me to it was Garry who stood with me at my Confirmation. When the priest reminded him that he was now responsible for encouraging me in the faith and for providing an example of how to live in Christ, Garry looked at him, then at me, then back at him and said, "Man, he's in really big trouble!" But Garry did encourage me, and he did provide an example in that he continued to grow in faith and to walk closer with our Lord in spite of the many obstacles and trials and temptations that prison life provides in abundance. Garry would be the first to admit that it wasn't easy for him to stay on his feet, so to speak, but every time he fell he would get right back up and continue his journey.

"Garry loved to pray the Rosary and the Divine Mercy chaplet, and he was faithful in praying the Liturgy of the Hours each day. He was devoted to the Blessed Mother, and I would often hear him trying to sing the Ave Maria and the Salve Regina - I say, "trying" because he couldn't carry a tune in a bucket, but he never let that stop him. His favourite hymn, regardless of the time of year, was "O Holy Night". He loved Christmas and the idea that the Christ Child is forever being reborn in our hearts as we die more and more to the world. He also had no illusions about who and what he was or where his help came from, and he always looked forward to receiving the Sacraments of Reconciliation and the Eucharist. He was strong enough to admit he was weak, and he gladly - even eagerly - took advantage of the graces provided by our Lord's love and mercy.

"In the last couple of years of his life, he developed a very strong devotion to St. Benedict. He began to live in strict observance of the Rule of St. Benedict, and more and more he devoted himself to prayer and penance, but without ever losing his fun-loving sense of humour. And when, a month before his death, he was accepted and enrolled as an Oblate by a Benedictine monastery, he knew his life was complete. He was sorry for the pain his death would cause his family and friends, but the only thing left for him at that point was to meet his Lord face to face. He had no worries or fears, because he firmly believed in the Communion of the Saints and the resurrection promised by Jesus, and he had confidence that for him there was no death, only life.

"Garry committed a terrible crime, accepted responsibility for it, and paid with his life, but in spite of what the secular world has to say about him, I knew him to be a very gentle and loving person. His life remains a powerful testimony to the loving redemption that Christ freely offers to each of us, and his death was a holy one. Garry was my friend, closer to me than my own brothers, and I miss him. I thank God for the blessing of having known Garry, and I know that he now sits at Jesus' feet with all the saints, asking for us all the graces that he himself enjoys."

Garry's ashes were carried to the door of the old oak-beamed church that had witnessed and sheltered so many different emotions over the years. The comfort and feel of the wood and the cold, stone floor inside changed dramatically as the heavy, dark-oak door opened and let in the pale sunlight. The wind whistled in the bare trees, making the yellow daffodils dance and sway among the grass growing in between the rows of grey headstones. Dark green moss, weeds and white pebbles surrounded the purple slates that whispered the names, dates, love and anguish of friends and relatives resting peacefully there. I recognised many of the family names having taught in the district for some years. It was comforting to see that Garry was amongst old friends of both Joy and I.

The sounds of the lambs and sheep from the surrounding fields and hillsides mingled with the wind and Father Gordon's voice as Garry was laid to rest. A year later, when the earth had settled, a Welsh purple slate was placed on top. The white inscription reads: "Garry Miller 1969-2000 Now At Peace."

Garry's ashes now lie safely, far from home, below a thick slice of Welsh slate. Pantasaph, North Wales. Easter, 2002.

Chapter 29
Ave Maria.

I tried to turn my ship around,
But the helm would not respond.
I even tried to swim for shore,
But my ship and I had formed a bond.

As Ted reported on May 1st, being incarcerated did not mean in isolation away from petty human grievances – and he was not referring to his fellow inmates either:

"There is, as usual, very little going on in here. I expect a small war to break out soon, but it will be between the first-shift guards and the second-shift guards! As our new Warden continues to dream up new ways to harass us, the guards find that the harassment just means more work for them. And you know from your own experience here just how lazy these people are – well, the first-shift guards have started working slower and slower, and doing less and less, and then the second-shift guards are left with more than their "fair" share of the work to do. There have already been two fights between guards (that I know of) when the two shifts are together at shift change. I fully expect it to get worse. The fact that they're fighting amongst themselves shows you how stupid they are. They ought to get together and figure out how to get rid of this new Warden who's causing the problems!

"According to the new rules the guards have to search our cells every day when we go to the shower. Lately it seems that every little thing they do is designed for the sole purpose of pushing us that little bit closer to the edge. The only time my nerves are not on edge is when I'm lost in a book."

Two days later, on May 3rd, while we were giving a talk to social work students in Liverpool, Ted was happy to relate a new development in his literary "career":

"I am now the unofficial 'Assistant Editor' of the Carmelite Review. Before publishing each issue, Father Bill has been sending half of the Review to me for correction of spelling and grammar, and the other half to the Carmelite nuns near him, but he hasn't been real happy with the results he gets from the nuns who are so busy with other things (they're in charge of a school and an 'assisted living' home for elderly religious). I make the time to actually read the material, which is the only way to put each word in context, and to see if it says what it's supposed to say.

"Well, I'd originally started doing it because it was a way to pass the time, and it made me feel useful. But, I figure if I am going to help with 'mistakes', then I might as well do the job properly – I would tell him if something didn't make sense, or if a word, or words, seemed to have been left out (many of his 'reporters' are priests from Mexico and Peru, and their English is sometimes less than perfect) – and he has gradually been sending more stuff to me, and now I get the entire Review for correcting! I enjoy it, of course, but it does take up a lot of time.

Ted was able to explain some of the terms he uses in his letters: ""General Population" – it's both place and person. You have the "population" of the prison system – some are Death Row, some are Ad–Seg (administrative segregation), some are "close custody" or "protective segregation", and everyone else is "general" population. It doesn't matter how much or little time they're in for, if they enjoy the limited freedom of being able to go to the chapel for church services and the dining room to eat and the gym to play and work out... they're all general population. They're also the ones who have jobs. Ad-Seg is people who refuse to work, are trouble makers, or gang members. Protective–segregation is for folks who, for one reason or another, would be in danger in general population: ex-police officers, very feminine gays, people who are known as "snitches", and so on.

"There's still not much going on around here that's worth talking about. Several "population" at this unit were locked down this morning. Rumour has it that someone was cut or stabbed in a fight, but I don't know that for a fact. For all I know, the guards may have decided they wanted a day off work, so they locked it all down tight and went fishing. What I do know is that there's no one working in the kitchen today – for lunch, we had a cheese sandwich and a tuna sandwich (if you want to call a spoonful of frozen tuna between two slices of bread a 'sandwich'), and we'll probably have the same for supper. But, they are still allowing Death Row to "recreate" and shower, so the lockdown didn't reach us, except for us not getting hot meals. They didn't bring me more library books today, either, and we probably won't be able to make our Commissary orders Monday morning. I guess we're "locked down" even when we're not "locked-down!""

In Spain, John and I viewed some of the small villas in the area of the flat but we saw nothing affordable where we wanted to live. I was unable to buy a hat for the wedding of our year, which was approaching fast. I had managed to find a lovely dress, shoes and bag in Puerto Banus, Marbella. We both concentrated on our work. It was a treat to be able to sit down quietly and think. My asthma had improved significantly and I had stopped taking the cortisone tablets that I had needed regularly. The temperature in Spain suited me.

On Death Row, however, things were not so sunny as he wrote on May 11th:

"We haven't had access to a tape player in almost three years. Chaplain McKinney provided me and Garry with one along with several tapes of Gregorian chants, and one of Pope John Paul praying the Rosary. He also gave us some tapes of Marian hymns and that was how Garry learned the Ave Maria. We lost the tape player and all the cassettes right after the escape attempt at Ellis, though, and I don't know if we'll ever have them again. (And if we have to depend on this so-called Chaplain we have now, I know we'll never have them again!).

The sheer futility and emptiness of prison life was evident in Ted's letter of June 8th:

"I'm getting really tired of all the shouting and banging and clanging that goes on here all day and everyday. The guys here are getting more bored, frustrated, and restless with each passing day, and it shows in the noise level and the increased use of profanity by men who used to be very careful of what they said and how they said it. Everyone seems to be changing for the worse, and I sometimes wonder if I am too but just can't see it. I hope not!

"I finally got a reply from our new Bishop. I was hoping for a better response but what I got from him was about what I really expected. It was the usual: "Sorry, we're doing the best we can, but all our priests and deacons are busy elsewhere!" Why do the clergy think – or seem to think – that they're the only one's in "the Church"? I specifically asked the Bishop to consider a lay-ministry to death row, because all the priests and deacons are busy. He totally ignored that and then simply repeated what I'd said to him. I don't know if he's just stupid or if he didn't bother to really read my letter. Well, as I said – it wasn't totally unexpected.

"If you ever get to Avila to see the sketch by John of the Cross, be sure to take your camera with you. If photos are allowed I'd definitely like to have one. I would love to be able to visit Spain and to see all the places that are connected with St. John and St. Teresa. I guess I'll have to settle for their words instead, but even that is more than a lot of people are able to enjoy.

"Well, you should have had your meeting by now, about the problem of young people drinking and taking drugs at the back of your church garden. I hope the problem can be solved without those young people feeling rejected by the church and the community. I remember being so frustrated when I was a kid – 13 and 14 – when the adults were always telling us "don't do this", "don't do that", "go away!" but they never suggested anything that we could do, or anywhere we could go. I don't remember any drugs being around, but we had alcohol and cigarettes and there were always fights. Our parents were all at home watching TV and didn't have time for us, so all we had was our own miserable company and nothing to do. That's life though."

Ted was referring to our local Justice and Peace meeting. It was held in the entrance hall of the Holy Family Church and was well attended by parishioners, neighbours and local councillors. A community policeman described solutions that had calmed other local trouble spots. He talked about identifying the ringleaders, talking to their parents and helping them to find a hobby in the new local youth hall. He also said that the police would be more vigilant with off-licences and shops that served underage teenagers.

Joy and I were invited to give a talk to the Mother's Union at Eglwysbach, a small hamlet in the Conwy valley. The wooden floored, cosy building, the scene of many a parish social event, was tucked out of sight down a narrow side road. I have a special feeling for the village as my paternal grandfather came from farming stock there.

We were listened to intently. Many of the ladies there had no idea what went on in a Death Row prison. It was a privilege to meet these industrious ladies who do so much good in their local community.

Our next Malaga interlude took a dramatic turn when we returned there to continue our rest and writing period. Two excited estate agents took us round to see the "perfect little house" for us. We were told not to look at the stark exterior walls and untidy front garden, as the vendor seemed to love cement. The spacious interior was just what we wanted - two bedrooms, salon and huge sun lounge. Outside there was a small garden and swimming pool. Some of the garden and entrance porch would have to have some tender, loving care. The kitchen, bathroom and bedrooms did not need any refurbishment. What a great June birthday present. We decided that we would have it but there were many obstacles to overcome. Fortunately we had a good solicitor. John has also read many books on "How to Buy a House in Spain." It is not easy.

In his letter of June 19th Ted relayed a palpable sense of isolation:

"When Father Bill visits, he comes in as a minister and ministers' visits are altogether different from any other type of visit and don't interfere with them.

I haven't seen or heard from my sister in almost two years, and she's no longer on my visitors' list anyway. I haven't seen my step-dad since November of 1999 – the last letter I got from him was back in April and he finally came right out and admitted I was a problem for his new family. He said it would be best "for all concerned" if he no longer sent money or letters, since it could be embarrassing if it came out that he had two step-sons: one on Death Row and one a sergeant near Houston. He also told me in the last letter that my nephew Everett, had died in February. That's all he said – nothing about how or where, just that he was dead. He was only 13."

I was devastated with the sad, cold, heartless way that this was relayed to Ted. Everett had never met his uncle, probably as Ted said, he might not even know that he had an uncle, but he was thought and prayed about there on Death Row. The sadness of it all must have been yet another trial for Ted to bear, which he did stoically and inside himself, not divulging his feelings to anyone.

Everett Marsh, the nephew Ted never saw. 1992.

Chapter 30

White Wedding

Does the heart of a buttercup
know love for its maker?
Does a rose offer thanks
for sunshine and rain?
...yes!

For John and I things were hectic. It was almost time for the Wedding, John and I packed all our accumulated possessions from the rented flat in Spain and left them with Salva, our Spanish help.

First we had to go to Richard's third graduation, his MBA from Warwick. We left after a splendid lunch and drove home to be with Tanya for her birthday. We celebrated it all at the Sunflower Ball in the beautiful gardens of St. David's School, Llandudno, with some of our friends.

On 20th July 2001 John and I put our glad rags in the car and made our way down to Cobham for Richard and Carrie's wedding. The weather was fairly stable and I remembered to bring all the necessary clothing. We stayed in the lovely old manor house that had been converted into a country club. It had a superb golf course, amazingly spacious gardens, and a heated swimming pool in a walled rose garden. The cobbled, totally secluded and gated

306

stable area had been converted into a modern complex of bedroom suites. The heated pool, surrounded by comfortable chairs and sun beds, looked enticing. Nearby, people played tennis on modern courts. That evening we had a dinner party in the manor house. It was a good start to the weekend.

The next day the sun managed to appear sporadically as the clouds were shuffled around a windy sky. It was lovely to see Father John McKay who had known Richard since he was a small altar server. He had always had a soft spot for Richard and the two teased each other whenever they met. He welcomed all the guests and married Richard and Carrie, who looked stunning with her slim figure and beautiful white dress and train. Francesca and Charlotte looked adorable in their cream dresses and blond hair. William and "Peter Wabbit" were in command at the end of the procession.

I gave an account to Ted as well as sending him some photos. He particularly enjoyed William and his "body-guard". Francesca looked like an angel, he said.

For Ted things were becoming particularly arduous. He was finding that being a practising Catholic on Death Row was difficult in the extreme:

"No, we didn't have Mass on Pentecost Sunday, but then we haven't had Mass in almost two years, except for "last masses" for individual inmates. There also wasn't any sort of Communion service, and there weren't any priests, deacons or chaplains here either. Pentecost is a lot like Easter and Christmas – they don't

307

really exist in prison except in our minds. I expect it to be this way from now on.

"We just got off a ten-day lock-down, from the 2nd of July through the 11th. Since there was no one in the day room trying to hold impossible conversations with people in their cells during those days, it was nice and quiet for a change. The sandwiches seemed to be even worse than usual, but we were expecting the lock-down so I was able to stock up on instant soups and saltine crackers and corn chips. I know, that doesn't sound very appetising either, but it's a lot better than those half-frozen sandwiches!

"The Gestapo showed up – with the Visigoths and Vandals in tow – on the morning of the 8th and, as usual, they made a terrible mess of things. I'm seriously considering just tossing out any and all old papers and letters that I don't absolutely need. I don't know which I dislike more: the way my cell looks after a shakedown, or the self-satisfied smirk on the guards' faces when they stalk away to their next victim! But getting rid of a lot of this stuff would possibly reduce both.

"I do still have the Missals, and I use them daily. Fortunately, they're very well made books! My day begins with Morning Prayer from the Liturgy of the Hours, and then I read and pray the Mass for the day. And I end each day with reading from the Scriptures, Night Prayer and then my rosary. And throughout the day I have all the other prayers from the Liturgy of the Hours, of course, but it seems to me that when I start and end my day "properly", everything else seems to go smoothly. (Well, everything except shakedowns, that is – those are still pretty rough!)

"Father Walsh was here on the 3rd of July. He visited a bit longer than usual, almost an hour, because he was going back to Boston for the summer and won't be back till October. My Profession has also been put off until then. Father Bill just can't seem to get any cooperation from our Chaplain when he tries to make arrangements to come in, so he said in his last letter that he won't try again. Father Walsh said he would be happy to accept my vows on behalf of the Carmelites, but I haven't got all the necessary paperwork yet. Well, everything in its own good time, I reckon, right?

"My August issue of the Catholic Digest came in the evening and contains an article titled "A Saint who killed?" It seems, a Frenchman Jacques Fesch, who was beheaded in 1957 for killing a police officer, after a bungled robbery, is being considered for beatification by the Church. And it's causing a bit of controversy, of course, as many people (and more than a few of them are police officers) are opposed to the idea of a mere criminal being raised to that level. I thought it was an interesting article and hope that those who are promoting his cause succeed.

"We made out our Commissary orders last night. I have $33 and some odd cents left and most of that will go towards stamps and a new typewriter ribbon. I've spent a bit more than I intended to in the last couple of months. I have a neighbour who gets no money at all, and every week when they bring our orders around he stands at his door looking at all the "goodies" everyone else is getting. Well, thanks to you I no longer have to do without, but I still remember what it's like so I've been buying extras to send to him when no one's watching. He's been here six years (he's only 24) and when we were at Ellis he supported himself by making clocks and jewellery boxes, but here he's got nothing. Keep him in your prayers – his name is Joe.

On July 24th Ted wrote with some more disappointing news: "By now, you should have gotten my last letter telling you that my Profession has been temporarily postponed, due to Father Walsh going back to Boston, until the end of September. Well, you know what they say about "the best laid plans of mice and men!" But, I love the card of congratulations that you sent. I've tucked it away in my Bible, and on the day that I finally profess my vows, I will bring it back out, and we will celebrate!

"Father Bill was here for a visit this afternoon. He seemed a bit surprised to find that they actually let him through the gate this time! We had a nice visit though. He was only here for a couple of hours, and then he had to go to San Antonio for a convention of Carmelites that he's "hosting". He said that he'll try to be back after Christmas for another visit.

"I've been "asked" by the Provincial to rewrite the formation books, so they'll be more relevant to prisoners, and others who are so isolated that they're unable to attend the regular formation meetings in their area! Truth be told, I think they are just tired of hearing me complain about how meaningless the formation lessons are to someone in my situation, so they decided that if I didn't like their books, I could just write my own. Father Bill said the Province has already put aside enough money to have 500 "special editions" published whenever the new manuscript is ready. It's kind of exciting, in a way, to know that future "isolates" will be studying from my version of the books."

On Thursday August 16th, the same day that John was admitted to Stanley Hospital for treatment to his eye, Ted wrote to me: "Well, you can see by the envelope, the Terrell Unit has now been renamed "The Polunsky Unit". I knew that Mr. Terrell had asked the Prison Board to remove his name from the Unit, but I didn't really expect them to do it so soon. Maybe they were afraid that he might use the media to raise a big stink! Anyway, I hope that Mr. Terrell can now sleep with a clear conscience, though I don't see how it really matters – as long as he is a voting citizen of Texas, every execution is done in his name!"

"Speaking of unpredictable rules, did I tell you that as of August 1st, visitors are no longer allowed to bring paper money into the unit? I think I told you, but I don't remember.

"I recently joined the Prisoners' Poetry Workshop, coordinated by Liz Hoyle of Human Writes. She is also the Coordinator for "Prisoner to Prisoner" correspondence. I'd asked her about finding an English prisoner pen pal for me, but I haven't heard from anyone yet. I haven't quite decided yet what I think of the Poetry Workshop. We're all amateurs, of course, and Liz encourages members to submit poems, which she distributes and then we are to critique each other's

311

work. Well, that doesn't sound like such a great idea to me – I don't mind being criticised by someone who knows more about poetry than I do (Okay, I do mind, but not terribly so!), but I might have a hard time tolerating that sort of criticism from someone who doesn't know the first thing about poetic style or form! I don't know how much longer I'll be a member.

"I'm still getting "fan-mail" from people who have read my essay on Titus Brandsma. I received a short letter from a man in New Jersey who just wanted to thank me for opening his eyes to the fact that he has for a long time now been taking the Church, the Mass and the Eucharist for granted. I like those sorts of letters, as they make me feel sort of useful! I wish I could get more letters like that!"

The "Catholic People's Week" organisation had asked Joy and I to give a talk at their annual conference that year, to be held at Noddfa, a convent in Penmaenmawr. This we did on the 29th August. We spoke to people who had come from all parts of the country for a week in pleasant surroundings to pray, listen and contemplate and to hopefully enrich their own spiritual lives.

As Ted related on September 8th he was keen to show that his imprisonment did not mean that he could not at least attempt to be a useful and productive member of society:

"I've been trying to stay busy, too, and so far I think I have been fairly successful. I think I told you about the project I've been given by Father Bill and his "boss" to rewrite major portions of the Lay Carmelite formations books, so that they are more suited for the use of prisoners and other isolated members. The Carmelites put considerable importance on "community"; so many of the formation lessons are concerned with the "reasons" for community and how to live in a community, and so on. So, I'm rewriting those sections to show how to build an "extended community", and how to cultivate a sense of community with the larger and unseen Carmelite family. I've already finished the first book and started on the second. Only twenty lessons to go!

"I'm also writing an article on the Carmelite Charism, what the Order claims it is "traditionally", and what different professed members say it is in their own lives and ministries. So far, it's coming along well. Right now, I'm waiting to get replies back from several priests and nuns in Spain and France, so I can incorporate some of their ideas into the article.

"I'm also working on what I hope will become an article, sooner or later, about why the Church and so many "Justice & Peace" groups tend to ignore prisoners who are guilty of their crimes, and concentrate more on political prisoners, or those unjustly confined. It's nowhere near being an article yet, and is mainly just notes with statistics and ideas."

Chapter 31
Ted C. Cole T.O. Carm.

Only in a world of shifting shadows
Can things ever again come my way;
That's why each night I dread the coming
Of the harsh cold light of day

Although the Western World was still reeling by the events in New York City a month earlier, "9-11", for Ted things were progressing satisfactorily, as he conveyed on October 13th 2001:

"Father Walsh was here yesterday and he said that he finally received all the necessary paperwork from the Lay Carmelite Office and he will be able to accept my profession on behalf of the Carmelites. He also asked the Warden about a Mass for my profession and the Warden has given his permission as a Mass has been scheduled for October 18th, the feast of St. Luke at 6.00 p.m..

"My article on the Carmelite Charism is coming along well. I've received responses from several Carmelites and lay Carmelites – including one lady near Liverpool who is a Lay Carmelite and a "Spiritual Director". The poor woman is supposed to be living the Charism continuously but she wrote and said that she couldn't give me a reply because she's much too busy and she would have to spend "two or three days in intense prayer in order to give a proper reply." (She also told me that I wasn't qualified to write such an article because I've only been a member of the Church for just over three years.)

"Yet my formation lessons ask over and over again, "What is the Carmelite Charism?" "Where does the Charism come from?" "How does one utilize the Charism?" and on and on. But that poor confused woman, who has been a Lay Carmelite for years, needs to spend days in prayer to find out what the Charism is!! You can be sure that I will use her reply in the article.

"I may have trouble getting the article published in the Carmelite Review, though, as Father Bill is no longer the editor of the magazine. During their Chapter Meeting in Rome last month, he was elected as the Assistant General of the Carmelite Order for North America and North and Central Europe. He'll be in Rome for the next six years."

Perhaps one of the most petty minded and inexcusable traits of Ted's guardians are their occasional, and apparently pointless, "search and destroy missions" as Ted related on November 29th:

"Well, as I said, today is the 15th day of our current Lockdown. The Gestapo (and I believe they were accompanied by the Wehrmacht (at least a full battalion), the Abwehr and the S.S.) invaded on the 25th and promptly began to destroy anything that looked like it might be breakable, tearable, or water-soluble. Well, we knew they were coming, so most of us were ready. Or we thought we were ready. I'd gotten rid of most of my "excess" property – all those little books and magazines that I thought I might be able to live without – and I packed everything else I owned into two bags, which is the amount they said we were allowed to have. They took my two bags, dumped everything out into the middle of the floor, and just sort of scattered everything around. When they were finished playing, they made a feeble attempt to cram everything back into the two bags, but, of course, there's a big difference between my packing and their cramming – what had previously fitted perfectly into two bags now had to be "thinned out" as I obviously had more than two bags of belongings.

"So, they proceeded to throw stuff out, mostly books, but also some items of clothing, all my old letters (I have the worst luck in the world when it comes to keeping letters!), a few recent letters that I hadn't answered yet (when those folks write again wanting to know why they haven't heard from me, it won't be the U.S. Postal Service's fault, will it?), and even some of my Commissary items! The Sunday and Weekday Missals you sent are gone (again – I give up, as it seems to be apparent that I'm not supposed to have them, though why Divine Providence wants it that way is beyond my understanding), the Dictionary of Catholicism that I got from Garry is gone, all my books by and about Titus Brandsma are gone, all of my books by and about St. Therese are gone, all of my books by and about Edith Stein are gone. In fact it would be easier and quicker to simply list the books that I have left: the works of John of the Cross, my dictionary, my Spanish books (they left me all those, for some strange reason), and a book of St. Teresa's poems.

My Lay Carmelite formation books are gone, as well as the notes I'd made for the rewriting of them for the benefit of "isolated" members. Well, maybe someone else will find the time to rewrite them. Anyway, when they finally left and had everything back in their cells, it looked as if we'd been bombed by the Luftwaffe."

It was evident that Ted has also no say in what he was allowed to keep in his bags. The guards seemed to have the right to choose.

Ted had some much needed good news to relay about his Profession and Mass: "The ceremony was held in the dayroom in my section. A four-person table in the dayroom was used for the 'altar' and the four of us (Father Walsh, Deacon Al O'Brien, Chaplain Stanley and myself) sat around it for the Mass and ceremony of profession. There was only one guard in the dayroom, and most of the other men in this section watched from their cells. I'm really surprised it was so quiet, but I guess we put on such a good show that their interest was held. At any rate, there were no interruptions from either inmates or staff – and I was really afraid that everything would somehow be spoiled for me! – and, the Mass was great! When I was first taken to the dayroom, I was able to give Father Walsh a big hug and to shake hands with the Deacons; the first human contact I've had since coming here, except for some member of the Gestapo clinging to my elbow as I'm "escorted" to and from the shower or the visiting room.

"They gave us plenty of time and didn't try to rush us at all, so Father Walsh was able to hear my Confession before Mass. And even though neither of us really knew what we were doing during the profession ceremony, I read off the "official formula" of profession, and Father Walsh read the "official response" accepting my promises, so it was all legal and binding. I tried to pay close attention to every little detail during the Mass, because I've got a feeling that the next Mass I have the privilege of assisting, will be the day before my execution.

"I wrote to Father Bill a few days ago and conveyed to him your congratulations on his election as you asked. Did I tell you that he's the first American Assistant General in more than 65 years? I think that makes his election sort of special. And there's already talk being spread about that he's almost sure to be elected Prior General at the next General Chapter. I don't know if he visited other areas of England and Wales, but he was frequently at Whitefriars, the Carmelite Priory at Faversham, Kent. Prior to his election, he was in charge of "communications" for the American branch of the Order, and he will probably still have much to do with that aspect of the Order's business, but on a much larger scale."

On the feast of the Immaculate Conception, December 8th, Ted wrote giving us the benefit of his knowledge of Hispanic culture:

"Your house in Spain sounds quite nice. I would especially enjoy the patio and the garden. I hope you will be able to take some photos of the place for me. I have to admit that I got a good chuckle from your letter where you were describing the "wrecker" that had to be taken off the window in order to put the new window in. But it also provided me with another clue as to how the words are pronounced in southern Spain. Many of the Spanish-style homes in West Texas have the grills over the windows of the lower floor (though they're more to keep burglars out than wives in) and here and in Mexico the grill is called a reja ("ray-ha"), but I'm told the "j" is more guttural and harsh in some parts of Spain, so apparently your "wrecker" is actually a "reja" ("ray-ha"). The iron foundry where I once worked used to make these sorts of grills, but they were a bit more elaborate than usual, with vines and leaves entwined in the base, and sometimes birds and butterflies."

Ted had taught me, in his casual way, something, neither the builder, John or I had known.

Ted had had a setback: "I've abandoned writing anything for the Carmelite Review. Father Bill is no longer the editor of the magazine since being assigned to Rome, and the new editor – Father Greg Houck of Houston – doesn't seem willing to answer my letter. Father Bill had suggested I write to Father Houck and send him some of my poems, and I did that more than a month ago. Maybe someday, when he just hasn't got anything better to do, he'll get around to writing a response. Then again maybe not.

"My attorney, Rob Owen, was here this afternoon. He didn't really have much to say – there's no news on my appeal yet – and he just stopped by to let me and a couple of others know he was still alive. I spent about three hours talking to a law student from Britain who has been working on several cases in Mississippi. His

319

family live in Surrey, but he has an apartment in Nottingham. We had a really nice visit and he said he would write after he goes home on the 20th December.

"I'm still trying to get a copy of the one-volume Liturgy of the Hours to replace the four-volume set that was confiscated. I've got two different people looking for one, but apparently that book is no longer being published (in anticipation of a new and revised version) and that makes it difficult to find. I really miss being able to pray the Hours each day, and I'm on the verge of wearing out my rosary, but hopefully one of them will find a copy of it pretty soon.

"Almost all of the "cards" I'm sending this year are of the homemade variety. At previous Christmases the chaplaincy always distributed cards for us that were donated by different charities, mainly the Sacred Heart League, but apparently our warden hasn't allowed that this year. And by the time our Commissary gets them in stock it will be too late to send them overseas in time for Christmas. I hope the card I sent to you arrives in time."

Two days later, on December 10th, Ted was finding his services were very much in demand:

"I got a letter from Garry last night, one that he had written before his execution, with a list of about 20 people he wants me to write to with messages. That ought to keep me busy for a while. And I still have my third Titus paper to write (it's due today!), but my instructor is in Portugal for two weeks so there's no big rush. I'll write again as soon as I find a spare moment or two.

Despite the approach of Christmas there was little on the horizon to cheer Ted up, as he wrote on December 18th:

"As usual there's not much news to report. There's nothing going on here now that the lock-down is over with and they've already taken most of everything we own. I still haven't heard from my step dad or my sister, nor from my attorneys. In fact I haven't heard from very many people at all, so I've just about stopped writing letters. I just spend most of my time reading – Spanish in the morning and whatever I can get in English during the afternoon and evening. After the Gestapo came through, good reading material is a bit hard to find. (Even bad reading material is hard to find!)

"I got a couple of Christmas cards tonight – one from Garry's Dad and one from Garry! I'm not sure how many Birthday, Easter and Christmas cards Garry scribbled messages to me in, but Clare has been seeing to it that I get them on time. I guess Garry just couldn't see any reason why a little thing like death would stop him from sending a few cards to his favourite cell-mate.

"That was all the mail I got today, though, but it's just as well I guess. I really don't feel like writing a bunch of letters to a lot of folks mainly because I don't really have much to say. Seems as if everything that happens around here (which usually is only lock-down or shakedown) is just an excuse for me to complain, and I guess that after fourteen years of it I'm just tired of complaining. But I can't find much to write about that's cheerful either. (Well,

321

that's not entirely true – I got a new pillow from Death Row Supply yesterday.)

"Deacon O'Brien was here for a few minutes yesterday. He's the head of the diocese's "Criminal Justice Project", which means that he works for the Bishop in prison ministry and (technically at least) is our chaplain's "boss". But, since our chaplain refuses to have anything to do with Death Row, Deacon O'Brien now drives up from Beaumont every two weeks or so to visit and bring Eucharist. Anyway he was here yesterday for about ten minutes. He's still trying to find a copy of the one-volume Christian Prayer for me, but he's not having much luck, so far. I'll have it soon, though, I hope.

"Thanks for the article, The Pope's Favourite Poet, from the Catholic Herald. I'd never heard of Cyprian Norwid before, but the article has piqued my curiosity about his work. Besides if Papa John Paul likes his poetry, it can't be so bad! There is an address at the end of the article for ordering a book of his poems and letters.

Chapter 32

Life goes on

As quickly as it began,
The storm passes over.

Christmas 2001 in Wales was hectic and fun. Carrie's family came up for the celebration at our house. This was the first festive occasion for Richard and Carrie since their marriage in July. Everyone had something to do during the day such as sightseeing, and then met in our house for dinner. Afterwards we played team games like charades. The house was decorated for Christmas. We had a cosy fire and it was great fun. James and family were delayed in York due to coughs and colds. Towards the New Year the house emptied only to be filled with Francesca, William and Bee. James stayed in bed as soon as he arrived, feeling ill.

John and I went back to Spain for a break after New Year. Little did I realise that I would not see Wales again for a long time. How suddenly everything can change. Disaster struck very quickly one evening, after putting down my tapestry work I felt a terrible pain in my neck. It continued throughout the night. It was so bad that by morning I asked John to drive me to hospital. It was x-rayed. Nothing seemed to be amiss. I was sent home with painkillers, which were useless. The next day we returned. This time I was kept in for a few days of tests, including a lumbar puncture.

The results of this delighted the specialist. He told me gleefully, "You do not have Meningitis you can go home."

Armed with antibiotics and injections for pain relief I went home to the administrations of a local GP and a daily nurse, but still none the wiser and all to no avail. Gradually I realised that my right arm was becoming paralysed. My shoulders and then the left arm stopped functioning. A magnetic scan was arranged for early the following week. Meanwhile the pain and paralysis was too much to endure. I was sent to a Malaga hospital and sedated.

John and I were to have visited Ted in February 2002, but instead he only received intermittent letters written by whoever came to visit me in Clinica Galvez. I felt very sad about this state of affairs but I was struggling to combat the pain, regain my life and use of my limbs. Ted was safe for the moment so I had to concentrate on myself for a change, I realised. I did not tell Ted just how ill I was. On January 28th, the day I was to have a magnetic scan, Ted wrote to me:

"I'm glad you have Salva there to help you. I hope you are not spending all your time in front of the TV (that's what my Mom did when she was ill and confined to bed). If I was there, you could teach me to play bridge and I could teach you how to play Texas style poker (which is best played over a big plate of spicy nachos and vodka and iced lemon-tea!!), but I don't think our warden will let me come take care of you. The man has no heart at all."

"I had asked him [Father Bill] to find something – anything! for me in Spanish, and he sent me a real gem: El Principito (The Little Prince) by Antoine de Saint-Exupéry. I first read it when I was nine or ten and living in the Children's Home in Oklahoma. And this book includes the watercolours and pen and ink illustrations that were in the original, so a lot of memories came flooding back when I looked through it. Father Bill couldn't have chosen a better book if he'd tried. I saw an animated film version of the story a few years ago, but they had changed the words and added scenes to the story, so I didn't really care for it. And I usually like animated films too.

"Still no word from my attorneys. They're either working very hard or they've fled the country. Personally I think I would choose the latter – I hear the south of Spain is nice this time of year! Or maybe they are just depressed, as one of their "clients", Jeffrey Tucker, dropped his appeal and was executed not long ago. I guess he just couldn't take any more of the nonsense of this place.

Still no words or visits from my wonderful family, either. I got a Christmas card from my step-dad; no note or message, he just scrawled his name under the printed verse. That's about what I've come to expect from him though. But I haven't heard from my sisters or brothers at all. I don't even expect or look for letters (to say nothing of visits) from any of them now."

Ted's letter of February 2nd revealed that there was to be no letup in either the number of executions or in the toll it was exacting on his chaplain friend:

"Father Walsh was here yesterday, Friday, with Communion. He wasn't doing well – he witnessed the execution of Windell Broussard on Wednesday evening, and then the execution of Randall Hazdahl on Thursday. Windell was Catholic and Randall "wasn't sure" what he believed. Father Walsh said that only minutes before he was executed, Randall asked to be baptised "just in case". Randall Hazdahl was the fourth executed this year, so it looks like Texas is off to a roaring start. Father Walsh said he won't be going off to Boston until after Ash Wednesday, so I'll probably see him a couple more times before he leaves. I'm glad he's going to be here for more than just a few days, because it's almost a sure bet that the priests from this area won't be coming around again until after Easter (if then)."

Despite Ted's depressing news about the number of executions, an American Gallup Poll in Spring 2002 was to have encouraging news for us all. It showed that public support for capital punishment had fallen from 80% in 1994 to 65%, largely because of DNA tests proving that some Death Row inmates were innocent.

In Málaga hospital the magnetic scan showed that the pain that had suddenly attacked my neck, shoulders and paralysed my arms was osteomyelitis. A virulent streptococcus infection was growing in my cervical vertebrae bones and around my nervous system. I had to have an emergency neck operation.

Two months in hospital passed vaguely. Clouds of flies cascaded and swirled around the room above my head after the operation. John assured me there were none. It was all a morphine-induced hallucination. Every morning after being fed some croissant with jam, I heard the sound of footsteps along the corridor. It was Juan, the physiotherapist. He was very optimistic that I would regain the use of my arms. My head and neck were encased. Tubes sprouted from my body. The top half was static but my legs moved. Gradually my left hand was able to pick up some bread and so I was able to eat. I drank through a straw but could not hold the vessel.

Clinica Galvez, a former convent, is next to Málaga Cathedral. The bells have a special ring to mark the passing of each quarter of the hour. Most useful when one cannot move. Night time always dragged the most. Spring came in the shape of a dove or una paloma who strutted along the window ledge outside the grey shutters. Juan told me about the nest that the couple guarded, one sitting, whilst the other searched for food. It was so sad one morning, after a stormy night, to be told that the doves had flown. Left in the nest was the tiny dead body of the baby. How or why we could not guess.

Easter week, or Semana Santa, was noisy every evening. Hundreds of people, it seemed, talked, ate and sang all night long in the square and gardens beneath my window. These were members of the brotherhoods who carried the many heavy floats or tronas around the streets of Málaga during Holy Week. I had seen a part of the daily religious processions many years previously with my father.

The renowned religious spectacle of an Andalucian Easter was far removed from Death Row, Texas, as Ted recounted in his letter of April 6th:

"Easter this year was the same as always - all the priests and deacons are too busy at different parishes to have the time to bother with us. Father Walsh was here on the 19th March, but he also had to go back to his parish in Boston. Deacon Pete started here the day after Easter – of course! – so there wasn't anyone at all for us.

"I haven't heard anything from my attorneys lately. All the paperwork and arguments have been sent to the Fifth Circuit Court and now we're just waiting for the judge to make a decision. I'll let you know as soon as I hear something. My attorney says it could be as soon as a couple of months or as long as a couple of years. We'll see."

In the same letter Ted also developed his views on the obligations of the Church towards those on Death Row:

"Deacon O'Brien has been here several times recently. He's in the process of making a video about Death Row and the suggested stance Catholics should take concerning the death penalty and he says he wants me to "star" in it, so now he's trying to find some common ground between what he wants me to say and what I'm willing to say. I don't think there's much common ground to be found though! I want the Catholics in Texas to know and understand that, as voters who elect the officials who pass the laws in this State, they're responsible for what those officials do, and also that – as citizens and Catholics – they have an obligation to teach and heal, as well as "punish", not only those of us on Death Row but all prisoners.

"After all, if a prisoner isn't given an opportunity to better him-her/self and eventually goes back into society the same (or worse) person than he/she was – society can only blame itself. The same is true of religious instruction – Catholics have an obligation to provide spiritual teaching and guidance, as well as the sacraments, to the people they plan to kill. If they insist on sending us to meet our maker, they have to provide us with the opportunity to prepare ourselves for that encounter, rather than leaving our "salvation" in the hands of a Franciscan friar who comes from 2000 miles away each month!

"Deacon O'Brien, on the other hand, doesn't want to hurt anyone's feelings, doesn't want to make waves, so he wasn't really happy when I told him that I'm not interested in making folks believe that everything will be okay if they just do away with the death penalty. Everything won't be "okay", because conditions in the general population are just as bad – both physically and spiritually – as they are here. Well, we'll see what happens. He's already interviewed the Bishop and Sister Helen Prejean, as well as the heads of a couple of anti-Death Penalty groups and victims' rights groups, and the Bishop told him that the only way the diocese will pay for the video is if there's an interview on it with a Death Row prisoner, and none of the other Catholics here will even consider giving an interview. I think I'll end up having my way."

I was eventually allowed home to the villa after Easter. Recuperation and physiotherapy were the order of each day. Unable to do anything for myself, Salva, my Spanish friend, became my hands. Thanks to her, nearly a year later, I am now almost fully recovered. During this time John was my mind and my inspiration. Without him I would not have survived physically, let alone recovered.

Being still for such a long period gave me time to think and pray. I was able to turn my situation round to positive thought. I too, like Ted, was a prisoner and I too had hope. Unlike Ted I was given daily Holy Communion by the resident priest at the hospital. The wonderful, cheerful people whom I met in the hospital contributed enormously to my gradual recovery. The two neurosurgeons who performed the operation came to see me constantly, enquiring, examining and assessing my progress. I was told to go "Slowly, slowly, it will take time."

On April 24th Ted wrote, grateful to hear some welcome good news:

"Many thanks for the literature from the local church that you sent. I always enjoy reading the Diócesis newsletter, not only because it gives a chance to improve my Spanish, but because it contains nothing but good news and reasons to praise God. I am so tired of reading and hearing about the scandals in the Church – one would almost be tempted to think there's nothing good left in the Church to write or talk about!

The Spanish climate agreed with me. My asthma had vanished. My recovery from osteomyelitis although slow was sure. I had a change of collar. This third one was soft. My right arm responded to daily physiotherapy. I could lift my right hand slightly. I finally came off antibiotics. I was saddened though by the figures for June 2002 that Ted sent to me. The population of Death Row, divided amongst the 38 US states that allowed Capital Punishment, had reached 3700 inmates. But, I was thrilled that Illinois and Maryland, both advocates of the death penalty had declared a Moratorium.

Ted's letter of July 2nd showed the usual uncertainty prevailing in the life of an inmate:

"I'm expecting the big, twice a year, lock-down to begin just any day now. Maybe they'll wait until after the July 4th celebrations, though. You can never tell what they're going to do in this place until they've already done it. We're supposed to be able to make orders for Commissary tomorrow, but if they lock us down tonight I think I'll still have enough stamps to last me for a while, if I'm careful."

Ted's letter of July 17th once again touched on a scarcity of a very common commodity outside prison walls:

"I wish I had some of your fresh tomatoes (large, small, I don't care) and onions. We never have fresh vegetables here, just canned stuff. I know what pimentos are – sort of. I'm familiar with "pimento-cheese spreads" and the little red pimentos that are stuffed in olives, but do they grow on bushes or trees? I have no idea."

With the villa we inherited, Jésus, a gardener. He loves to grow vegetables, successfully planting tomatoes, peppers, olives and garlic. Now we have planted spring onions and they are flourishing. He had put down an orange and a mandarin tree a few years before. The white blossom was beautiful to see and smell. Now they bear fruit. We planted lemon trees that grow fruit in abundance and an avocado that does not seem to be flourishing and also a pear tree that now looks very sad. He assures me that new leaves will appear next spring. It was the peppers though that Ted did not know about. They grow on small bushes that Jésus grew from tiny plants in the Spring. Supported with bamboo canes, in a small vegetable patch in our garden, they grew as tall as the tomato plants.

While we concentrated on our horticultural endeavours, Ted was still living in a world of uncertainty. As he wrote: "We're still not locked down yet. I don't know why not. They're supposed to have that state wide lock-down and shakedown at the beginning of July, but…? There are a lot of rule changes going into effect on September

332

1st, and maybe they're waiting for that. After the new rules go into effect, they'll be able to confiscate more of our belongings since a lot of stuff that's allowed now will be considered "contraband" then: my electric razor, my rosary (because it has metal parts), my John of the Cross medal (because it's "too large"), and lots of other stuff.

"They're determined to leave us with nothing but our four walls to while away the time with. We're almost at that point now. But that's the only thing I can think of that might cause them to delay a lock-down (when most of them can sit around and do nothing) and shakedown – and you know how they just love to trash our cells!

"There's really not much going on here, as usual. We all just sit and wait, and most of us aren't real sure what we're waiting for. That being the case, I think I'll shut up for now and get this in an envelope. It's 10:46 p.m. and way past time for prayers and meditation!"

One big decision that I had made whilst lying in bed and reiterated when I was able to move about was that Sea Mist, our yacht, would have to go. I was totally incapable of sailing in the near future. I hoped to recover the use of my arms and the strength to use them again. But for the foreseeable future I would not be able to handle that big boat or cope with the rolling sea. Sadly the boat was sold, but I was too busy struggling with my muscles to worry. I had some beautiful memories and had learnt a great deal during the sailing period. No regrets. It had been a great adventure.

According to Ted's letter of July 29th, the opportunity of a video interview, something that Lesley had experienced, would have to be put on hold:

"The video that was/is being made by the diocese – well, it has indeed died, but I wouldn't call it a natural death. Deacon O'Brien, who is actually in charge of making the video, had received permission from both Huntsville administration and the Warden here to interview me in front of the camera, but then someone in Huntsville said, "Wait a minute! You're not part of the "real" media are you? Oh no, - you'll have to get permission from someone else, because we only deal with "real" media!" So he tried to find for a couple of months whoever it is that's supposed to deal with "unreal" media ("fake" media, "artificial" media???), but no one knows anything about anything – whether they're truly ignorant or merely stupid is open to debate, but the end result is the same regardless of the reason for the lack of knowledge. So – the diocese (meaning the "Bishop", of course) has decided to finish shooting the video without my smiling face. And I was just so sure I was going to be a star!! Maybe next time.

Ted had discussed the problems surrounding the September 11th terrorist attack with Father Walsh: "Ever since 9/11 he's been sending or bringing articles from several different Catholic magazines and papers, condemning Islam and Muslim teachings and explaining

334

to Catholics what the Qur'an "really" teaches. Well, I write to a Muslim family, and a lot of what I was reading in the articles just didn't sound right to me. I asked my attorney to get me a copy of the Qur'an so I could read these teachings for myself.

"I started looking up the references in the footnotes and I found that the authors of the articles had done the same thing that the Church is always accusing anti-Catholic writers of doing: taking things out of context; quoting the first half of a verse, while ignoring the second half that makes the verse clear; and in quite a few cases they quoted verses from the Qur'an that don't even exist! I thought at first that the verse numbers had been misprinted so, in order to find the verse in question, I just read the whole book. Twice! (I'm working my way through it for the third time now.) Those verses are simply not there.

"I may have been out of mainstream society for a while but I'm no dummy and I still know the difference between what's real and what's fantasy! When a man writes an article saying that a certain book says "such-and-such", and then I read the book myself and find it doesn't say any such thing then, that man is either a liar or a fool – take your pick!"

So Ted and Father Walsh had fallen out. Ted was unsure what upset Father Walsh the most: the fact that he had dared to question the scholars or that he would defend the "murdering pagans".

The Spanish postal system, which is none too reliable, became problematic for me. I did not receive several letters that Ted had sent to me in August and September. He said that the problem lay in the Houston sorting office.

Ted had been ill with a stomach upset since the middle of September. He had the nurse come to his cell, as he was unable to keep any food down. He had sent an official "request for sick–call" asking to see a doctor, but by the time they got around to taking him to the clinic, he no longer needed a doctor.

Ted wondered what had happened to the annual state-wide July "lock-down." New rules had been implemented in September and still no lock-down by October. He had not seen Father Walsh for some time but was pleased to see Deacon O'Brien every fortnight for a quick chat as he passed Ted's cell. He did not think that there was much that Deacon O'Brien could do with the current administration. The Baptists were the official Chaplains and there did not seem to be any room for other denominational clergy on the board.

The other person that Ted had seen in the last few months was Father Long, a Houston Carmelite. Ted had given up on ever seeing or hearing from Lay Carmelites.

A new rule again came into force, which could result in limited correspondence. A two-ounce letter requires more stamps than an ounce letter. This matters when inmates are only allowed 30 stamps every two weeks now instead of the previous 50 stamps a week. What was the point of changing this particular rule? The one rule that is totally enforced is that nobody can send stamps to prisoners. They must only be purchased at Commissary. The same applies to stationery. If I even send in a picture postcard I must write on it or it will be impounded. I send photos of the house and garden to him with explanations on the back.

By the middle of November 2002 Ted wrote that the prisoners had been on lock-down for 26 days and he thought that there would be another week more. He wrote:

"The Gestapo raided my section on the 25th October and once again I lost everything. They came around to each cell carrying a wooden box that measured 1ft tall by 1ft wide by 2ft long. Whatever could fit into that box we could keep and everything else was confiscated. I have three shelves here in my cell and everything I now own will fit on half of one shelf."

I felt heartbroken for Ted as now many more of his treasured letters and belongings, including his Spanish books and prayer missals, were destroyed. He had to keep all his records of dates and law notes. There would not be much room in that box after radio, shaver, toothbrush and cleaner had been fitted in along with stationery, his art materials (which had hardly been used) his tapestry and the articles that he had written. The hardship of losing books that had become a part of their lives must have been psychologically very damaging for them all on the Row.

In November James, Bee, Francesca and William came to see us in Spain for their Christmas visit. They enjoyed the deserted beach, building sandcastles and moats. The sea was cold but the weather was warm. We would stay in Spain until the warmer weather came to Wales. I had been unable to overcome five or six bouts of bronchitis during the summer and autumn.

David had now changed jobs, and was doing locum work in Crawley as an occupational therapist. He had accepted a permanent job in a Bristol hospital for January 2003. He would be able to visit us for Christmas. Richard and Carrie would spend Christmas with her parents and join us for Boxing Day and New Year. Changes all around, made all the more apparent by Ted's burgeoning interest in Arabic.

He wrote: "The Qur'an I've got [from his lawyer] has the Arabic text on one side of the page and the English translation on the other side, when I would read it I would find myself being constantly distracted by the little "squiggles" and I would wonder which squiggle meant "God" or "heaven" or "peace". It started to look more and more like a puzzle that I needed to solve!

"I lost all my Spanish books in the shakedown, though I still have the dictionary that you sent. I am finding Arabic to be much simpler than Spanish. I have an Arabic vocabulary of about 160 words, I can read and write them in both Arabic script called the Urdu alphabet."

As the rubric of Ted's daily life had abruptly been "confiscated", his enquiring mind began to examine new cultures. Again he astounded me, but I understood that his mental survival needs spiritual nourishment. He wrote to me and said:

"I think that Father Walsh is still upset with me. He'll be even more upset when he discovers I'm studying Arabic rather than a good "Christian" language like Italian or French. Do not do as Father Walsh has done and confuse true Islam with the fanatical mumbo-jumbo of those so-called "Islamic" terrorists. After several readings of the Qur'an and the "Sunnah" or teaching and sayings of the Prophet Muhammad, I can't find any basis or justification for those sorts of actions."

Ted added that his attorney had visited. He still did not have an execution date or any news from the judge or courts. His health had recovered. He was pleased with my steady progress along the road to convalescence. I will soon be strong enough for a return visit to Texas, I am an optimist, this time with John, who has now become more aware and more understanding and would like to meet this intelligent, spiritual man on Death Row.

Chapter 33

Consequences

Salaamul-laahi 'alaikum

The peace of God to you all!

Ted's hardships on Death Row had not abated, as his letter of December 2nd showed:

"The lock-down was finally lifted on 16th November. After that first lock-down in July of 2000, I learned my lesson about keeping plenty of stamps on hand, but since September of this year we've been restricted to only purchasing 30 every two weeks, so I'm no longer able to keep enough postage on hand. This last lock-down has been the longest one yet!

"I've mainly just been sitting here doing my Arabic lessons and when the letters start to run together and my eyes cross, then I sit and talk to my walls. A wire in my headphones got broken during the shakedown so I'm not able to listen to my radio, and our Commissary manager doesn't seem to be in any hurry to get more headphones in stock. It will probably be a while before I can listen to my radio again. It's this way after every lock-down and shakedown, though, because we have to get rid of nearly all our books due to the restrictions on how much property we can have. It's really tempting to just sleep the days away, but that can be too depressing."

In Spain I had been writing my Christmas cards for John to post on his return to Wales on 10th December. I had included a Christmas letter to my friends that was short, succinct and hopeful. Despite all my setbacks I am thankful to God that I have had this extra time, which I am using as well as I can each day. I could always do better I know.

In a very minor way my health problems remind me of Ted and his daily struggles to keep his life balanced as he faces mindless life-altering challenges. He has to accommodate, constant, new, relentless rules that seem to make little sense. For example, the new rule that minimises his allowed personal possessions to a 1ft x 1ft x2ft box. Choices had to be made. Most of his treasured books that gave him a prayerful, peaceful hopefulness in God each day were "trashed" as "contraband". For what reason? The man is going to die soon. He is quiet, self-controlled and well behaved. Why add to his already heavy burden? It makes no sense. Ted says that the proponents of the death penalty will cheer when they read of all the deprivations that go on in prison. But there will be many more who, like me, say, "Poor things. This cannot be right."

Ted, as usual, was receiving little in the way of direct human contact:

"I still haven't seen or heard from the good Father Walsh, or from Father Bill Harry either, for that matter. I guess they are busy with clerical duties – or else they're still irritated because I don't see a terrorist hiding behind every copy of the Qur`an. Father

Felix has been by my cell a couple of times in the last month and he always brings Communion with him. He's an elderly grey-haired man who is from Nigeria. He's always smiling and cheerful.

"I just finished observing the Ramadan fast in solidarity with my Muslim friends in New Mexico. The fast began at dawn on November 6th and ended at sundown on December 5th. Each day, from dawn to sundown, they neither eat nor drink anything and an amount of money equivalent to the cost of what they would have eaten each day is given to a charity to feed the poor. I used to think the Lenten fast was difficult – eating just one meal during each Friday! – but that's nothing compared to the 30 days of Ramadan. And even the youngest children of the family in New Mexico observed the entire fast, and they're 8 and 10 years old! It was an interesting experience."

‘ John brought some Christmas mail back from Wales. It was wonderful to hear from friends. Many of them now send annual letters relating the good and the bad events of their families during the past year. Two friends had died, and I read that I was not the only one to be ill and operated on.

For Ted there was no news from his family. He had little enthusiasm for Christmas. It was usually due to circumstances beyond his control, as he explained:

"I hate being stuck in this cage without access to television, e-mail or a 'phone, and not knowing what's going on just outside these walls. All I can do is sit here and wait for someone to write to me, or to visit, and tell me what's what. Most frustrating!

"Most of my time I still spend studying Arabic. Keeps my brain from getting lazy.

"I still have not heard from anyone who claims relationship to me by blood or marriage, but I know you will be wondering. I'm not sending Christmas cards to any of them this year, either – partly because I don't have any "extra" cards, but also because I have decided that "enough is enough". I've sent Christmas and birthday cards to all of them every year, and had none in return for the past four years. I can take a hint. I may be a little slow but I catch on eventually."

The weather in Texas was wet and humid. The ceiling of Ted's cell leaked. He watched as water dripped from the drab concrete ceiling to the concrete floor. He studied Arabic and thought a little bit about the past. He no longer has library access. His own stock of books had been decimated. The order of his day is again in turmoil so he reaches for new avenues of knowledge and fulfilment.

"When we first got here from Ellis, Garry and I would both donate our books to the central library when we finished them, but after several months the Warden decided that would no longer be allowed. He didn't offer any sort of reason or explanation for his decision – probably because he didn't have one to offer. Now when they "confiscate" our "excess" books (or anything else) no one ever sees them again, unless we have a family member or friend who can come and get them. If not, they are supposedly destroyed.

"I'm finding my thoughts and opinions about religion are constantly changing and being revised as I learn more about other faiths and religions. Only Jehovah/God/Allah remains unchanging and constant. I believe He is the essence of love, truth and justice, and we should praise Him daily and try to live in such a way that His essence can be seen and experienced through us by others. Not because we "have" to, and not because He "demands" it, but simply to show our gratitude to the Lord and Cherisher of Mankind for giving us life and the opportunity to know Him in this world and the world to come.

"I have to admit that my reading of the Qur'an has made a deep impression on me. I have absolutely no problem at all in believing that the Qur'an is a divinely inspired scripture. Even its English translation is inspiring and thought provoking. If I live long enough (God willing) I hope to read it – and understand it – in the original Arabic.

"I'm sure you will be happy to know that I'm no longer forced to talk to my walls in my search for "companionship". I managed to get some more headphones from the Commissary so now I can go back to listening to my radio, and just in time for the Christmas programmes and all the carols.

"It's getting late and I suppose I should go have my supper – "Hunan Vegetables" (carrots, celery, onions, bamboo shoots, mushrooms, peas, water chestnuts and soy sauce) on rice with

344

cheese and crackers (saltines) on the side. Garry would have loved it!"

Although Ted had asked me these questions before he again wrote to ask me if I had ever given any deep thought to the Trinity? My reply to him in short explained that the Trinity had always been a part of my life from my mother's knee. The Father has always been there for me, even when my own father had not always been present. The Son gives me guidance by the example of His own life here on earth showing the way with love, mercy and compassion. The Holy Spirit fills me with the power of His love, strength and courage. I feel fortunate to have this faith as it has guided me through life.

Ted thanked me for sharing my thoughts. I said that it was good to explore and try to understand other faiths. Islam came into being around 635 AD. Many Western religions are derived from Judaism. He misses human contact, and loved to discuss spirituality with Cliff Boggess and Garry. Now he has no one close at hand and I am unable as yet to make the long journey there but I will soon go and see him.

With Christmas came a change of diet: "8:22 a.m. Merry Christmas. The guards have just brought the first half of my Christmas dinner: a "cold tray" – three black olives, two tiny sweet pickles, a spoonful of chopped white onion, coleslaw with raisins, a spoonful of cranberry sauce, two sugar cookies and a piece of spice cake. I'm not too sure it will survive until the rest of my dinner arrives (the olives and one of the pickles are already gone), but maybe it will help if I concentrate on my cup of coffee and your letter.

"You obviously understand that the continuance of that relationship [with God] depends on the love and mercy of God, because even our very best efforts at righteousness can never quite measure up to what He makes us truly capable of doing. A true "relationship" requires effort by both parties involved – we constantly fail in our efforts, and on His part there really is no "effort" involved. He loves His creation and He forgives us as often as we ask Him to (and sometimes without our having to ask) simply because He wants to and He can.

"I read too much about too many inter-related subjects, and each subject brings a slightly different focus to all the other subjects. Everything mixes and mingles in my brain – "simmering" on a low flame – but when it's all cooked up and ready to be served, there's no one around who wants a "taste" (can you tell that at least a small part of my mind is thinking about food?).

"I think you folks on the other side of the Pond are much more open-minded and tolerant of others than the vast majority of Americans are. Especially concerning religion, race and/or politics. Most of us Yanks act as if we were only allowed to associate with those who look like us, talk like us, dress like us, act like us and who believe what we believe. And that last one is of course, the most important of all. Silly Yanks!

"It's now 10:46 a.m. and the rest of my very grey-looking dinner has finally arrived. It looks much like what I had for

346

Thanksgiving, except that this is cold. Well, could be worse, I suppose. Back in a bit –

"Okay, that didn't take long: a slice of roast beef (I could almost, but not quite, read this through it!), a slice of turkey, cornbread dressing with giblet-gravy, creamed corn, sweet peas, candied yams and two dinner rolls. Cold, but still better than boiled link-sausage! Better luck next year, maybe.

I had written to tell Ted about the Nativity play that William was in at Acorns playschool. William told his parents that he did not want to be a shepherd. He did not want to look after sheep. Ted replied:

"I never really cared to be on a stage either. When I was in school and a class was putting on a play, I nearly always managed to have myself assigned to making props and costumes. I had very little self-confidence as a child and was always terrified of being made fun of or laughed at. I got enough of that from my stepfather at home."

Father Walsh had been round to see Ted and wish him well for Christmas. I think that the situation was uneasy as neither would bend to listen to the other's point of view.

David, John and I had a Christmas lunch with friends near Benalmadena Pueblo in contrast with Ted's solitary meal. It was interesting to speak with and meet expatriates. Everyone had a lot to talk about.

347

Our builder had remodelled the large fireplace in the house in Spain. When I originally sent Ted a photo of it he had laughed at the size of the fireplace and the tiny little travelling clock that I had placed on the mantelpiece. Then, it was the only timepiece that we had in the house. He remembered it on Christmas day a year later and wrote to ask me if we used the fireplace with a real fire now that the nights were cold. He reminisced:

"I used to love to sit by the fire in the evenings (I had gas "logs" but they looked real), listening to the stereo with a glass of wine. There's just something soothing and relaxing about watching the flicker of firelight."

I hated to disappoint him but we had had radiators installed, as a fire was too much work this year. Maybe another year we would have a fire.

A couple of days after Christmas and all its poignant memories, Ted wrote:

"A guard just came by and said that we're all locked-down again, this time because one of the guards "working" in general population lost his ID card. I don't know what that's got to do with Death Row, but apparently the entire unit is locked down until the card is found. I swear if it's not one thing – it'll always be another."

I had asked whether this year's Christmas Dinner was an improvement on former years:

"The cooking is probably about the same as it was last year, which means everything is either over or undercooked and always served cold. Still the same. And all the "cooks" in the prison are prisoners – though, before they came to prison, I think they were all truck drivers, mechanics and oilfield workers, because they obviously know nothing about cooking!

I had taken out a subscription to The Tablet for Ted some years previously. Usually I heard little about the articles that he had read but now restless, lonely and grumpy he wrote:

"I don't know about you, but I'm real tired about clerical sex scandals, the evils of Islam, and how terribly wrong a war with Iraq would be. If – and personally I think it's only a question of "when" and not "if" – we attack Iraq, it won't be about right or wrong or oppression or even about "weapons of mass destruction". It will be about oil. Dubya tried to repay his oil-baron buddies by opening up the Alaskan oilfields for new drilling but Congress (and the environmentalists) told him flatly that it wasn't going to happen. His oil-baron buddies promptly reminded him that he may be the President, but the power behind his "throne" is money – and they have it all - so he'd best come up with something else. So now he's going to give them Iraq and the Iraqi oilfields.

"And don't let them fool you with this talk about going in and outing Saddam, and then getting out again. No, once Saddam is no longer a "threat" and the oilfields are secure, it will "suddenly occur" to Washington that if they leave Iraq without an American (and British?) military force, the poor civilians are going to be caught between rival factions of Kurds and Shi'ite Muslims. So – if and when we invade Iraq we're going to be thore for a long time, and –

as long as we're in the neighbourhood – we might as well help the Iraqi oil business get back on its feet…

"I find Arab/Muslim culture and religion fascinating and I'm thoroughly disgusted with my own country and culture (if the US can even be said to have a "culture").

"I'm not real happy with the Church right now. Well, actually I haven't been real happy with the Church for quite a while now, as I'm sure you're aware. It would probably be more accurate, though, to say that my problems are with the Clergy and the hierarchy – the so-called leaders of the Church. They really should get out of the way and leave the Church to the "common" people, as I believe Jesus intended.

"Some of them- maybe even most of them – try to be true shepherds to their "flocks", but I can't help but feel that way too many of them, especially after they reach the ranks of Bishops, feel their main responsibility is to the institution that has come to be called "the Church", rather than the people who are the real Church.

"I enjoy pomp and ceremony as much as anyone, particularly on special truly holy days, and on those days I think we should even go back to using Latin instead of the vernacular because I think it exhibits more powerfully the majesty and mystery of God. But for everyday worship I think Catholics should meet and celebrate the Mass in one another's homes, with the head of that household being the main celebrant, and not some priest who has been provided by Rome. That's the way it was done in the early days of the Church and it should still be done that way.

"True, we all need direction and Leadership, but people will naturally follow the lead of someone they respect, someone who is devout (if not actually "holy") and who practises what he (or she!) preaches, but take a good hard look at the clergy we're saddled with today – does it appear if the "laying on of hands" and the giving of the "gift of the Holy Spirit" really accomplishes anything? (Well, Scripture does say that the Spirit goes "where it wills" and not necessarily to the place – or the person – to who it's directed!).

Our Bishops can ordain as many priests as they wish but not one of them can make a man holy or righteous simply by laying his hands (which may, or may not be holy and righteous themselves!) on the man's head. I've met several truly devout people, men and women both, who will never be ordained because they are not eligible – not "worthy" – of the priesthood; and I've met a few priests and deacons (and one bishop) who should never have been ordained (or even confirmed for that matter!).

"Father Walsh was here this morning, still hoping to convince me that Arabs – and particularly Muslim Arabs – are evil incarnate.

"Today he stopped to lecture me about the Qur'an and, judging by his expression and body language, you would have thought he was confiding a truly important secret that was for my ears only. He looked around, as if to ensure that we were alone, and then leaned towards my door and said, "Muslims will try and tell you that the Qur'an is original. Don't believe it – most of it comes straight out of the scriptures! Islam is about as far from the truth as any religion can be!" And he was just as sincere and serious, too! It was sort of funny, actually.

"As for the first part of his statement, the Qur'an itself states that it is "only proclaiming the divine message that God has sent down to Mankind from the very beginning of creation." Well, that's about as far from "original" as any religion can be and no Muslim would say it's original because a Muslim would never dare to contradict the Qur'an itself.

"But take his statement in its entirety – you would think that a religion whose scripture is composed mostly "straight out of the scriptures" would at least be closer to the truth than a religion that totally denies Christianity, wouldn't you? But, nope – it apparently doesn't work that way.

"I'm not going to agree with him just to placate him. I could understand him going on and on about it if the Vatican was being invaded and the Pope was in danger, but I can't see that Islam is any threat to the Church – not the institution or the people. (you and I both know that those radical and extremist splinter groups and suicide bombers don't represent true Islam!)"

In a way this outpouring of frustration and divisiveness from Ted is an after-effect of 11th September 2001. Our world has changed. Uncertainty cripples the international economy. Circles are still expanding round the "pond." They are becoming wider and more extensive. The ripples are now stronger and threaten every part of our globe.

Those on Death Row are affected. The threat of terrorism has lead to the outbreak of war with Iraq. Even less time will be taken over each case. Sadly, men and women will still be murdered in Texas in the name of justice, which really reads as "revenge". Women, even young women, with postnatal depression who have killed a wife beater, will still be put to death. Such is the nature of mob hysteria. It gets "results" and re-election. It is called "Justice".

At the same time as both Ted and Iraq were in turmoil, Ted became interested in an article about St. Winifred that he had read in "Catholic Life":

"There are some nice pictures with the article: Henllan Church tower, the spring at Holywell, a landing stage and boats below Holywell and an early tombstone at Gwytherin. I thought of you as I was reading the article because of your past connection to Holywell.

"There is also an article entitled: Saint Dwynwen: Patron Saint of Welsh Lovers," I thought of you as I read that one too, as she is connected to the Isle of Anglesey. The article says that her feast day is on the 25th January."

I was impressed that Ted had remembered that I used to teach at St. Winifred's primary school in Holywell, near the famous shrine. That was before I was married and my name then was Miss Jones. He also remembered that my maternal grandmother came from Cemaes Bay on the Isle of Anglesey. Such small connections to me that he had retained for five years astonished me.

Ted spoke of that wonderful peacemaker, Martin Luther King Jnr. He did so much work for the people and his country, that his memory is commemorated in America by a national holiday. He demonstrated that trust goodness, humility and love are all-important even though the result for him had been his murder by a fellow American.

Chapter 34
Muhammad

A dream can take you to mountain tops,
or beyond, to the Milky Way;
There is no place a dream can't go -
No music a dream can't play.

Meals at Livingston's Polunsky Unit, that is now home to all Texas's Death Row inmates, are brought to the one-man cells by the guards. The Commissary has improved, selling better quality and more varied food to those who have the cash, as Ted wrote:

"The vegetables come in an aluminium packet that I "cook" in hot water. I have a "hot pot" - a coffee pot looking container that has a handle and pour spout and an electrical heating element in the bottom. It almost heats up to a boil, but not quite. Commissary also sells "Oriental Beef and Vegetables" and "Chicken and Vegetables," "Turkey and Dressing"… Two sorts of cheese spreads, sauces and tortilla chips and bread."

The Spanish postal service is still very slow. We usually have one delivery a week, sometimes not even that, just a bumper pack when they feel like coming down our road. My letters were reaching Ted, but as he explained, he sometimes had difficulty receiving mail inside the prison:

"Not too long ago someone sent a letter (junk mail, actually, wanting a donation for some charity.) addressed to "Ted Calvin 000906" and the mailroom had written my cell number on it (12-ce-67) and sent it with the rest of the mail. The guard passing out the mail wouldn't give it to me, though, claiming it was for "Ted Calvin" and not "Ted Cole". He sent it back to the mailroom and naturally they just put it back in the mail bag for the next day. The next evening - same thing - the guard (a different guard) wouldn't let me have it.

The THIRD time there was a guard working who was able to use her head for something besides keeping her ears apart, and she gave it to me. I didn't really want it after I saw what it was, and I promptly tossed it out with the trash, but it was three days before I could toss it out! Sort of funny, sort of frustrating."

Perhaps some of the most revealing (and poignant) details of a person's life appear in apparently throwaway lines:

"I have noticed the letters "T.O. Carm" on some of my letters. The guards always frown and want to know what it means. I like seeing it after my name. Sort of makes me feel I've accomplished something, you know?"

Changes in prison bureaucracy had resulted in a minor easing on restrictions for the inmates – for a change, as Ted related:

"The administration here has decided that it's no longer necessary for us to have "craft cards" in order to purchase paints and coloured pencils, sketch pads and watercolour paper. I haven't used watercolours since I was about twelve. The brushes they sell us here aren't much good, and they have stiff plastic or nylon bristles – sort of like painting with a fistful of toothpicks!"

On a more serious note Ted was unchanged on his views on life without parole:

"The only thing that makes life bearable for most of us is hope, big hopes, major events in life. Everyone gets through life looking forward to reaching the next goal or the next milestone. Doing things, going places, accomplishing dreams. But what happens with life without parole? You go to prison and… that's it! The only problem is that it takes years ands years to finally die. There's no hope of ever doing anything or going anywhere and there are no dreams to accomplish because all your dreams suddenly become useless and frustrating fantasies. (And do you know what is really sad? I've just described the "lives" of a lot of people who have never been to prison at all).

"It doesn't really matter. Very few people actually have control of their own lives. People in faraway cities, who don't know us and don't really know anything about us – but who are convinced that they know what's best for us – create laws that tell us what we're allowed to do and how we are allowed to do it, where we can and can't go…

"And then there's that other source of legislation: public opinion. There are all sorts of rules and regulations that determine what we are allowed to do based on whether we're too old, too young, too fat, too skinny, too poor, too sick, too white, too black,

357

too male, too female – and we accept and go along with it and encourage our children and relatives and friends and neighbours and hired help to accept it and go along with it because what would people think if we went against social conventions?"

"If I were to be given a sentence of life without parole, I would be transferred to another unit and would continue to get up every morning and do what ever I'm supposed to do (just like folks outside). And if I stay on Death Row I continue to get out of bed every morning and go to bed every night until the day comes that God says: "Time's up!" (Just like the folks outside). So it doesn't really matter one way or the other (though I may change my mind tomorrow!).

Ted had received an article I had sent him from The Times about the development of faith:

"I have always believed that whatever doesn't grow and respond to what is around it will decay and die and soon become only a memory. Every living thing changes and improves itself striving for perfection in whatever niche it has in God's creation. To remain forever the same, unthinking, not growing or expanding in meaning or relevance, is to be in violation of natural law – God's law.

"Unfortunately too many people feel that not changing is synonymous with safety and security and change is an uncomfortable risk to be avoided at all costs. (Which is a further argument against life without parole, since the unchanging day-to-day monotony of that sort of existence is in direct opposition to true "life".)

358

"Truth, too, is a living thing, and while truth doesn't change, what we know of truth and religion and God does change, because our ability to grasp and understand new concepts regarding truth is constantly expanding and growing."

Ted compared God to "being like a huge multi-faceted and sparkling emerald":

"You can't cling to one facet of the emerald and declare: "this is all there is!" You study the facet and then allow yourself to move to the next facet, while experiencing the truth that both facets – and many more besides – are all aspects of one single reality."

It is important to remember that Ted's thoughts evolve in the shadow of regular executions as he notes:

"There are executions scheduled for both tonight and tomorrow night, but I don't know either one of these guys. It wasn't too long ago that I knew almost every man being executed. Most of the "old-timers" have either been killed or have gotten new trials. I'm beginning to feel a bit like a dinosaur – I keep expecting one of those cavemen in Austin to stop polishing his club long enough to look up and say: "Hey, y'all! Looks like we missed one!""

I had asked Ted if there was anyone in the world of Islam who was inspirational besides Muhammad? He replied in his letter of February 10th 2003:

"Personally I think Muhammad is the single greatest individual to have lived since the time of Christ, because once you understand the time and culture he was born into and realise just how he changed everything about the whole Arab world in only 20 years, it seoms nothing short of miraculous. Every true Muslim since the birth of Islam has done nothing more than attempt to live up to Muhammad's example, so I think most Muslims would think it's crazy to look for inspiration in the lives of those who are or were looking to Muhammad for inspiration."

The threat of war was having a direct effect on the lives of the inmates:

"The guards here have gone from working three eight-hour shifts to working two twelve-hour shifts, and since most of them have been unhappy with their new hours, guess who they're taking their frustration out on? A lot of the younger guys who work here are in the National Guard and have been mobilised for deployment overseas, so I guess all the prisons are understaffed at the moment.

"The shifts change at 6 a.m. and 6 p.m. and these sorts of hours are hard on one's family life and as the tensions and difficulties with their families increase, so will the tensions and difficulties they bring to work with them also increase. They started the twelve-hour shifts on February 2nd and the day shift is already grumbling that they have to do most of the work! I'm sure they would be much happier if I had my supper at midnight and my shower at 2 a.m. just so that all the work is spread out over the full 24-hour day.

Despite his incarceration, Ted was aware of his own personal development:

"I've never been very good at meeting strangers. I'm just too self-conscious and always worrying about what people will think of me, and what they'll say about me after I've gone. It's been a while since I had a chance to meet anyone in casual surroundings. I might not nearly be as self-conscious as I used to be – I'm much more sure of myself, of my worth as a person, than I was several years ago. "

Conditions in Ted's Unit were less than conducive to good health, as Ted noted on February 22nd:

"As I write this there are trails of brown rainwater creeping down my wall here and at my elbow from the leak where my wall and ceiling meet.

"It seems as if I'm catching a cold every time I turn around in the last three months or so. Everyone is handcuffed each time we leave our cells, the showers, rec. yard, etc. and these guards just go from one of us to another, touching everyone's hands. Sometimes I forget to wash my hands when I come back to my cell and that's why I know it's my own fault that I've always got a cold."

Ted had sent a copy of Worship Aid, a Catholic newsletter for the Polunsky Unit, listing an unexpected variety of activities for the week ahead. However, Death Row inmates are always excluded. Ted commented:

"I finally met the new priest last Saturday, Father Charles Atuah. He is from Mozambique. He is friendly and smiles a lot."

Ted, a voracious reader, had requested a copy of My Life and Travels: an anthology by Wilfred Thesiger, which he had seen reviewed in The Tablet and detailed the author's time with the Marsh Arabs of Iraq. He said:

361

"It was only a couple of weeks ago that I read an article about the Arab marshes and how they're rapidly being drained and filled because so many Shi'ite Muslims are evading Saddam's wrath by hiding in them. Most of the marshes are in, I believe, the eastern part of Iraq and are home to a huge number of bird species that will soon be endangered if more of the marshes disappear."

Ted had just begun a new book: "I was up late last night reading the Seven Pillars of Wisdom [by T.H. Lawrence]. Although I've only just begun the book I think I am really going to enjoy it. I had no idea it was such a large book."

Ted was cynical about America's international role: "Why is Bush suddenly so intent on ousting Saddam and "liberating" the Iraqi people, while at the same time he's trying "diplomacy" with the North Koreans? Because Saddam has oilfields that can produce five million barrels of oil a day, that's why. The US will gladly liberate the Iraqis, but only in exchange for their oilfields

"I'm not much of a patriot. America is supposed to be the home of democracy and freedom, but "the people" don't run this country and they never have. "Big Business" runs this country and the average American citizen is a slave to the almighty dollar – busily spending what he hasn't yet earned and then working him/herself into an early grave while trying to pay for it all."

GENERAL INMATE
CORRESPONDENCE • TEXAS
DEPARTMENT OF CRIMINAL
JUSTICE — INSTITUTIONAL
DIVISION

☆ I-290 (07/93)

Chapter 35
Till we meet again.

I read and write and talk and listen....
I know those things don't sound like much,
But in here they're life and I'd give them all
For a single warm and heartfelt touch.

One will never change the mind of the fanatic, or the fact that some people are inclined to "mob hysteria". The mood of the people of Texas has become ambivalent about capital punishment however Governor George Ryan of Illinois, originally an exponent of the death penalty, had declared a moratorium. It was proved that several prisoners about to be executed in his State were innocent. They were freed and in one or two cases the real culprit was found.

In January 2003 he commuted the sentences of all the State's Death Row as a final end of term gesture. Those who have been found not guilty, 13 in all, have been freed. The rest are still in prison. But they will not be murdered there in the name of the State of Illinois. George Ryan said:

"Our capital system is haunted by the demon of error: error in determining guilt and error in determining who among the guilty, deserves to die. What effect is race having? What effect is poverty having?"

The lives of one hundred and sixty seven men have been saved. It will be interesting to see if Rod Blagojevich, the new Governor, will re-introduce the death sentence at some stage. At the moment his comments are that "It [the repealing] is a mistake."

In February 2003 the International Court of Justice urged the United States Government to halt the execution of Mexicans. There are more than fifty on Death Row in America. The court was set up by the United Nations in 1945. It is the highest body for settling disputes between states, but it's ruling is not binding. The Mexican Government has complained that the United States has persistently failed to make Mexican lawyers available to those accused of capital crimes. Mexicans are routinely given court-appointed lawyers who do not speak Spanish.

What of the guilty? DNA testing should be standard procedure at trials. Some defendants charged with capital murder avoid the death penalty by plea-bargaining. An innocent man will be reluctant to plea-bargain and usually insists on a trial. The jury though, will not include anyone who, on principle, will not impose the death sentence.

Some Death Row inmates are there because they had the wrong lawyers. It is not unknown for a lawyer to fall asleep during a trial. One such, was awoken, on the orders of the Judge, to hear the verdict.

Some attorneys are on contract to the Public Defender's Office (P.D.O.). They have to defend a certain number of cases per year for a specified sum of money. One of these assignments has to be a capital case. This is not an experienced murder trial lawyer, in most instances, or he would be in private practice making a great deal of money. Usually it is an end of fiscal year lawyer taking a case to fit in with his portfolio. He will do a minimal amount of investigative work for the specified sum of money assigned to him.

Many defendants mistrust attorneys, prosecutors and the police. Some defendants already have a "record". Some just want to be "left in peace". As they do not trust the system, they do not trust the justice that they will receive and will not therefore fight for their cause.

There is a wide variation in the serious nature of the crimes that have put people on Death Row. There is also a wide variation in the equally serious crimes that have given people sentences other than death.

After a harrowing crime a frightened, angry public demand results. This pressure can lead to questionable behaviour by some police and prosecutors, who understandably can overreact.

Execution ends any chance that a man or woman has to be found "not guilty" later for whatever reason i.e. new evidence or a true confession. Execution also ends any change of heart towards sorrow and repentance that may come with time and reflection.

Some inmates remain intractable. They have severe problems and it seems that violence stays with them and is used at every opportunity. Fortunately they are in the minority. They are also held in Maximum Security cells.

Most murderers are genuinely sorry for their actions. They must live with this knowledge, which can be torment in itself.

What of Ted? Ted has grown in love and hope and has left his burden of hatred behind him. He has a constant desire for knowledge, to solve the puzzle of life. His penalty is the death sentence. There is no case for petty daily punishments, metered out thoughtlessly, viciously and indiscriminately. There is a case for civilised, dignified, treatment and for good behaviour, a reward system, within the prison regime.

His development over the years has been particularly encouraging especially when one sees the constantly deteriorating situation in the Polunsky Unit becoming rapidly harsher and unfair. Sadly this now results in inmates feeling broken and frustration is endemic.

There should be hope that even the most casehardened criminal can be helped to lead a more worthwhile life given the opportunity and encouragement.

It has to be remembered that Ted's development is and was undertaken without the help of the State, and despite the State. This poses the question, "What could be achieved if the State played a more active role in re-educating its convicts instead of trying to break their spirit as well as to take their lives?"

At the time of writing Ted still waits for his execution date, which he knows will come soon. Even this year Ted has kept me focused, as I needed to return to health to write to him and about him. He has given me one of the most disturbing, profound and enriching encounters of my life.

A year ago my arms, neck and shoulders were paralysed. I had been in hospital for two months. I came home unable to do anything for myself. A year later, thanks to my wonderful friend Salva, who washed, dressed and fed me, and Paula the physiotherapist, who came every day and worked hard with me for an hour, I am mobile again.

Without John I would not have survived at all. My children are a constant inspiration to me. I am always amazed that they are a part of me. Our grandchildren are also a gift from God, whom I thank constantly.

As I walk towards the sun setting on the breakwater of the Marina, I review my small world in this pleasant place. The tranquil sea stretches out to distant, unseen shores. Cats play, love, fight, eat, sleep, preen themselves on the multi-shaped rocks that divide the sea from the Marina. Boats of all shapes and sizes sway in the gentle swell as other craft putter past. The fishermen mostly stand or sit silently by their long rods that have one end drowned in the sea. Here, today, all is peace and tranquillity. On a rough day it is all changed. Nothing lasts forever.

The lengthening, dark shadows hide the opposing world of anger, greed, envy, jealousy, petty squabbles and violence that could be in all of us but have to be somehow controlled.

I thank God for my life. I thank Him for my family. I thank Him for my place on this earth and my trials of the past year. I thank God for Ted and enabling me to meet him and his world.

Thank God for all the people who pray. I try to make my life a thanksgiving. Sometimes I succeed sometimes I do not. Meanwhile, across an ocean, Ted sits in solitary confinement waiting for his execution date.

To my newest
friend, Margot.

I'm happy to be able
to share my joy with you
through these pages

My words are all I have,
& I share them with love.

Ted

SHIFTING SHADOWS

The daylight hours are hardest of all
When you live in a world of dreams;
The harsh cold light of day is not
Conducive to dreaming, it seems.
That's why, when I wake each morning,
I look forward to the coming night,
For it's only then — at the end of the day
That my fantasies leap in delight.

Only in a make-believe, storybook world
Are you here when I need you with me;
It's only then things turn out the way
That I always felt they should be.
Chances I missed don't pass by me again,
Some things that I said — I don't say.
Things that should have been said, and weren't,
Are easily spoken at the end of the day.

Only in the fantasy world of my dreams
Does the love that we shared seem real;
Only in darkness can I look in your eyes
And tell you the way that I feel.
Only in a world of shifting shadows
Can things ever again come my way;
That's why each night I dread the coming
Of the harsh cold light of day.

T C Cole 7/13/88

THE SEARCH

I'm not sure what I'm searching for,
I'm not sure where to look.
I wish I could find a secret map,
or instructions in a book.
I wish I had a crystal ball
So I'd know which way to go,
Or a crow's-nest in which to perch,
So I could see both high and low.
I need a guide to show the way,
I'll never get there on my own
And I need a magic carpet
Cause my poor legs are worn to bone.
I've searched for years and years on end,
From the hunt I've never strayed —
I've often felt close to this mystery goal,
But just out of reach is where it's stayed.

————————————

You know, I may have fooled myself
With this idea of an endless quest.
If I reached the end I wouldn't know it —
It's the search itself I like best!

T C Cole 8-16-88

I still don't know what I was searching for happiness, my soul-mate, God, myself... I don't know. And I'm still searching. I've been assured that what I want Can only be found in God — and I believe that — but until He reveals Himself in all His glory, the search goes on!

372

MESSAGE IN A BOTTLE

I built a ship of shadows
To escape out on the deep.
I built it big, and built it strong,
Then climbed aboard and went to sleep.
And while I slept aboard my ship
A nightmare crew came on;
They cast off lines and spread the sails
When I awoke, safe port was gone.

I tried to turn my ship around,
But the helm would not respond.
I even tried to swim for shore,
But my ship and I had formed a bond:
My ship couldn't sail without me;
I couldn't leave without my ship —
And the nightmare crew sailed on and on;
My ship had wings I couldn't clip.

But now my ship has run aground
And I'm busy building a new one.
My crew says there are other seas
To sail on when at last she's done.
I guess the ocean's gotten in my blood,
And my blood's gotten into the sea.
It seems no matter what I do,
My crew will never set me free.

I tossed a bottle in the ocean
With a message just for you —
I sure hope the gods are smiling down on me.
If they are and you should find it,
This is what you ought to do....
WAKE ME UP
And make things like they used to be!!!

T C Cole 10/10/88

This one is pretty obvious, I think. At the time I wrote this, I was in the middle of a lot of court appearances (in fact, I'm not absolutely sure, but I think this was written in the courtroom), and life was not good. Outwardly, it really hasn't improved much! Inwardly, it's a whole new ballgame!!

373

IT ISN'T EASY

I read and write and talk and listen...
I know those things don't sound like much,
But in here they're life and I'd give them all
For a single warm and heartfelt touch.
The people are cold and brittle here —
The air is even crisper —
And if there's any warmth at all,
It comes sealed in a written whisper.
I reach and grab for happiness...
My hands — ten thumbs — they fumble.
I try to walk toward the sunlight...
My feet, they slip and stumble.
I hear in far-off corridors
The tinkling of bright laughter,
But this maze of steel and rotting brick
Stands tween me and the goal I'm after.

The cruel and ugly games we play
In our struggle to survive,
I know will someday haunt us
But they make us feel alive.
And I'd rather hear the screams of another,
Than listen to my own dark sounds.
(It takes, at least, an angry scream
To drown the baying of the hounds.)

It isn't easy for a man to be brave
When he stands in the shadow of the grave.
T C Cole 1/25/89

I wrote this one specifically for a prison-poetry contest so, while the thoughts and words are mine, the sentiments aren't necessarily my own. I was trying to write as the voice of Death Row as a whole, and not as an individual.

BEGGAR MAN

"Nobody loves me," I hear you say,
"Nobody cares at all.
Nobody knows that I live and breathe,
No one cares if I stand or fall."
But...

If I love you and never say the words,
Will you feel small and hated?
And if I feel no love, but say I do,
Will your heart then feel elated?
You see...

You live for empty, shallow words,
When the only love you'll ever know
Is that which flows inside yourself;
That which you're afraid to show.

So, tell me this, my precious friend,
What difference does it make?
Will you become less special
If you give instead of take?

Would a rich man become a beggar?
I think not, so why have you?
Don't ask for more — just give your love,
Even if only to a few.

I can see the love behind your eyes,
And I can hear it in your voice;
You can sit and cry, or share the wealth –
Such a very simple choice.

Give it all away, my friend;
Just give (then give some more!),
And pretty soon the Lord of Love
Will knock at your heart's door.

                              T C Cole 8/19/89

I wrote "Beggar Man" for a friend of my Mom's who felt as if her husband didn't love her "enough" and she was thinking about leaving him. Later she wrote and said that, after she'd read the poem and thought about it, it wasn't really her husband who was the problem. She felt as if no-one loved her and just put the blame on her husband because he was more "available" than anyone else. She said in her letter that she felt silly and selfish at the way she'd been thinking, and she talked about it (finally) with her family and her husband, and now everything's okay.

ALL MY THANKS

Oh Lord,
You Who are the
Creator, Sustainer, and Destroyer;
Christ Jesus,
Savior of the world — hear my song.

You created a new being from the wreck that I was,
        replacing my despair with hope
and giving life where there had been only death;
You sustain this new being
with a love and joy most people
have only dreamed of and wished for;
You've already begun the task
of destroying those things
that kept me from You for so long:
envy and hate, doubt and confusion,
greed and selfishness
All my thanks goes out to the Destroyer
Who,
brick by dirty brick,
tears down the wall of my blindness
to lay the foundation for a
Temple of Light.

No date. Sant Mat teaches that there is one single God who has three different "manifestations" of Himself: Brahma, the Creator of the world; Vishnu, who sustains and blesses the world; and Shiva, who will ultimately destroy the world and start creation all over again with a "new world". It occured to me that those three aspects or manifestations can also be found in Jesus, as well as in the three Persons of God

HANDFUL OF MIRACLES

I woke up this morning complaining —
    and missed a whole handful of miracles!

Sweet birdsong seemed only noise,
and it woke me so I ranted;
I opened my eyes and looked around,
and I took my sight for granted.
I was thirsty and drank cool water,
and ignored its fresh, sweet wetness;
I was hungry for companionship,
and didn't notice our dear Lord's presence.
Someone greeted me with "Good Morning!";
in irritation I replied with a growl.
Christ - in - man prepared my breakfast -
    I accepted it with a scowl.

I am an ass.

Amen.

MEMENTO MORI

Remember that you must die

Death. A Grim Reaper?
To some perhaps.
To some, Death is a great, black void;
a nothingness; a total non-being,
to be avoided at all costs.

To some, Death is the "other" face of God.
The gate to a Golden City where
                              (they say)
  they'll spend eternity singing praises
                    to a Deity they've no time for now.
          (maybe tomorrow)

Death. A Grim Reaper?
I think not.
For me, Death is an old and faithful friend.
Hand in hand we've raced
            through this game called life;
            challenging the unknown
            with no thought of tomorrow.

Tomorrow comes soon enough,
and mounting that pale horse
will be just another adventure
shared with an old friend.

When Azreal points his bony finger
at yours truly,
I'll just hand an obolus to Charon
and be on my merry way!

T C Cole 7/27/90

LIFE!!

You'll never find a single place
In all this wondrous Earth
That's happy in, and of, itself
It's people who give it worth.

Ordinary, simple folk
A lot like you and I
Folk who laugh, folk who frown
Folk who live and die.

Men and women, boys and girls
Who've hopes and dreams and fears
Mere mortals striving to survive
In a world where life is dear.

But survival alone is worthless
When happiness is denied
It takes a full and balanced life
With love on ever side.

And it doesn't really take a lot
To have a life worth living
It only takes a minimum
Of taking and of giving.

Someone to love and care for
To tell your troubles to
Someone whose arms are open
When you're feeling down and blue.

Someone who knows and understands
That we all have ups and downs
Someone who'll wait out life's storms
When the tempests come around.

Someone who'll take a helping hand
Without feeling guilt or shame
And who's eager to reach out in turn
As we play life's crazy game.

But then, no matter where you are
In all this wondrous Earth
It's love — and Love alone —
That gives your life it's worth.

10/25/90

TRIVIAL PURSUIT

Words
And words
And more words.
Will they never cease?
Must I always be inundated by
These inane and asinine noises?
"Stop!

"Have you heard
"You should
"You can't
"Did you know
"You must
"Quit!
"By the way
"You shouldn't
"You have to
        etc.
                etc.,
                        etc.,

Oh! What I wouldn't give for a small respite from the endless drivel that constantly
pounds against the senses —
finally reducing the mind to mush!

T C Cole 4/15/91

AN ODE TO ERATO

The Elusive Muse

Many who read the words I write
Will see only the ramblings of a lonely man.
Perhaps they'll be right,

For I've only the company of my own mind
And I can only converse with my soul
I live in a world of dreams — speaking to
the moon and stars,
and to a darkness that surrounds and caresses me in a way that human hands
can't, and never will again –
But only my spirit answers.

I've tried to preserve those things my soul speaks of,
That I might return to better times
When the days seem darkest and my spirit refuses to answer my pleas,
But the magic and mystery that I feel -all the joys and sorrows,
The many emotions which yearn for release.
They all elude my pen.
I can't find the words to express
the depth and fullness
of what my soul tells me.

Only when the words have taken form on the page
When I can see their shapes and recognize their meanings —
Only then do the whisperings of
My spirit take on a fragile reality.
But it's a reality seen through a dark,
shifting mist.
My words show only a shadow
without substance.

(Published in Lucidity; awarded an "Honourable Mention".)

T C Cole 5/17/91

FOR THE MOMENT

Poets say that love is blind,
But I know that isn't true.
Love sees with much more clarity
Than most mere mortals do.

Love sees beyond the surface —
Love looks from heart to heart.
It sees the truth that's hidden,
And it tears the lies apart.

Love doesn't recognize the past,
And the future may never be;
Love lives only for the moment,
And today is all it can see.

T C Cole 10/3/91

TURNING POINT

I looked up to the sky tonight,
Through chain-link fence overhead,
Just to whisper one small prayer
Before I took myself to bed.

"Dear Lord," I said, "You know my name,
Though Yours, I thinks are many
You know my needs and all my wants,
And heaven knows they're plenty.
But tonight I have a question —
I need an answer before the dawn:
O God, please tell me, if You can,
What's the use of going on

"The odds seem insurmountable,
My foes are full of lies.
My fate looks quite predictable,
Though blurry, through these teary eyes.
Are You not a God of mercy and grace?
Didn't you say that we've only to call?
Then give me a reason to continue
As I sit and wait for the axe to fall."

With a heart brim-full of self-pity
I paced the rec-yard for a while.
Not a single soul seemed to give a damn;
My troubles were jumbled in one big pile.
The cool wind couldn't quench the fire
That raged deep down within,
And a bright full moon only showed more clear
The walls of this man-made, man-filled pen.
I knew tomorrow would be more of the same
None of the misery, or pain would be gone
"So," I asked the Lord again,
"Just what is the use of going on?"

I don't suppose the wind really spoke,
Though at the time I thought it might have.
"Hey! God sent me to calm you, Friend;
If you'll let me, I can be a soothing salve.
And I can promise it won't cost you a thing;
It's just part of the job that He Save me.
If you'll just sit quietly here in my embrace,
You might be amazed at how clearly you'll see.

The moon spoke too, in its small, still voice;
"God sheds my light on one and all;
Not to illumine your misery, Friend!

He just doesn't want you to stumble and fall.
I reflect the Sun's magnificence
Day-in and day-out, without fail,
And when my duty — and His will — are done,
Then He will cause my lustre to pale."

Suddenly I was no longer alone
And life wasn't quite so grim,
So once again I bowed my head
And I offered up a prayer to Him:

"Lord, I don't know what the future holds
Whether pain and death, or freedom,
But I'll live each day to do Your will —
I only want a small place in Your Kingdom.
Just fill me with Your love and joy,
Let me live each day without fear;
Fill me with Your peace, O Lord,
Let me live in Your presence here."

Later I sat and watched the horizon
As the sun appeared — a bright gold light;
I knew it was the Hand of God —
He'd come to take away the night.

T C Cole 11/3/91

I wrote this one in collaboration with Martin Draughon, who was my cellmate at
the time. He — like most of us at one time or another — was thinking about
dropping his appeal, so I started the poem and then asked him to help me finish it.
His question, had been, "Man, what's the use?" I only helped him find an answer.

IT'S TIME . . .

For so many years I lived
in fear of the world,
of its thoughts and many opinions.
I felt so small and ugly;
never worthy of being a
"Person" in my own right.
I lived behind a facade which
        showed to the world what
        I thought it wanted to see.
But never did I truly understand
        that in order to really "belong,"
I had first to accept myself —
        just exactly as I was.
I thought happiness was something
        you got from other people,
        never understanding that
        true happiness comes from within.
Happiness, pleasure, contentment –
        they're just mental attitudes,
        and we are what we think.
Everything we could possibly need
to be truly "human" and "civilized"
can be found within our hearts.
It's time to throw away the masks,
throw away the labels,
        and be who we really are.
Only then can we become
what God intended us to be.

T C Cole 11/8/91

This is the rather lame result of a talk I once had with Lesley on the subject of "Just Who In The Hell Do You Really Think You Are?" Lesley had found an article by a Buddhist lama that talked about the face of God and he asked the question, "How can you hope to know God; you don't even know yourself!" Lesley, and I decided that we really didn't have any idea who we were!!

POINT OF NO RETURN

I stand here alone atop a treeless hill,
    the wind cutting through me
    with fingers of ice.
I've stood here for a short eternity,
    staring in silent terror as, below
    me, steam rises from a new grave.
The mourners are absent,
    but they haven't left –
    they just never showed up.
As if in a trance, I slowly shuffle
    toward the dark mound of
    freshly turned earth;
Drawn against my will, against my better
    judgement, but unable to turn
    from the path my feet have chosen.
The sun begins to set and twilight descends,
    but the small white crosses
    can still be seen.
Row upon row of cheap, flimsy plastic.
    They're all that's left to show where
    once-living beings now lay.
My terror mounts as I get close enough
    to read the names. These
    were people I knew;
People I once worked with
    and played with
    and lived with.
Suddenly, one name stands out from
    among the rest, and I become
    the terror I only felt before.
It's the name of the man who
lies beneath the broken
brown earth —
the name is mine!!

T C Cole 11/9/91

This one was written for a poetry contest of a university's "arts" magazine. It only
won third place, but I figured that was better than not winning at all. I got the idea for
it from a dream that Cliff Boggess told me about. At least, I think it was Cliff.

A GARDEN IN WHICH TO ROAM

There is a silence here amid
     the din and confusion, which
     no man can take away;
A peace that seems strange
     and out of place,
But which is our natural
     birthright, for it
     comes from within.
I have glimpsed the secret
     of being in the world,
     but not "of" it.

From the world I receive
     scorn and derision –
     they see the man who was;
Here I've found a serenity that
     I'd only dreamed about before
     my Maker sees the man who is.

Through the Grace
     of the Almighty,
I can accept the pointing fingers
     while loving the unseen
     faces behind them.
I've made my mistakes; they're
     entitled to some of their own;
     God forgives one and all.

I have found that — even here –
     the Earth is a Garden
     in which we are meant to roam
     with love and contentment;
Let other men fight their petty
     battles of, word and deed –
My God and I need only to
     dwell here, where...
There is a Silence amid the
     din and confusion, which
     no man can take away.
                T C Cole 11/13/91

This was written after I'd gotten involved with Siddha Yoga. I think, if someone is sincerely seeking God, it doesn't really matter where he or she starts looking — God Himself will lead the way to the full Truth.

ALWAYS!

I wanted to bring happiness to the world...
        but I wasn't happy!
I wanted to bring peace to my neighbours...
        but I had no peace!
I wanted to bring love to the universe...
        but I could find no love!

When happiness, peace, and love fill my
        being, from my head to my toes,
Then I'll have something to give the
        World - I won't be able to stop it!
When I can smile in the midst of my troubles,
And speak softly to those who despise me;
When I can be patient and gentle with myself,
Then I'll change the world...
        without even trying!
But — until then... ?
        Change the world... ?
"Physician, heal thyself!"

But, an old man told me,
When happiness, peace, and love fill your being,
You'll find that nothing needs to be changed;
This beautiful and curious drama we know
        as 'life'

Is unfolding just exactly as it should.

So!

I'll relax, enjoy the show as well as I'm able,
        and put my fears and worries behind me.
Those who truly want happiness –
        will find it;
Those who truly want peace
        will get it;
Those who truly want love
        will discover the secret!
The things we yearn for will
        always come to us.
If we truly want them and if we truly yearn.
        They will come.
        Always!

This poem came about as a result of a meditation experience. It occurred to me that until we have everything we can give nothing to anyone. But if we would stop trying to give and would just concentrate on "being", then the same God who is working on us (the "old man" of the poem) will also work through us so that others can "receive" from us, but without us actually "giving". We can't give what we don't have, and since all things are God's — do we ever really "have" anything at all?

AMBROSIA

Once again, a cold Spring rain
Beats its rhythm against the glass
Of windows over-long unwashed,
Spattering mud onto bright green grass.
The hypnotic tattoo of its lively play
Presses against my drowsy senses,
While its clean and earthy aroma
Comes floating on cool May breezes.

Miracles are taking place around me;
The magical power of life is everywhere.
Mother Earth no longer lies sleeping,
And her love songs are filling the air.
Like ambrosia falling from heaven
Is this downpour just outside,
And I watch in quiet fascination
This beautiful, life-giving tide.

T C Cole 5/19/92

Ellis One was notorious for having all the power knocked out whenever even a small storm came over. I always liked to sit and watch the rain late at night when nearly everyone else -was asleep and the only sounds were the occasional slam of a door and the beating of the raindrops on the windows. Electrical storms were always exciting of course, but there was just something soothing or calming about watching the rain against the bright backdrop of the security lights.

BLESSINGS

Bright blooms of red,
    of blue and green and yellow,
      cling to the branches
      of a newly—leaved tree.
Suddenly, without warning,
      they spread their petals and
      scatter on a cool spring breeze.
A living bouquet, they flutter
        their delicate wings -
        visible blessings and prayers -
        pastel and neon, blending
        and finally merging with
        another glorious sunrise.
Once again a still, small voice
      has spoken somewhere
      inside my heart and soul.
His subtle whispers always
      seem to echo loudest.

6/7/92

One Saturday morning I was watching a program presented by National Geographic Society, that was about leopard cubs. The narrator was telling about the natural beauties of the African landscape and the camera was trained on a lone tree sitting in the middle of an otherwise barren plain, and I thought how strange it seemed that this tree with all its bright flowers was out there in the middle of nowhere. It occurred to me that perhaps God liked beautiful things too, and that some things He may have created simply because He could - like this tree. Then suddenly some sort of bird flew into the tree and all the "flowers" took to the air. Thousands of butterflies seemed to just explode onto the breeze, and I thought that was just the coolest thing I'd ever seen! They seemed to hover around the tree for a second or two, and then they all moved away in a group until they were lost in the glare of the morning sun.

    I was thinking about it later and decided that if prayers could be seen by the human eye, that's what they would look like - all of our hurts, desires, hopes and anxieties resting in our hearts until we release them to God in prayer.

391

THE PLAYWRIGHT

Have you ever wondered about the meaning of life?
Have you ever asked yourself, "Why am I here?"
Well, I'll tell you a long-kept secret, my friend:
You were blessed with life because He holds you so dear.

Our universe, in all its myriad parts,
Is merely the setting for a celestial Play.
And God, the most awesome Playwright of all,
Wrote a script just for you on that first wondrous day.

The timing was perfect when He led you onstage —
The assembled cast cheered your debut —
And the Playwright Himself, from the balcony,
Sat awaiting your first rave review.

You looked good on the stage, you played your part well;
From the critics, kind words you soon earned.
But you grew discontented with your part in the Play;
For a bigger, more important role you yearned.

It wasn't too long til you'd forgotten your lines,
And when the cue was "stage left", you went right!
You started to think that your character was real —
You forgot the Director as you sought the spotlight.

The Play, though, is still far from over;
The Director's glory you still can reflect.
He wants to give you your cues and your lines,
And those rave reviews he'll still help you collect.
Birth —
         it's a glorious gift from the Almighty,
A gift that's renewed each and every day.
Birth is a miraculous awakening to life —

And life?
         It's just God's most enchanting Play!

T C Cole 6/8/92

This one needs a bit of work before it reflects Catholic theology accurately. But I kind of like it anyway. And I think you can get some sort of idea about what I'm trying to say here, even though it's not quite correct.

AWAKENING

It is early morning and the
                fresh spring air frolics
                through open windows,
                greeting me with a kiss.

Sitting for meditation, I close
                my eyes — once again
                turning within to sing out
                "Good Morning"
                to the Lord of my life.
He, too, greets me with a kiss,
                and my heart swells with
                a Love so vast and all –
                encompassing it can only
                be a gift from God.
As I mentally kneel at the feet
                of my Beloved, I thank Him
                for once again providing
                an opportunity for me to
                experience His Grace and
                awe-inspiring compassion.

Blazing with the brilliance
                of a million suns, He
                smiles and lifts me to
                my feet, sending me out
                into a Garden of such
                beauty and fragrance that
                I'm constantly reminded
                of His sacred Presence.

Suddenly the Sun peeps over
                the horizon, its radiance
                multiplied a thousand-fold
                by tiny diamonds of early-
                morning dew that bedeck
                the bright green grass.
Already the day has been blessed
                with a miracle of light and colour.
Birdsong mingles with the sounds
                of voices as others rise to
                meet another day, each a living
                vessel containing a spark
                of God-given divinity.

Oh Lord, breathe Your sweet breath
                upon each of us, fanning this
                spark until it becomes a flame

we can't possibly hide.
Protect us from the selfish desires,
        fears, and compulsive actions
        that would smother this spark
        if only given a chance.
Shower us with Your Grace and Love,
        never allowing us to forget that
        our fate lies in Your Hands alone.
Grant us Your Blessings, Oh God,
        for without Your Blessings each
        breath we'll breathe today will
        be as air given to a corpse.
Only by resting in Your Shadow
        can we truly become alive.
Thank You Lord, just for being. Amen.

T C Cole 6/07/92

This one doesn't exactly mesh with the mystic doctrines of St. John or the Cross or St. Teresa of Avila, but it is an accurate representation of one of the "way-stations" along my path to the Church. What I mistakenly refer to here as "Beloved" is only the first stirrings of my heart in response to the Holy Spirit, but it was so totally different from anything I had felt before and so alien to what was "normal" to me... Perhaps I can be granted a bit of leeway due to my sincerity?

DANCING

On a distant horizon
        I watch them gather,
Dark and brooding — too heavy
        to stay aloft, it seems —
Yet graceful and beautiful
        in their own way:
Storm clouds, called together
        by forces unseen.
Quickly they approach and my mind
        is swept up in Mother Nature's
        dazzling show of mock anger.
A brilliant flash and
        lightning skips to Earth;
A sudden clap of thunder and
I jump, startled.
As the first patter of raindrops
        strikes against my window,
I witness yet another miracle
        as buttercups and roses
        lift their faces,
Gazing into the darkened Heavens
        as they drink their fill.

Watching them as they sway
        in the quickened breeze,
        I wonder .   . .
Do they dance in joy to music
        my ears can't hear?
Does the heart of a buttercup
        know love for its Maker?
Does a rose offer thanks
        for sunshine and rain?
I believe the answer to each
        is a resounding yes!

As quickly as it began,
        the storm passes over.
Grey clouds give way to blue skies
        and cheerful sunlight,
As the buttercups and roses
        continue to dance beneath a rainbow-adorned Heaven.

T C Cole 6/09/92

HARMONY

Waiting for the sun to rise,
      I sit alone and listen to
      a symphony of creation.
All around me I hear
      the music of life:

A choir of sparrow chicks
      call for their breakfast
And a soft breeze, whispering
      through oak leaves,
      joins in on the refrain.
Crickets and cicadas compete
      for places in the orchestra,
Each being directed by waving
      tendrils of sweet
      honeysuckle.

While trying to blend in with
      the brick wall behind me,
I watch a grey squirrel scamper
      across the dew-sprinkled lawn.
He appears to be dancing
      to the symphony as he tries
      to keep his dainty feet dry.

Soon human voices will add a
      different texture to the music -
Wives and husbands
      seeing each other off to work;
The greetings of friends;
      the laughter of children
      at play.

A familiar melody, yet I strain
      to catch each and every note.
I can dance to the music
      only as long as I can hear
      the orchestra play.

T C Cole 6/17/92

I used to go outside early in the morning (as soon as they opened our rec-yard, usually about 6:30 or 7:00) while everyone else was still trying to wake up or was at work. It was always quiet, and I could watch the squirrels play on the other side of the fence, and sometimes I would just sit with my eyes closed and listen to the world to wake up.

THANK YOU, LORD

Dear Lord Who dwells within us all,
Ignore my words, I pray,
And hear instead, O Perfect One,
The things my heart will say.
My mind is oh! so fickle, Lord,
And wants what shouldn't be;
Ignoring all You've blessed me with,
Wanting more and more from Thee.
But my heart, O Precious Saviour,
Cannot lie to One so True,
So listen, Sweet Beloved,
As it offers thanks to you:

Thank You for another day
To spend here at Your feet;
Thank You for another chance
To hear Your words so sweet.
Thank You for my enemies —
By loving them I grow;
Thank You for my many friends —
Through them Your blessings flow.
Thank You, Lord, for everything
You've given to me here,
But thank You most of all, Great God,
For living in my heart so near.

T C Cole 6/09/92

This one pretty much explains itself, I think, but it occurred to me one day that when most of us pray we have a tendency to say what we think God wants to hear, instead of what we really think or feel. Which is pretty stupid (or just plain silly) when you think about it, because He sees through what we say to what we mean, anyway! Lying to God... oy vey!!

UNITY

Sitting on the beach,
      my mind wandering,
And I notice there's no horizon.
Blue sky meets blue ocean –
      and they merge, becoming one.

This thought leads to another:

The sky —
      Heaven; the realm of God.
The ocean
      Earth; the realm of men.

How often have the two met –
      and merged, becoming one....
      and no one noticed?

T C Cole 6/9/92

The answer to the question is that they've merged only once, in the Incarnation of our Lord. The merging of the ocean and sky is something that I saw in a photo once. The photographer had caught the scene at just the right angle so that the ocean perfectly reflected the sky - I think it was somewhere in the South Pacific — and the only way you could be certain that it wasn't simply the ocean alone (you could see a few whitecaps) is that there were birds flying in the distance. I kept that photo on my wall for a long time before I finally lost it in one of our shakedowns.

398

A SEASON OF DREAMS

A man with a dream is a wealthy man,
And a child with a dream has hope;
But a man who has no dream at all,
At his best, can only cope.

A dream can take you to mountaintops,
Or beyond, to the Milky Way;
There is no place a dream can't go –
No music a dream can't play.

It seems I've always been a dreamer,
But I've never liked dreaming alone.
I think dreams were meant to be shared
They were meant to be built upon.

Our dreams are like rose gardens –
With care, their beauty will grow;
But they also need the light of day
So their beauty all others can know.

You can't lock them up inside your mind
And expect to see them bloom;
It's only when they become reality,
That you can smell their sweet perfume.

Sometimes dreams, like roses,
Must wait for the proper clime,
But when at last the planting's done –
You'll see blossoms in due time.

T C Cole 6/27/92

MY BEST

O Lord, when I am weary
And think I need to rest,
Remind me, Sweet Beloved,
That I've promised you my best.

I can't do Your work, Lord,
While sitting or lying down;
There are many in this sea of sin
Use my hands, lest someone drown.

Give me access to Your strength,
For I have none of my own.
Lend me courage also, Lord,
On this path of thorn and stone.

Give me songs my heart can sing;
Let me do Your work with zest....
And remind me, Sweet Beloved,
That I've promised you my best.

T C Cole 7/03/92

Again, I'm not sure what I may have been doing or thinking when I wrote this one.
There was nothing significant going on at the time that makes this one stand out. I
may have written it for a contest or a magazine, but I'm not sure.

FINO

When time has finally run its course,
       and flowers bloom no more;
When birds no longer sweetly sing,
       and the lion's ceased his roar;
When fish no longer swim the seas,
       and trees put forth no fruit...
Will we have found the rainbow's end
       and shared with all its loot?

When no more chances come our way
       and all is said and done,
Will we have tried our very best?
       Will we have played and won?
Will we step into eternity
       as family — one and all?
Will we be able to say "We made it!"
       when, at last, the roll is called?

T C Cole 7/21/92

FRIEND AND COMPANION

Lord, You existed before the
                foundations of the world,
And Time itself will cease
                before Your reign will end.
In spite of Your glories, Lord,
          will You be my Friend
           and closest Companion?

Walk by my side through this world,
         Sweet Jesus,
And allow me to see its beauty
           with new eyes.
Let me hear Your Voice
           in gentle breezes, and
Hear Your Laughter in the
          voice of a child.
Teach me to walk softly,
         to speak softly,
And to reach out tenderly
           to those around me,
Just as You so gently and
           tenderly reached out to me*

Take my hand, Lord, and keep me
           close to your precious side,
For the road seems smooth and easy
          in Your presence
And life itself becomes a game.

Grant me faith and wisdom, Lord,
         and let my love for You
           grow stronger and sweeter.
Let the peace that comes from
           knowing you fill my soul,
And spill over into the hearts of those
           you send into my life each day,
And may the joy that comes
         from serving you
         never end.
         Amen.

T C Cole 2/27/93

A "COMMON" MAN?

Christ Jesus,
>> born in a stable and
>> destined to die as a
>> common criminal,
Chose to walk among the
>> common people.

He was God Almighty and had
>> the power of all Creation
>> at His command,
Yet He mingled with the poor
>> and the sick.
His companions simple men
>> with simple ways,
Yet He was truly one of them.
He was a King Who commanded
>> a celestial army,
Yet His uniform was a dusty robe
>> and worn sandals, and Truth
>> was His only weapon and He
>> sharpened it with Love.
He raised the dead and healed the lame,
>> accepting nothing in return;
He gave sight to the blind
>> and hearing to the deaf,
>> and caused the mute to speak.
Yet He allowed Himself to be bound,
>> to be spat upon, beaten and mocked.
He lived a life of love and compassion,
>> showing mercy and tenderness
>> and teaching charity and forgiveness...
Oh, what a fool I've Been!

I sought the company
>> of the rich and powerful,
Feeling flattered whenever
>> I was noticed.
I considered myself
>> to be sophisticated,
And avoided my more
>> simple neighbours.
I was proud of my health
>> and personal appearance,
And shunned those who couldn't
>> live up to my "standards".
I took from everyone
>> and gave nothing in return —

God, forgive my ignorance.   4/02/93

403

A PALACE OF GOLD

Oh, Lord of Mercy and Compassion,
I have built for You a throne.
It's made of purest gold, Lord,
And adorned with precious stones.
It rests upon a dais
Where only You may go,
And round about it is a river
Where sweet milk and honey flow.

I have laid for You a table,
Spread with fruit and fresh baked bread;
A feast of cakes and pastries —
At this table, You alone will be fed.
All the Saints — past, present and future
Are gathered to sing just for You;
Please tarry here at Your leisure
For the Lamb, all this I do.

For You, Lord, I've built a palace
On the foundations that You laid.
Of purified gold, it glitters,
And on its lawns Your angels play.
Its floors are strewn with rose petals
A carpet to ease Your way;
I've prepared these in my heart with love
-Lord, please accept them, I pray.

4/04/93

I don't know what to say about this one. Its not one of my favourites. I think I was just
playing with images and words, and this is what I came up with

404

THE MASTER

There was a man
      who walked this earth,
      two thousand years ago.
A man who owned
      not so much as a shack,
      and who had no wealth to show.

A carpenter
      by trade was he;
      a lowly man he seemed.
And yet, today,
      He rules Supreme —
      amid splendor no man has dreamed.

A man by birth,
      He lived and died
      as a servant to the world,
But now He sits
      at His Father's right hand –
      my Master,
      my King,
      my Lord!

4/05/93

THE MAN IN THE DEN

There is a man
        hanging on a cross
        above the mantel
        in the den.
I hear him at night,
        begging, pleading:
        "Please let me down!
        You don't know what
        you've done."
I hear him sobbing
        and the small wooden cross
        rattles against the wall
        as he writhes in pain.
The small brass tacks
        hold him securely
        (he was made in Hong Kong -
        too dangerous to be free).
He wears a thorny crown
        and a plaque calls him 'King",
        but his blood isn't blue
        it's red like mine.
He's hung there for years,
        day—in and day—out.
        How despicably evil and
        horrendous his crimes
Each morning I creep
        silently downstairs
        to see this criminal
        this half—naked "King".
He doesn't move or speak,
        but I know he watches.
        His expression is blank,
        but his eyes are not empty.

One night there's only silence;
        in the morning
        he was gone.
        He left a message:
"You will find me in your heart.
        Follow your heart,
        whatever the cost
        My suffering must not
        have been in vain!"

11/13/93

I WILL BUILD AN ALTAR

Precious Saviour,
      Lord, God Almighty
Please hear my prayer:

I have sinned, Lord,
      and broken my word to You.
Allow my tears to mingle
      with your grace
      and make me whole again.

I asked You to walk beside me –
      then left You standing alone
while I followed my pride.
      I will build an altar
      and lay my pride upon it;
      destroy it with Your might.

I asked you to catch me when I fall
      then refused Your aid so
      all would see my strength.
I will build an altar
      and lay my strength upon it
      humble me through your mercy.

I asked to hear Your Voice
      then ignored your words of caution
      while I listened to the world.
I will build an altar
      and lay my ears upon it
      purify them with Your wisdom
O It will be a very large altar lord!!

Upon it I must lay my eyes,
      my mouth and hands and feet
      this temple is impure Lord.
Cleanse it of all that is ugly and mean
      of all that would separate
      me from Your Presence.

I will build an altar
      in my heart, Sweet Jesus,
And rededicate this temple to You.
      Rekindle that flame within
      that burns with Your Light.
So I might walk
      by Your side
      once more.
Amen.
                              T C Cole 3/28/93

CATCH ME WHEN I FALL

Lover of Life,
      Lord of Light,
Guide my steps as I travel
      Life's rocky road;
Leave the stones in my path –
      just catch me when I fall.
Sweet Beloved,
      as we journey toward eternity,
Be patient with me, I pray.

You know my fears, Lord
      push me beyond them.
You know my demons, Lord
      give me strength to resist them.
You know my enemies, Lord –
      together we can love them.
You know me better
      than I know myself!
Sweet Jesus,
      mold me into what I should be,
And fill me with Your Love
      and Your Light.
Amen.

T C Cole

A prayer, as you can see. I didn't date it for some reason, so I have no idea when it was written. Most likely, though, it was after August or September of 1997.

JUST KNOWING YOU'RE THERE

There is a disease in the world
        called loneliness.
It's a killer,
And I'm dying.
There is a cure in the world
        for this disease.
It's you,
But I'm still dying.
What I need — your love –
Is too precious, too pure.

I'm afraid my bitterness
        would destroy us both,
So you'll never know
How important you are to me.
I can't ask you
        to stop my dying,
But knowing you're there
Eases the pain.

T C Cole

No date, no dedication, no hints — you'll just have to wonder!

TEACH ME, LORD

Teach me to wait on You, Lord,
When my patience begins to fray
You alone have perfect timing,
Yours alone is the perfect way.

Teach me to listen to You, Lord,
When my mind begins to stray;
Help me heed Your Words, Lord,
Let me hear what You have to say.

Teach me to talk with You, Lord,
When my tongue begins to bray;
Let me speak only worthy things,
As I kneel in Your Presence to pray.

Teach me to be more humble, Lord,
Help me to keep my pride at bay;
Let me be more like You, sweet Jesus,
With each wonderful passing day.

T C Cole

And — again — no date, but probably written after I started studying for my
Confirmation. I kind of like this one because it's nice and simple.

NOVA

Another star has gone nova,
Destroying itself in one final
         dance of self - annihilation -
The shock of its death
Is felt immediately:

Those in its orbit are stunned —
Others watch from a distance,
         unbelieving.
A world is gone, shattered
         beyond repair,
And my heart falters —
         crying out in pain
As this young, beautiful star
         ceases to exist.

to R.P.

This was written for a friend who died of a drug overdose. No one even knew that he'd been doing drugs!

...BLESSED ART THOU....

I knelt one night by my bed to pray,
My beads the colour of desert sands.
But before I'd whispered one decade,
I found I held dear Mary's hands.
So I prayed there with Our Lady:
"Hail, Mary, full of Grace!"
And when I dared glance up again,
I saw my Lord had taken her place.
No longer was I on my knees
At Mary's feet, intent on prayer.
No, now her Child and I were walking,
And the Blessed Lord alone knew where.
He said, "I'm happy you met my Mother;
She's brought many like you to me."
He smiled and firmly grasped my hand,
"She's our Mother — we're brothers, you see!"

I said, "Little Brother, where are we going?"
He stopped suddenly in mock surprise.
Then he laughed as he turned to me,
And I saw an ocean of love in his eyes.
"Why, we're going to the Temple, of course!
Where else could we possibly go?" he said.
"Our Father's business needs tending to —
There's work to be done, lambs to be fed."
"But, Jesus, I don't know your lambs.
Your sheep and the goats look alike to me!"
He simply laughed again, "It doesn't matter.
Just feed them all — the meal is free."

"And how do I feed them, Little Brother?"
In my frustration I turned away.
"My hands are empty — I've nothing to give!"
"You can give them me," I heard him softly say.
I turned and saw the tears in his eyes,
And his disappointment cut me like a knife.
"How can you say you have nothing to give?
You have everything. I gave you my life!"

" Show unto us the blessed fruit of thy womb...."
Again I knelt beside my bed in prayer.
The Virgin's Child, the Son of God, was right:
Even here, I have everything to share!

T C Cole 8/25/00

412

ON EAGLES' WINGS

Of all the creatures
        which grace our world
I can think of none so free,
        so light-hearted and joyful,
As those who soar so effortlessly
        between Earth and Heaven.
And of all the birds of the air
        surely there can be none
More noble and majestic, more
        splendid of bearing, or more
Heart—thrilling and soul—stirring
        than the eagle.

Whether gliding high among rocky peaks
        or just above a valley forest,
To catch sight of an eagle is to see
        a miracle on the wing.

We too can be eagles,
        with just a little faith and love.
But all too often we seem afraid
        to leave the security of the nest.
We're content to remain eaglets,
        depending on others for our needs,
When we should just spread our wings
        and trust a merciful God
To bestow compassion and grace,
        and to support us in our flight

Many, like myself, who dare the leap,
        will spend a whole lifetime
Fighting madly against winds which,
        if just given a chance,
Would carry us gently and safely
        to what we truly want and need.
We too could soar effortlessly,
        with grace and so much joy,
If we would only trust the Almighty,
        Whose breath supports our wings.
"I carried you on eagles' wings
and brought you unto myself."

Exodus 19:4

Appendix 1

Manchester Medjugorje Centre, 5 Oaklands Drive, Prestwich, Manchester M25 1LJ England.

Information Centre "Mir" Medjugorje.
http://www.medjugorje.hr/

Appendix 2

Human Writes

Enquiries:

Membership Secretary
Hill Farm, Little Ryburgh
Norfolk NR21 OLR

Web site: www.humanwrites.org
E-mail: humanwritesuk@yahoo.co.uk

Appendix 3

Lethal Justice by Sr. Joy Elder (Published by New City 2002)

Appendix 4

The following article appeared in the Carmelite Review (April 2001), edited by Father William Harry, O.Carm (Father Bill).

Carmelite Blessed Titus Brandsma as a Role Model on Death Row

By Ted C. Cole
Livingston, Texas.

The saints and blesseds of the Church serve as models for Catholics in all walks of life and, as a. Catholic prisoner on Texas' Death Row, I find myself in need of a role model at almost every moment of every day. Having come to the church less than three years ago, this walking of the straight and narrow is a new experience for me and old habits die hard. I find myself constantly faced with the hatred and cruelty of my jailers at best, with their simple contempt and indifference to my physical and spiritual needs and meek acceptance of the situation does not come easily. Fortunately, there is a man whose example speaks directly to people in my situation: Blessed Titus Brandsma.

Titus had no crime or wrong doing on his conscience, but he didn't rant and rave about the injustice of his imprisonment. He was fully aware of the evil he was defying, he knew he would eventually be arrested, and he calmly and cheerfully accepted the consequences of his words and actions.

Titus' first lesson to me was that all words and actions have consequences and, depending on the times and circumstances, anyone anywhere can end up with a prison number on his or her chest. And once the gate has slammed shut behind you, it really doesn't matter whether you're guilty or innocent, a political prisoner or a criminal. The reality of prison life is the same for everyone regardless of who or what you are. How that reality affects you is the important thing you can wallow in outrage, or in shame and guilt, or you can get over it by turning to God.

Titus brought the message and example of Christ to his fellow prisoners. He brought hope and comfort even though he was a prisoner himself. and he can still bring inspiration to prisoners today Titus encouraged his fellow prisoners to pray for their Nazi captors, and he preach and lived forgiveness. I've been sentenced to die for my crime and, according to the laws of Texas, rightly so. But our guards seem to feel they have a right perhaps even duty to help us "pay" for our crimes by making us as miserable as possible until the time comes when, like Titus, we will be given lethal injections. My first instinct is to lash out physically and verbally at these people who don't know me and don't know anything about me. But Titus says to me: 'Accept it. forgive it, and let it go!" That can only be done through prayer and self-discipline, but if a man as virtuous and holy as Titus Brandsma says that this is the right thing to do, how can anyone as ignorant and guilty as I am possibly argue with him?

Titus' second lesson to me is that forgiving and letting go can be very empowering. My peace of mind depends entirely on me and the way I react to those who are in positions of authority over me. The only power anyone can have over my mind and emotions is the power I give them. and' following Titus' example puts power over me back into God's hands were it belongs. Titus knew this, and it was his intimate relationship with a Power much greater than the Nazis' that enabled him to live and die as he did.

Titus also confirms for me the fact that I will find God where I am, and not necessarily where I expect Him to be. We on Death Row in Texas are no longer allowed to have religious services. The last Mass I had the privilege of attending actually a very hurried and haphazard Communion service was more than a year ago. But Titus' life in prison is a poignant reminder that, regardless of how our actions may seem to prove otherwise, God is not confined to a church or a chapel or to any other physical place, nor is He confined to any rite or ritual, even one as sacred as the Holy Mass. Even as he lay dying at Dachau, Titus was himself a chapel where God was alive and well and still reaching out to others. Titus assures me that I can also be a chapel dedicated to God and that's ones duty to serve others and to influence others to do good does not stop simply because "home" is now a prison cell.

He also shows by his example that the solitude and loneliness of prison, far from being a burden or a frustration, can

417

be an asset in one's spiritual life. Time alone with God is so very precious. and it seems to be something that very few people are able to take advantage of. Titus wrote. "I am here alone, but never was our Lord so close to me." I firmly believe that what was accomplished in one man can, with the grace of God, be accomplished in me. If being able to sit attentively at Jesus' feet is, as He said, the "better part" then along with Titus, I have indeed been blessed!

So, by following Titus' example I have a model of how to live with myself, how to live with others, and how to live with God. What more could anyone possibly need to know?

Appendix 5

St. John of the Cross

By Ted C. Cole

"St. John of the Cross is my hero, because he was a tremendously charismatic person and that shows in his writings. He was a little man, just four foot eleven. Frequently, he was described as small and delicate, but he commanded great respect from everyone. Well, everyone except his superiors, but that was because he had joined with St. Teresa of Avila in bringing reforms to the order, those in power are seldom happy with "trouble makers" like John who see the need for reform.

St. John always thought of himself as a priest and servant of the poor. He often went door-to-door begging for food and alms for the nuns, so they would be spared the humiliation of begging for themselves. He would frequently do the nuns' chores - washing, cooking, scrubbing floors and tending the garden so they would have more time for prayers and recreation.

St. John was a priest, of course, with all that goes along with that: preaching; counselling; hearing confessions and celebrating Mass. But he was also a poet; writer; artist; architect; bricklayer; schoolteacher; housepainter and tailor, etc. He did his own work and then he did all the things that his religious friends couldn't do, didn't have time to do, or just simply didn't want to do.

I think all those things make him an ideal person to take as an example of how to live a Christian life of service to others. Most important for me is the fact that he was a mystic who knew God very intimately and who was blessed with the knowledge of Divine Union. He was given the ability to write books of "instruction" concerning the spiritual journey. Now I know that there are a fairly large number of saints both "official" and unofficial, who have written about their mystic experiences and visions. There's an even larger number of Catholic authors who wrote about their theories concerning Divine Union. But John's works provided for me, at least a tried and true spiritual path that can prepare a person to live in "perfect love" should God see fit to grace a person with Union.

It's difficult to put into words just why St. John is so "special," but his writings speak to my heart in a way that no one else's works ever had. I'm also impressed by the fact that some of his best poetry was composed during the nine months he was held in prison in Toledo, when he was repeatedly beaten and humiliated by his fellow friars! I guess the best way to understand how I feel is to read his works for yourself, if you ever have the time and inclination. He's not everyone's "cup of tea," of course, but he tells me what I need to know and not what I think I want to know.

Appendix 6

Statement by the Catholic Bishops of Texas on Capital Punishment

As spiritual leaders in the community, we Catholic Bishops of Texas, are acutely aware of the violence in our state. Despite a growing reliance on long sentences, more prisons and more executions, our state's crime rate has escalated.

Since the reinstatement of the death penalty in the United States in 1976, the Catholic Bishops of the United States have repeatedly condemned its use as a violation of the sanctity of human life. Capital punishment, along with abortion and euthanasia, is inconsistent with the belief of millions of Texans, that all life is sacred.

It is important that we address this issue at this time. Since 1976, Texas has executed more than 100 men, some of whom were mentally retarded or mentally ill. We currently have more than 400 men and women on Death Row. We sympathize with the profound pain of the victims of brutal crimes. Nevertheless, we believe that the compassionate example of Christ calls us to respect the God-given image found in even hardened criminals.

We must now take bolder steps to change the attitude of the American people regarding capital punishment as a means of dealing with a complex issue. It is unfortunate that a large majority of Americans, including Catholics, support capital punishment as a means of dealing with crime, even in light of strong evidence of its ineffectiveness, its racially-biased application, and its staggering costs, both materially and emotionally.

Capital punishment has not proved to be a deterrent to crime. States which have the death penalty do not have lower rates of violent crime than states without the death penalty. All other Western democracies have abolished capital punishment and have lower rates of violent crime.

The imposition of the death penalty has resulted in racial bias. In fact, the race of the victim has been proven to be the determining factor in deciding whether to prosecute criminal cases. Of those executed, nearly 90% were convicted of killing whites, although people of colour are more than half of all homicide victims in the United States. More than 60% of the persons on Death Rows in California and Texas are either Black; Latino; Asian or Native American.

In the State of Texas, it cost $2.3 million on average to prosecute and execute each capital case, as compared to $400,000 for life imprisonment.

Tragically, innocent people are sometimes put to death by the state. It has been proven in 350 capital convictions over the past 20 years that the convicted person had not committed the crime. Of these cases, 25 people were executed before their innocence was discovered.

Capital punishment does nothing for the families of victims of violent crime, other than prolong their suffering through many wasted years of criminal proceedings. Rather than fuelling their cry for vengeance, the state could better serve them by helping them to come to terms with their grief. We applaud the work of support groups of victims' families who have joined together to work toward reconciliation and rehabilitation of the people who caused tragic loss in their families.

While human logic alone seems to support the abolition of the death penalty, as moral leaders, we call for alternatives because of its moral incongruity in today's world. The Catechism of the Catholic Church states, "If non lethal means are sufficient to defend and protect people's safety from the aggressor, authority will limit itself to such means, as these are merely in keeping with the concrete conditions of the common good and more in conformity with the dignity of the human person.

Today, in fact, as a consequence of the possibilities, which the state has for preventing crime, by rendering one who has committed an offence incapable of doing harm – without definitively taking away from him the possibility of redeeming himself – the cases in which the execution of the offender is an absolute necessity are very rare, if not practically non-existent".

In our modern society, we have means of keeping the offender from harming others. Although, in previous times, people of faith have employed capital punishment, today, we have the ability to realize better the principles of mercy, forgiveness, and unconditional love for all people, as evoked in the Hebrew Scriptures by the Prophet Ezekiel: "As I live, says the Lord God, I swear I take no pleasure in the death of the wicked man, but rather the wicked man's conversion, that he may live. Turn, turn from your evil ways!"

We believe that capital punishment contributes to a climate of violence in our state. This cycle of violence can be diminished by life imprisonment without parole, when necessary. The words of Ezekiel are a powerful reminder that repentance not revenge, conversion not death, are better guides for public policy on the death penalty than the current policy of violence, death for death.

As religious leaders, we are deeply concerned that the State of Texas is usurping the sovereign dominion of God over human life by employing capital punishment for heinous crimes. We implore all citizens to call on our elected officials to reject the violence of the death penalty and replace it either with non-lethal means of punishment, which are sufficient to protect society from violent offenders of human life and public order.